Cross-Channel Modernisms

Cross-Channel Modernisms

Edited by Claire Davison, Derek Ryan
and Jane Goldman

EDINBURGH
University Press

Edinburgh University Press is one of the leading university presses in the UK. We publish academic books and journals in our selected subject areas across the humanities and social sciences, combining cutting-edge scholarship with high editorial and production values to produce academic works of lasting importance. For more information visit our website: edinburghuniversitypress.com

© editorial matter and organisation Claire Davison, Derek Ryan and Jane Goldman, 2020, 2022
© the chapters their several authors, 2020, 2022

Edinburgh University Press Ltd
The Tun – Holyrood Road
12(2f) Jackson's Entry
Edinburgh EH8 8PJ

First published in hardback by Edinburgh University Press 2020

Typeset in 11/13 Adobe Sabon by
IDSUK (DataConnection) Ltd

A CIP record for this book is available from the British Library

ISBN 978 1 4744 4187 2 (hardback)
ISBN 978 1 4744 4188 9 (paperback)
ISBN 978 1 4744 4189 6 (webready PDF)
ISBN 978 1 4744 4190 2 (epub)

The right of Claire Davison, Derek Ryan and Jane Goldman to be identified as the editors of this work has been asserted in accordance with the Copyright, Designs and Patents Act 1988, and the Copyright and Related Rights Regulations 2003 (SI No. 2498).

Contents

List of Figures		vii
Notes on Contributors		viii
	Introduction: Cross-Channel (Transmanche) Modernisms	1
	Claire Davison, Jane Goldman and Derek Ryan	
	Interlude: Translating	14
	Derek Ryan	
1	On Unknowing French? *Rhythm* and *Le Rythme* on a Cross-Channel Exchange	19
	Claire Davison	
2	Impressions of Translation: Ford Madox Ford's Cosmopolitan Literary Crossings	50
	Max Saunders	
3	Sydney Schiff and Marcel Proust: Table-talk, Tribute, Translation	69
	Emily Eells	
	Interlude: Fashioning	91
	Claire Davison	
4	Cross-Channel Modernisms and the Vicissitudes of a Laughing Torso: Nina Hamnett, Artist, Bohemian and Writer in London and Paris	96
	Jane Goldman	
5	Jean Rhys's *comédie anglaise*	120
	Vassiliki Kolocotroni	
6	Betray to Become: Departure in James Joyce's *A Portrait of the Artist as a Young Man*	138
	Naomi Toth	
	Interlude: Mediating	155
	Jane Goldman	

7	*Close Up* and Cross-Channel Cinema Culture *Laura Marcus*	162
8	Debussy at the Omega Workshops *Charlotte de Mille*	184
9	Across the Other Channel: Elizabeth Bowen and Modernist Mediation *Lauren Elkin*	199
	Coda: 'You, who cross the Channel': Virginia Woolf, Departures and the Spectro-Aesthetics of Modernism *Patrizia A. Muscogiuri*	215

Index   243

Figures

1.1	First-issue cover pages of *Rhythm* and *Le Rythme*, designed by J. D. Fergusson and Camille Schuwer respectively	24
1.2	Cover page for regular issues of *Le Rythme*, from no. 2 onward, designed by G. Lecornu	25
1.3	Page layout and visuals in *Rhythm* 1.1, p. 12 and *Le Rythme* 2, p. 7	27
1.4	André Derain's 'Creation' in *Rhythm* 1.3, p. 28 and G. Lecornu's 'Dessin' in *Le Rythme* 4.10	28
1.5	Jessie Dismorr's 'Isadora' in *Rhythm* 1.2, p. 20 and Marcel Gromaire's 'Clair de Lune' in *Le Rythme* 2, p. 17	29
1.6	Cover page of 'Special Issue – Maurice Maeterlinck', *Le Rythme*, June 1911	32
4.1	Torsos: Henri Gaudier-Brzeska, letter 3 November 1912	111
4.2	Henri and Sophie Gaudier-Brzeska dancing: Henri Gaudier-Brzeska, letter 3 November 1912	113
8.1	Toy design (Jellicoe) (verso), attrib. Winifred Gill, 1914–16	189
8.2	Toy design (Jellicoe) (recto), attrib. Winifred Gill, 1914–16	189
8.3	Toy design (fat military man), attrib. Winifred Gill, 1914–16	190

Notes on Contributors

Claire Davison is Professor of Modernist Studies at the Université Sorbonne Nouvelle, Paris, where her teaching and research focus on the borders and boundaries of modernism; this includes the translation and reception of Russian literature in the 1910s–1920s; cross-Channel modernist dialogues, and literary and musical modernism. She is author of *Translation as Collaboration: Virginia Woolf, Katherine Mansfield and S.S. Koteliansky* (Edinburgh University Press, 2014) and editor of the Edinburgh Edition of Katherine Mansfield. Her current research bears on modernist soundscapes and broadcasting in the 1920s–1930s.

Charlotte de Mille is a film curator, writer, lecturer and arts educator who works freelance at the Courtauld Gallery. She specialises in European modernism, and intersections of art, music and philosophy. Among her publications in this area she is co-editor of *Bergson and the Art of Immanence: Painting, Photography, Film* (Edinburgh University Press, 2015).

Emily Eells is Professor of Nineteenth-Century British Literature at the University of Paris at Nanterre. Her monograph *Proust's Cup of Tea: Homoeroticism and Victorian Culture* (Ashgate, 2002) was followed by several articles on questions of intertextuality relating to Proust and writers and artists from the English-speaking world. She is co-editor, with Naomi Toth, of *Son et traduction dans l'œuvre de Proust* (Champion, 2018). She has published on *fin de siècle* aesthetics and Anglo-French cultural transaction and is currently working on the cosmopolitan salon of Natalie Clifford Barney as a site of transnational cultural exchange.

Lauren Elkin is a critic, translator and writer. She is author of *Flâneuse: Women Walk the City* (Chatto & Windus, 2016). Her writing on books, art, culture, travel and fashion has appeared in many publications, including the *New York Times*, the *Guardian*, *Le Monde*, *Vogue*, the *London Review of Books*, the *Times Literary Supplement*, the *FT* and *frieze*, and she is a contributing editor at *The White Review*.

Jane Goldman is Reader in English Literature at the University of Glasgow. She is General Editor of the Cambridge Edition of the Writings of Virginia Woolf; author of *The Feminist Aesthetics of Virginia Woolf* (Cambridge University Press, 1998), *The Cambridge Introduction to Virginia Woolf* (Cambridge University Press, 2006), *With You in the Hebrides: Virginia Woolf and Scotland* (Cecil Woolf, 2013); *Modernism, 1910–1945: Image to Apocalypse* (Palgrave Macmillan, 2004); and co-editor of *Modernism: An Anthology of Sources and Documents* (Edinburgh University Press, 1998).

Vassiliki Kolocotroni is Senior Lecturer in English Literature at the University of Glasgow. She is an expert in international modernism and the avant-garde, with special interests in theory, surrealism, film, travel writing and the modernist reception of classical and modern Greece. Her book publications include *Modernism: An Anthology of Sources and Documents* (Edinburgh University Press, 1998) and *The Edinburgh Dictionary of Modernism* (Edinburgh University Press, 2018).

Laura Marcus is Goldsmiths' Professor of English Literature at the University of Oxford. Her research and teaching interests are predominantly in nineteenth- and twentieth-century literature and culture, including life-writing, modernism, Virginia Woolf and Bloomsbury culture, contemporary fiction, and literature and film. Her book publications include *Auto/biographical Discourses: Theory, Criticism, Practice* (Manchester University Press, 1994), *Virginia Woolf: Writers and Their Work* (Northcote House, 1997/2004), *The Tenth Muse: Writing about Cinema in the Modernist Period* (Oxford University Press, 2007) and, as co-editor, *The Cambridge History of Twentieth-Century English Literature* (Cambridge University Press, 2004).

Patrizia A. Muscogiuri is an independent scholar. She has a special interest in radical inscriptions of sea metaphors and has published widely on Virginia Woolf, modernism, film, the visual arts and cultural studies. Recent publications include 'Matchsticks out of their Boxes, from Arthur Melbourne-Cooper to Virginia Woolf', in *Modernist Objects*, ed. Xavier Kalck and Noëlle Cuny (Clemson University Press, 2020).

Derek Ryan is Senior Lecturer in Modernist Literature at the University of Kent and Director of Graduate Studies in English at Kent's Paris School of Arts and Culture. His publications in modernist studies include *Virginia Woolf and the Materiality of Theory: Sex, Animal, Life* (Edinburgh University Press, 2013) and *The Handbook to the Bloomsbury Group* (Bloomsbury, 2018). He is currently co-editing the Cambridge Edition of Woolf's *Flush: A Biography*.

Max Saunders is Professor of English at King's College London. He is the author of *Ford Madox Ford: A Dual Life* (Oxford University Press, 1996) and *Self Impression: Life-Writing, Autobiografiction, and the Forms of Modern Literature* (Oxford University Press, 2010); and the editor of five volumes of Ford's writing, including an annotated critical edition of the first volume of Ford's *Parade's End: Some Do Not . . .* (Carcanet, 2010).

Naomi Toth lectures in English literature at the Université Paris Nanterre. She has published a book-length study on modes of perception and stylistic innovation in the novels of Virginia Woolf and Nathalie Sarraute, *L'Écriture vive: Woolf, Sarraute, une autre phénoménologie de la perception* (Classiques Garnier, 2016). Her current research interests include conceptions of justice in documentary poetics and the politics of betrayal in modernist autofictional writing.

Introduction: Cross-Channel (Transmanche) Modernisms

Claire Davison, Jane Goldman and Derek Ryan

What better place to start than midway, in extracts from letters exchanged before and after a cross-Channel expedition?

> *To Vita Sackville-West*
>
> Rodmell
> Saturday 8 September [1928]
>
> Concentrate your mind upon this, and give me your answer. Suppose we start (you and I and Potto) on Saturday 22nd. Sleep in Paris. Get to SAULIEU on Monday ... Do you want to go 2nd or 1st (I insist on 1st on the boat) If first is much more comfortable, first is advisable. Not otherwise; because first class travellers are always old fat testy and smell of eau de cologne, which makes me sick. (Woolf 1975–80, vol. 3: 528)

> *To Virginia Woolf*
>
> British Embassy, Berlin
> Tuesday 11 September
>
> Your letter has caught me, as we leave early tomorrow morning. I am absolutely overjoyed to think that our France may really materialise, and I beg you to get the tickets before you have time to change your mind. (Sackville-West 1985: 298)

> *To Vita Sackville-West*
>
> 52 Tavistock Place W.C.1
>
> Oh there's a lot to talk to you about: Orlando: Radclyffe Hall: etc. I am getting a fish basket for Potto.
> Shall you be bored with me?
> As an experiment this journey interests me enormously. (Woolf 1975–80, vol. 3: 531)

> *To Virginia Woolf*
>
> Long Barn, Sevenoaks
> Wednesday 19 September
>
> I write in a hurry because I am just starting for Eton with Ben. Monday, – yes. Could you send a postcard to say
> 1) what time the boat starts,
> 2) how much I owe you for the tickets
> 3) the name of the hotel in Saulieu (Sackville-West 1985: 300)
>
> *To Virginia Woolf*
>
> Long Barn
> Friday night 5 October
>
> It was queer, reading some of your letters, in the light of having been with you so much lately. A fitful illumination played over them, – a sort of cross-light, – (do you realise that at Auppegard one is always in a cross-light? a symbolic fact which would, I feel, have had more influence on you or me, had either of us chanced to live there, than it has had on the relatively unimaginative natures of Ethel and Nan.) Well, a sort of cross-light, as I say, played across them, projected half from the rather tentative illumination of the past and half from the fuller illumination of the present. . . .
>
> Burgundy seems a dream. 'Before a joy proposed; behind, a dread.' I was very happy. Were you? I read Walter Pater on Vézelay. I say, that narthex that I kept worrying about is one of the glories of France, it seems. (Sackville-West 1985: 285, 286)

Here, within an epistolary exchange of thoughts practical, poetic, material and whimsical, heard in passing as they transit from Sussex to Berlin and back via London and Kent, is the epistemological and cultural framework that structures the present volume. The immediate context is the one, week-long, trip to France that Vita Sackville-West and Virginia Woolf made alone, in late September 1928. In symbolic, literary terms, at least, this marked the zenith of their love affair – their long-projected adventure had been organised so as to slot comfortably between any final editorial work on *Orlando: A Biography* (1928) and its publication on 11 October. Yet running through the sequence of letters written 'on the verge of my alarming holiday', as Woolf confided to her diary two days before setting out (Woolf 1977–85, vol. 3: 197), are the sorts of crossings and cruxes that index an offbeat topography of anglophone modernism as it set out across the Channel and came home across 'la Manche'.

These journeys, speculative and phenomenological, matter considerably more than place. First, the sheer practicalities of travelling: booking the tickets, choosing the degree of comfort – and thereby determining one's travelling companions – parking and getting to the boat on time. Second, the degree of fancy and fantasy that play as much a part in the move abroad as does long-acquired familiarity: the anticipation that 'our France may really materialise', and that 'Potto's' comforts have been catered for (more of whom shortly). Third, the real places on a real map that new turbine-propelled 'transmanche' ferry links had brought closer together than ever before – Newhaven, Paris, Saulieu, Dieppe and so on. Never, in peace time at least, had the Channel been so unintrusive, so easily bridged by civilians, especially for British travellers who were already so accustomed to the geography, lifestyle and language of France that even the 'relatively unimaginative natures' of their anglophone compatriots could settle easily there. Fourth, despite the cultural and practical ease of crossing the waters, the 'symbolic facts' that nevertheless infused writing about, thinking about and reliving travels to France: the 'fitful illuminations', the 'cross-light[s]', the play of dreams, intertextualities and times that refamiliarised the imaginary even as they altered and reinvented the familiar. The radical poetics of queering find their ideal space of resonance on the comfortable berths of the transmanche exchange.

Queer poetics is indeed inscribed in this modernist Channel crossing. Queer is after all aqueous, 'a continuing moment, movement, motive: recurrent, eddying, troublant', as Eve Kosofsky Sedgwick identifies: 'The word queer itself means "across" – it comes from the Indo-European root -twerkw, which also yields the German word "quer" (traverse), Latin "torquere" (twist), English "athwart"' (Sedgwick 1998: viii). And the *OED* cites as one of the earliest usages of queer in its modern sexual sense, Arnold Bennett's account of the weekly pacifist parties in Bloomsbury in 1915, hosted by Ottoline Morrell entertaining a cross-Channel crowd of Bohemian luminaries (see Bennett 1932–3: 550; Goldman 2017: 162–3). 'Potto' or 'Bosman's Potto' in full (a kind of lorisid) is Woolf's self-assigned Sapphic pet name: 'Bosman's Potto, *not* V.W. by arrangement – A finer name, don't you think?' (Woolf 1975–80, vol. 3: 456; see also Ryan 2016: 114–15). This creaturely and masculine persona (Woolf 1975–80, vol. 3: 468) peppers correspondence between the lovers. In these numerous billets-doux Potto is both co-author, with his own squiggly signature and erotic licks of the envelope (Woolf 1975–80, vol. 4: 232, 332, 388), and co-addressee (Sackville-West 1985: 300, 304). When Woolf falls ill in February 1929, Sackville-West saucily remarks on the curative qualities of their Channel crossing: 'Now look how well you were when I brought you back from France; all round and rosy, and Potto's coat a treat to see. Do you know what I believe it was, apart from 'flu? it was SUPPRESSED RANDINESS' (Sackville-West 1985: 318). Potto clearly marks a new queer subjectivity borne of their love affair, who apparently reaches his amorous apotheosis on this cross-Channel adventure, as Woolf later wrote to Sackville-West away in Porto Fino in 1930 and when passions were fading:

> Yes, it must be dull, travelling without Virginia – nobody to say Brusque – oh no Harold would know the word for rough, and so would the boys; but I daresay at Porto Fino . . . you've forgotten me, and Potto, and how we crossed the Channel, and how I wept as the white cliffs disappeared. (Woolf 1975–80, vol. 4: 197)

Woolf is referencing her own hilarious liberties with language on her Channel crossing with Sackville-West, who had overheard her lover 'asking a French seaman on the cross-channel steamer, "Est-ce-que la mer est brusque?"' (Woolf 1975–80, vol. 4: 197n2). In this context 'brusque' could be translated as 'sudden', whereas in French 'the rough sea' is more correctly 'la mer agitée'. Is Woolf here inscribing a new queer modernist discourse where the catachrestic 'mer brusque' or 'sudden sea' becomes a byword for queer erotic pleasures, an opening to jouissance, which in turn is obliterated by the white-cliffed front of hetero-normativity that the Nicolson family maintain on their cross-Channel travels? In the right company, then, Channel crossings can open travellers to the pleasures of radical experiment, thrilling and sudden aqueous plunges. Like Potto, 'brusque' is of 'a little language such as lovers use', as Louis in *The Waves* (1931) puts it (Woolf 2011: 112). Woolf, who believed she could 'cure' a bout of 'slight depression . . . by crossing the channel' (Woolf 1977–85, vol. 2: 308), resembles her canine protagonist in *Flush: A Biography* (1933), who 'was not happy until he found himself on the deck of the Channel steamer crossing to France' (Woolf 1933: 134). But in the wrong company, as also illustrated in this canine companion piece to *Orlando: A Biography*, written when ardours between Woolf and Sackville-West had cooled, a Channel crossing may turn one's sudden sea into precisely a rough one:

> It was a rough passage. The crossing took eight hours. As the steamer tossed and wallowed, Flush turned over in his mind a tumult of mixed memories – of ladies in purple plush, of ragged men with bags; of Regent's Park, and Queen Victoria sweeping past

with outriders; of the greenness of English grass and the rankness of English pavements – all this passed through his mind as he lay on deck; and, looking up, he caught sight of a stern, tall man leaning over the rail.

"Mr. Carlyle!" he heard Mrs. Browning exclaim; whereupon – the crossing, it must be remembered, was a bad one – Flush was violently sick. Sailors came running with pails and mops. ". . . he was ordered off the deck on purpose, poor dog," said Mrs. Browning. For the deck was still English; dogs must not be sick on decks. Such was his last salute to the shores of his native land. (Woolf 1933: 134–5)

If this 'rough passage' is a wink in English to Woolf's queer cross-Channel translation into the French 'mer brusque', it is nevertheless thoroughly English in its immediate context of Flush's departure in reverie from 'the greenness of English grass and the rankness of English pavements' – from, that is, the stereotypes of a pastoral imperialist ideology and the foulness of the class hierarchy on its streets, available in that pun on 'rankness'. And on this rough Channel crossing over 'la mer agitée', what gets Flush agitated to the point of vomiting is the sight of that Victorian personification of British imperialist heteronormative patriarchy, Thomas Carlyle, who so memorably stands on the other side of the vast cultural and political caesura that Woolf famously declares, in 'Character in Fiction' (1924), to have fallen 'on or about December 1910':

consider the married life of the Carlyles and bewail the waste, the futility, for him and for her, of the horrible domestic tradition which made it seemly for a woman of genius to spend her time chasing beetles, scouring saucepans, instead of writing books. All human relations have shifted – those between masters and servants, husbands and wives, parents and children. And when human relations change there is at the same time a change in religion, conduct, politics, and literature. Let us agree to place one of these changes about the year 1910. (Woolf 1986–2011, vol. 3: 421, 422)

The Channel, then, becomes a modernist caesura marking a radical, avant-garde break with tradition and the past. It is also, as the present volume explores, a chasm, a fold, a passage, a zone, and sometimes a blank, a buffer and a block, but always a site of action.

Thinking with nostalgia, apprehension, ease and anticipation across the narrow stretch of sea between England and France is of course a fundamental figure in any definition of English literature. 'In order to have ancestors by way of the mind he must cross the

Channel[,] his ancestors by way of the mind are the Greeks and the Romans' (1986–2011, vol. 6: 585), writes Woolf during the Second World War, in her unfinished essay 'Anon' (1940). She is considering William Harrison's view of the past in his book, *A Description of England in Shakespeare's Youth* (1577), where she finds his cross-Channel, abstractive classical (Greek and Roman) mind here ignores the local and contingent collective voice of the troubadour, 'Anon singing at his back door', in England. Woolf challenges this sidestepping ancestry to sketch out an alternative historiography of storytelling that could embrace voice, material change and the roaming life, albeit including other forms of Channel crossings.

Nevertheless, any sense of what the Channel represented and what was being transmitted from one side to the other was radically refashioned in the jagged context of anglophone modernism. The dawning years of the twentieth century saw the laying down of sub-sea cables that linked telephone exchanges in England and France; the 1904 Entente Cordiale celebrated the diplomatic bridging that brought an end to Anglo-French colonial tensions, even while the Edwardian pageantry that surrounded the event (and its marketing) foregrounded national pomp and glory; 1909 saw Blériot successfully fly across the Channel, an event whose imaginative expansiveness was abruptly countered less than a year later by the first cross-Channel air collision – a harsh reminder that the cross marks the intersection of lines. And indeed, this was but the first of the violent clashes that marked the geopolitical realities of the Channel that also severed the expanding, dazzling energies of emerging modernism from its haunted, haggard, post-war renewals. From 1914 to 1918, Channel crossings became markers on a complex map of submarines and mines, uniformed troops and mutilated bodies, nurses and newspapers, camouflage and conscientious objection, music and food parcels. Likewise, for the modernists whose lives, works and meetings are being traced here, the Channel had a decidedly amorphous geography and geometrics, as if in essence, form and regulations it were embodying the complex, critical intermesh of politics and aesthetics shaping the era. In a 1921 letter to Dorothy Brett, Katherine Mansfield bemoans 'that Channel which lies like a great cold sword between you and your dear love Adventure' (Mansfield 1984–2008, vol. 4: 269). By October 1922, it was 'such a big carving knife' (Mansfield 1984–2008, vol. 5: 287), but she was in France, burning her bridges and never intending to return.

However intimately familiar France as a 'garden of England' may have been, in other words, the imaginative, material and experiential markers of that familiarity were being radically destabilised, transformed and transposed as part of the drastic sociopolitical and technological upheavals of the early twentieth century. 'The queer feeling that the solid ground upon which we expected to make a safe landing has been twitched from under us', as Woolf (in a review in 1918 of Constance Garnett's translations of Anton Chekhov) says of the experience of encountering 'not known' languages, 'and there we hang asking questions in mid-air' (Woolf 1986–2011, vol. 2: 245). The renegotiation of territorial metaphors, political crisis and creative praxis that underpin the 'modernist forms of passing', which Pamela Caughie posits at the very core, the crux of the era, are thus perfectly encapsulated in the complex dynamics of change, 'more like a wave, a transfer of energy from point to point' (Caughie 2005: 401) being played out under, over and via the English Channel. Even the geometrical shaping and the naming of the treacherous waterway were apt figures of cross-currents and cross-purposes: the 'Channel' marks a waterway that is visible running west to east along the south coast of England and the north-eastern shores of France, but also a north–south sea crossing from Dover and Newhaven to Calais and Dieppe; the French 'Manche', the 'Sleeve', however, suggests a piece in a larger garment, a 'bras de mer', literally an arm of the sea.

New cheaper, quicker crossings and interlinked political alliances inevitably favoured a multiplication of crossings in the cross-Channel era that we are exploring here, as new classes of traveller, the newly defined indispensable paraphernalia of travelling and the cross-currencies of language and financial exchange along the way impacted upon the poetic forms best suited to recount the traversing of borders. Take, for instance, the 'little governesses' who began setting off on their own to take up employment on the continent – like those memorably depicted by Katherine Mansfield. Language itself inevitably misbehaves, as if revelling in the opening up of horizons and opportunities, especially for young, educated but still impoverished women:

> In the act of crossing the gangway we renounced England. The most blatant British female produced her mite of French: we 'Si vous plaît'd' one another on the deck, 'Merci'd' one another on the stairs, and 'Pardon'd' to our heart's content in the saloon. (Mansfield 2012: 226)

Take too the exponential growth of 'health tourism', as Thomas Cook and Robert Lunn designed new holiday packages for the frail, thereby seizing on more readily available, smoother and quicker transport to spas and other health resorts on the continent – which in turn fed into the narrative poetics and languages of modernism:

> The reason for poor Florence's broken years was a storm at sea upon our first crossing to Europe, and the immediate reasons for our imprisonment in that continent were doctors' orders. They said that even the short Channel crossing might well kill the poor thing. (Ford 2002: 13–14)

Within a decade, the novelty of the experience had been transformed anew with the arrival of the first car ferries, for example, and the huge shift they marked in the perception and practical experience of passing from one country to the other. Coincidentally, the service began in June 1928, the same summer that Woolf and Sackville-West planned their one and only unaccompanied escapade (if we discount the presence of Potto) to France, and in which Woolf had pictured Orlando lying in a spot 'crowned by a single oak tree', from where, occasionally, 'one could see the English Channel, wave reiterating upon wave' (Woolf 2018: 17).

There are, in other words, multiple reasons for pinpointing, conceptualising and exploring the specific paradoxes and alternations of Channel crossings in the modernist era; and the dismal state of transmanche imaginaries and Britain's ongoing constitutional crisis, which is founded on the political and cultural permeability of the waterway, makes our volume all the more timely (however distant such considerations were when the project first began). Not that we would make any claim to being pioneers in Channel crossing critical debate. In the lead up to 2004, in particular, and in the years following a host of publications looking back on a century of Anglo-French cultural exchange since the Entente Cordiale, there have been a number of essential contributions to the field. In *Bloomsbury and France*, Mary Ann Caws and Sarah Bird Wright produced a 'collective biography' detailing the influence on Vanessa Bell and Duncan Grant of French 'landscape and the light, so different from English "gloom"', and the 'civilized attitude' found there and appreciated by Leonard Woolf, as well as the numerous studies of 'French artists, writers, and historic figures' penned by Lytton Strachey, Clive Bell, Vita Sackville-West, and, perhaps most notably of all, John Maynard Keynes's ever relevant treatise, *The Economic Consequences of the Peace*, first published in 1919 (Caws and Wright 2000: 13–14). Central to Bloomsbury's relationship with French culture was Roger Fry, whose 1910 Post-Impressionist Exhibition has become emblematic of aesthetic influence across the Channel but had a very tangible effect on the artists of the time in England, being, in Vanessa Bell's words, 'a sudden pointing to a possible path, a sudden liberation' (quoted in Spalding 2016: 92). Matched to this wider influence was what Caws and Wright call a 'cross-Channel hospitality', where 'crossings and criss-crossings among friends, relatives, and domiciles are typical of modernism' (Caws and Wright 2000: 16). This is seen across modernist texts in *Franco-British Cultural Exchanges, 1880–1940: Channel Packets*, edited by Andrew Radford and Victoria Reid, which emphasises 'movement beyond, instead of consolidation within territorial borders' (2012: 16). Such cultural and especially literary movement beyond the national borders of France and Britain are placed in a broader historical context in Dominic Rainsford's *Literature, Identity and the English Channel: Narrow Seas Expanded* (2002), and *The Literary Channel: The Inter-National Invention of the Novel* (2002), edited by Margaret Cohen and Carolyn Dever, both of which chart the rise of cross-Channel formations and interchange from the eighteenth century onwards.

Like these earlier volumes, the present project stems from the double challenge of tracing and reassessing some of the key cultural partnerships and intellectual exchanges of the early twentieth century, and honing a set of critical concepts best suited to explain the networks of estrangement, alteration and reinvention that were flourishing in the modernist period. Here too, we would hardly present the challenge itself as trail blazing. If metaphorised as a form of traveller's guide exploring the workings and achievements of modernism as it crossed the border from Britain to France and back, Virginia Woolf herself had already drawn out the path even before anglophone intellectuals had taken up the term 'modernism' (which had been creeping in from France):

> Before going on a journey the question of a guide-book naturally suggests itself. Your need is not altogether simple, and, though many profess to supply it, few, when put to the test, are found to succeed. Baedeker settles your hotel and the amount you are expected to tip the waiter; but one suspects Baedeker as an art critic. The asterisk with which he directs you to the best picture and tells you to a superlative how much praise you must be prepared to expend seems too simple a solution of the difficulties of criticism. But though you consult him surreptitiously it is often solely upon him that you come to depend. His work, as generations of grateful travellers can testify, is a necessity, though hardly a luxury. . . . Sterne, when he invented the

title of Sentimental Journey, not only christened but called into existence a class of book which seems to grow more popular the more we travel and the more sentimental we become. It is their aim to provide all that Baedeker ignores; but as their aim is more ambitious so is their success very rarely so complete. (Woolf 1986–2011, vol. 1: 44)

Here then is a first sense of how setting off to the European 'mainland' entailed a redefining of manners, measures and impressions, and a new dovetailing of practical displacement and imaginary dislocation, concepts that, over recent years, have become constitutionally synonymous with modernism itself. Andrew Thacker's *Moving through Modernity: Space and Geography in Modernism* (2003), for example, and Susan Stanford Friedman's *Planetary Modernisms: Provocations on Modernity Across Time* (2015) see transport and geopolitical location as the essential components of the newly fashioned modern subjectivity. The paradoxes of transport, trespassing and translation were also the at the heart of the notion of dynamic, shifting modernisms sketched out during the agenda-setting 'Moving Modernisms' conference at the University of Oxford in 2012, or in books such as Rebecca Walkowitz's *Cosmopolitan Style: Modernism Beyond the Nation* (2007) and Jessica Berman's *Modernist Commitments: Ethics, Politics and Transnational Modernism* (2012).

Much as the present book acknowledges its debt of gratitude to these scholars paving the way, it also operates a new shift in the angle and focus of vision. It does not just seize upon the operative dynamics of passing metaphorically, or the multiple visions of estranged, deterritorialised, unfamiliar disclosures, but anchors the radical forms of modernist expression in the singular collusion of translation and movement, transport and spatial reimaginings, maps and self-reflexiveness. It works from the minor, micro odysseys that moving between degrees of familiarity on board the transmanche steamers entailed. It makes the shifting 'cross' of the 'cross-Channel' ferry into a disruptive complicating factor even as it marks a spot on a map: it looks at what gets crossed, crossed out, or just downright cross on the way – when wires and purposes are crossed and misunderstandings multiply, or when thoroughbreds and pedigrees are crossed. And even as it acknowledges that the complexity of cross-cultural encounters with their literal and metaphorical codes of translation date back to the very origins of cultural exchange, it posits a specific blend of heuristic and hermeneutic crossing taking place precisely where – precisely because – the English Channel (as well as, for writers like James Joyce and Elizabeth Bowen, the Irish Channel) ran midway.

This Channel, which had already been fantasised as an even more porous 'chunnel', was both a barrier and a bridge to artistic and cultural exchange in the first decades of the twentieth century. On the one hand, the movements, manifestos and innovations in France and the continent emerged in specific contexts and did not translate easily into a British culture emerging from the moral conservatism and realist conventions of the Victorian period. On the other hand, European modernism and its avant-garde impulses cannot, in a fundamental sense, be understood without attending to the cross-Channel 'adventures' of the writers and artists of the period. The Channel's history throughout the remainder of the twentieth century has continued this dual antagonism: from the violent exchange of gunfire and bombs (rather than swords, to recall Mansfield's metaphor) in the Second World War, to the signing of the Franco-British Treaty of Canterbury in 1986 which paved the way for the construction and operation of the Channel Tunnel. Today, the numbers of people travelling between Britain and France have never been greater, yet the politicisation of Channel crossing is part of an increasingly nationalistic and xenophobic discourse on both sides following terrorism and the Brexit referendum. At this time when swords are being sharpened, if not crossed, in the name of reactionary forces, the essays collected herein revisit and renew the radical potential of modernist cultural crossings in an effort to channel more positive, creative and collective intellectual and artistic exchanges.

Cross-Channel Modernisms is the fruit of our particular institutional cross-Channel links (between the Université Sorbonne Nouvelle–Paris 3, the University of Kent and its Paris School of Arts and Culture, and the University of Glasgow), as well as of numerous collaborations arising in the new modernist studies flourishing in transnational scholarly societies. That the editors of the present volume have chosen to embark on this cross-Channel modernist venture in the company of Virginia Woolf, above, will hardly surprise readers who know our work in Woolf studies, but the chapters that follow this Introduction consider and encounter, in focus and in passing, a host of other cross-Channel/transmanche modernists and avant-gardistes, including Mulk Raj Anand, Josephine Baker, Clive Bell, Vanessa Bell, Walter Benjamin, Henri Bergson, Elizabeth Bowen, Bryher [Annie Winifred Ellerman], Basil Bunting, Charlie Chaplin, Freddie Chevalley, Joseph Conrad, Aleister Crowley, H.D. [Hilda Doolittle], Claude Debussy, T. S. Eliot, Jean Epstein, Ford Maddox Ford, E. M. Forster, Roger Fry, Henri Gaudier-Brzeska, Winifred Gill, Nina Hamnett, Thomas Hardy, James Joyce, Roald Kristian, Valerie Larbaud, Wyndham

Lewis, Kenneth Macpherson, Katherine Mansfield, Filippo Marinetti, Christopher Nevinson, Wilfred Owen, Ezra Pound, Marcel Proust, Jean Rhys, Dorothy Richardson, Bertrand Russell, Siegfried Sassoon, Sydney Schiff and many more. The final chapter returns to Woolf in a differently imagined constellation of cross-Channel modes than those touched on here. Rather than attempt to introduce all ten essays from this first point of departure, the shoreline of the Introduction, we offer three 'Interludes' – 'Translating', 'Fashioning' and 'Mediating' – which may ferry our readers between these different modes of Channel crossing.

Read together, the essays that follow chart untold stories of artistic and intellectual endeavour back and forth across the Channel in the first decades of the twentieth century, while also examining some better-known journeys from fresh perspectives. Our contributors historicise the artistic connections and cultural exchanges between France and Britain, and propose a rich conceptual apparatus of 'crossings' and 'channellings' through which we can read modernist artworks and understand their aesthetics as emerging from, and intervening in, an always-already shifting, multivalent, transnational context. Yet, however enticing and inspirational the expanding metaphorics of crossing, transporting and dislocating, this book will constantly return to the cross-currents and cross-purposes of languages on the move: the 'cross' of the cross-Channel at Newhaven in the process of becoming the trans- of the 'transmanche'; the passageway of the Channel on the way to becoming the sleeve or handle of 'la Manche'; 'modernism' becoming always a little bit more than, a little bit less than, 'le modernisme'. The price of a return ticket, meanwhile, depending on the currency exchange, was more or less the same as an 'aller-retour'.

Bibliography

Bennett, Arnold (1932–3), *The Journals*, London: Cassells.
Berman, Jessica (2012), *Modernist Commitments: Ethics, Politics and Transnational Modernism*, New York: Columbia University Press.
Caughie, Pamela L. (2005), 'Passing as modernism', *Modernism/modernity*, 12.3: 385–406.
Caws, Mary Ann and Sarah Bird Wright (2000), *Bloomsbury and France: Art and Friends*, Oxford: Oxford University Press.
Cohen, Margaret and Carolyn Dever, eds (2002), *The Literary Channel: The Inter-National Invention of the Novel*, Princeton, NJ: Princeton University Press.

Ford, Ford Madox (2002), *The Good Soldier* [1915], ed. David Bradshaw, London: Penguin.
Goldman, Jane (2017), 'Review [*Queer Bloomsbury*, ed. Brenda Helt and Madelyn Detloff (Edinburgh: Edinburgh UP 2016)]', *Woolf Studies Annual*, 23: 161–71.
Mansfield, Katherine (1984–2008), *The Collected Letters of Katherine Mansfield*, ed. Vincent O'Sullivan and Margaret Scott, 5 vols, Oxford: Oxford University Press.
Mansfield, Katherine (2012), 'The Journey to Bruges', in *The Collected Fiction of Katherine Mansfield, 1898–1915*, ed. Gerri Kimber and Vincent O'Sullivan, Edinburgh: Edinburgh University Press, pp. 224–8.
Radford, Andrew and Victoria Reid (2012), *Franco-British Cultural Exchanges, 1880–1940: Channel Packets*, Basingstoke: Palgrave Macmillan.
Rainsford, Dominic (2002), *Literature, Identity and the English Channel: Narrow Seas Expanded*, Basingstoke: Palgrave Macmillan.
Ryan, Derek (2016), 'Orlando's queer animals', in *A Companion to Virginia Woolf*, ed. Jessica Berman, Oxford: Wiley-Blackwell, pp. 108–20.
Sackville-West, Vita (1985), *The Letters of Vita Sackville-West to Virginia Woolf*, ed. Louise DeSalvo and Mitchell Leaska, New York: William Morrow.
Sedgwick, Eve (1998), *Tendencies* [1993], New York: Routledge.
Spalding, Frances (2016), *Vanessa Bell: Portrait of the Bloomsbury Artist* [1983], London: I. B. Taurus.
Stanford Friedman, Susan (2015), *Planetary Modernisms: Provocations on Modernity Across Time*, New York: Columbia University Press.
Thacker, Andrew (2003), *Moving through Modernity: Space and Geography in Modernism*, Manchester: Manchester University Press.
Walkowitz, Rebecca (2007), *Cosmopolitan Style: Modernism Beyond the Nation*, New York: Columbia University Press.
Woolf, Virginia (1933), *Flush: A Biography*, London: The Hogarth Press.
Woolf, Virginia (1975–80), *The Letters of Virginia Woolf*, ed. Nigel Nicolson assisted by Joanne Trautmann, 6 vols, London: The Hogarth Press.
Woolf, Virginia (1977–85), *The Diary of Virginia Woolf*, ed. Anne Olivier Bell, assisted by Andrew McNeillie, 5 vols, London: The Hogarth Press.
Woolf, Virginia (1986–2011), *The Essays of Virginia Woolf*, ed. Andrew McNeillie and Stuart N. Clarke, 6 vols, London: The Hogarth Press.
Woolf, Virginia (2011), *The Waves* [1931], ed. Michael Herbert and Susan Sellers, Cambridge: Cambridge University Press.
Woolf, Virginia (2018), *Orlando: A Biography* [1928], ed. Suzanne Raitt and Ian Blyth, Cambridge: Cambridge University Press.

Interlude: Translating

Derek Ryan

'Much of Anglophone modernism was constituted by translation' (Piette 2018: 371). In his entry on 'Translation' in *The Edinburgh Dictionary of Modernism*, Adam Piette underlines the dizzying array of cultural and linguistic translation activity that influenced or was produced by modernists, primarily, though not exclusively, in Britain and Ireland. As Piette recounts here, and more fully in his introduction to an earlier special issue on 'Modernism and Translation' for *Translation and Literature*, aesthetic innovation and avant-garde creeds from the continent found homes in little magazines and small presses, while full-length works by the likes of Marcel Proust, Fyodor Dostoevsky and Anton Chekhov were given major translations. To mention only a handful of examples, writers including T. S. Eliot, Ezra Pound, Virginia Woolf and Vita Sackville-West were involved in translating the work of others, while Samuel Beckett translated his own work and James Joyce closely supervised translations of *Ulysses* and *Finnegans Wake* (see Piette 2003). France stands out in this story as the most important influence on the English literary and artistic scene, though what tends to be emphasised is that which anglophone culture belatedly learned from the continent – captured most famously, perhaps, in the example of Roger Fry collecting artworks to display at the 1910 Post-Impressionist Exhibition at the Grafton Galleries in London. Less attention has been paid, within anglophone modernist studies at least, to the back-and-forth nature of the relationship and how it was facilitated by various modes of Channel crossing. The question of how to account for the undoubted influence of France on specific instances of English modernism without reducing it to a one-way process is at the heart of this book's opening section.

Focusing on different practices and conceptualisations of modernist translation, each chapter here attends to francophone texts and contexts as much as to the anglophone. Claire Davison charts the changing significance of the slippery term 'rhythm' from the original philosophical texts of Henri Bergson through the publication of John Middleton Murry's *Rhythm* magazine. Max Saunders explains how Ford Madox Ford's efforts to find exactitude in translation could paradoxically lead to a sizable helping of translator's licence when it came to accuracy in description, illustrated by Ford's account of translating one sentence from Gustav Flaubert's *Trois Contes* (1877). Emily Eells looks closely at correspondences between Proust and Sidney Schiff, showing how the latter's desire to translate the former's multi-volume novel was finally realised after Scott Moncrieff's death with the much-maligned rendering into English, under Schiff's pen-name of Stephen Hudson, of the last volume of *À la recherche du temps perdu* (1913–27). Even when these essays are focused on translations from French to English, however, the story rarely follows a linear pattern. Taking her cue from Woolf's essay 'On Not Knowing French', Davison is interested in 'what can be gained, feared, lost and found *only* when texts, languages and cultural materiality are approached from outside *and* inside, and then side-by-side, crossing divides'. The to-and-fro nature of linguistic Channel hopping is underlined by Saunders, too, in his efforts to uncover how Ford would translate from English to French and then back to English in order to enhance his writing; what Saunders calls 'Fordian translationese' created 'a language which incorporates linguistic diversity'. This give-and-take of aesthetic crossings is placed in a more interpersonal light by Eells when she shows how the friendship forged between Proust and Schiff was one of 'mutual self-interest', whereby Schiff 'wanted Proust to help him get his own work published in France' at the same time as Proust saw an opportunity to sell his work in England through Schiff's associates.

The linguistic and personal encounters explored in the following essays do not, however, exist in a closed Anglo-French circuit. They instead open channels to the 'transnational' (see Berman 2012), 'global' (see Doyle and Winkiel 2005; Wollaeger and Eatough 2012) or 'planetary' (see Stanford Friedman 2015) dimensions of modernism. Readers will note that Davison's approach to (mis) translations of 'rhythm' is played out in little magazines packed with international contributors, while this transnational dimension is explicitly signposted by Saunders when he describes how Ford's literary impressionism is not only constituted via 'reverberations of languages, people and texts across the Channel' but that the '*trans-Manche* is always doubled, for Ford, by the transatlantic', notably through American expatriates such as Gertrude Stein, Ernest Hemingway and Djuna Barnes who contributed – and indeed 'who began to dominate' – alongside British, Irish and Europeans to the *transatlantic review* in post-war Paris. While Eells is most concerned with Schiff's connection to Proust, she importantly sets this relationship in a wider international context of the 'ostentatious promotion of modernism' which the Schiffs initiated through their 1922 dinner party at the Hôtel Majestic to celebrate the staging of Stravinsky's *Renard*. This gathering has become more famous as the site of the first and only (rather disappointing) meeting of Proust and Joyce, but insatiable appetite for the Ballets Russes is what enticed the international crowd.

If the Anglo-French focus of these three chapters channels centrifugal networks, however, the essays also reveal how translation sometimes leads to crossed wires. In this sense, they add weight to Miller and Rodgers's intervention in a 2018 special cluster of *Modernism/modernity*, where they caution that scholars within modernist studies should be alert to the limits of the very 'connectivity' that 'has been the catalyst that revitalized sizable quadrants of the field':

> We are scholars who, in our own work, have explored modes of interconnection across a number of sites, texts, and figures. But like many others before us, we also acknowledge the pitfalls of connectivity, and in a moment when the map of global modernisms seems increasingly networked, it seems timely to pause and consider the kinds of work connectivity does and doesn't do – and about connection's unintended effects. Furthermore, we want to consider how intertextual and linguistic disconnection formed both the modernisms that feel familiar (national, regional, and global) and those we have yet to recognize or have possibly misconstrued. If we set aside our predisposition to celebrate connection and to mourn disconnection, and instead view them as integral to one another's functions, the field before us can look refreshingly unfamiliar. (Miller and Rodgers 2018)

To return to the seemingly familiar territory of modernist connections between France and England is precisely to make unfamiliar crossings. The imperative in our contributors' essays may be to laud connectivity, but they refuse to shy away from the disconnections and cultural schisms revealed through their chosen cross-Channel relationships. Here we can consider Davison's point about the intellectual currency of 'rhythm' depending on a departure from its understanding and reception in Bergson's home country; or Saunders's reminder about how Ford's 'vision of literary transnationalism is a pre-post-colonial one' and therefore 'representative of the period in coming mainly from the imperial powers rather than the colonies'; or finally, how Schiff's translation was riddled with errors in content and style. 'Nowhere', Miller and Rodgers conclude, 'are the limits and risks of connectivity and networks clearer than in the fields and practices of translation – perhaps the quintessential act of connecting, while differentiating, two literary texts, figures, spheres, or media' (Miller and Rodgers 2018).

'Translating', then, is chosen as this opening section heading in order to emphasise the ongoing shifts in how the modernists read and wrote across linguistic and cultural differences, as well as how critics continue to make sense of these connections and disjunctions. In all three essays, the very writing about translation involves numerous acts of translating texts, contexts and concepts, whether the cross-Channel encounter under scrutiny was sparked by aesthetic experiment, intellectual collaboration, professional ambition or awkward dinner party conversation.

Bibliography

Berman, Jessica (2012), *Modernist Commitments: Ethics, Politics, and Transnational Modernism*, New York: Columbia University Press.

Doyle, Laura and Laura Winkiel, eds (2005), *Geomodernisms: Race, Modernism, Modernity*. Bloomington: Indiana University Press.

Miller, Joshua L. and Gayle Rodgers (2018), 'Only disconnect?: The flickering circuits of modernist translation', special cluster on 'Translation and/as Disconnection', *Modernism/modernity* Print Plus 3.3. https://modernismmodernity.org/forums/translation-disconnection (last accessed 30 September 2019).

Piette, Adam (2003), 'Introduction: modernism and translation', *Translation and Literature*, 12.1: 1–17.

Piette, Adam (2018), 'Translation', in *The Edinburgh Dictionary of Modernism*, ed. Vassiliki Kolocotroni and Olga Taxidou, Edinburgh: Edinburgh University Press, pp. 379–83.

Stanford Friedman, Susan (2015), *Planetary Modernisms: Provocations on Modernity Across Time*, New York: Columbia University Press.
Wollaeger, Mark and Matt Eatough, eds (2012), *The Oxford Handbook of Global Modernisms*, Oxford: Oxford University Press.

Chapter 1

On Unknowing French? *Rhythm* and *Le Rythme* on a Cross-Channel Exchange

Claire Davison

'On Not Knowing French' is a fascinating review which marked Virginia Woolf's official debut in France as a 'femme de lettres'. Published in French on the front page of *Le Figaro* on 10 February 1929, three days before publication in Britain, it was a commissioned contribution which followed her being awarded the 'Prix Femina – Vie Heureuse' for *To the Lighthouse* the year before.[1] It was Woolf's first opportunity to address an eminent French readership, demanding a theme, voice and mode of address suited to the occasion. Her essay's explicit purpose is to review *Climats*, a new novel by the French author, biographer, translator and staunch Anglophile André Maurois, who was then enjoying a successful literary career on both sides of the Channel. Rather than tackling the topic head on, however, the reviewer begins by reflecting on what reading and being read in translation, either side of the Channel, might mean. The opening gambit runs as follows:

> One scarcely dare say it, but it is true – nobody knows French but the French themselves. Every second Englishman reads French, and many speak it, and some write it, and there are a few who claim – and who shall deny them? – that it is the language of their dreams. But to know language one must have forgotten it, and that is a stage that one cannot reach without having absorbed words unconsciously as a child. In reading a language that is not one's own, consciousness is awake, and keeps us aware of the surface glitter of the words; but it never suffers them to sink into that region of the mind where old habits and instincts roll them around and shape them a body rather different from their faces. (Woolf 2009: 5)

It is an elegantly framed, somewhat deferential preliminary statement, paying homage to a form of 'exception culturelle française' – a national birthright bestowing linguistic finesse, Cartesian rationality and chic refinement on the French native speaker. However much one may aspire to proficiency in the French language, or savour their literature, Woolf seems to concede, one is doomed to fall short: there is no hope of attaining native competence.

But these are Woolf's opening remarks, launching one of her classic 'But' paragraphs[2] where commonplaces and contradictions are exposed so as to better dispel them. There is consequently much more to this courteous lip service paid to French linguistic and intellectual dexterity than meets the eye, as the final sentence quoted above had already subtly implied: the public face is 'rather different from' the hidden body. This mischievous ambivalence continues in a deft shift in the implied addressee – from the presumably native French *Figaro* reader to the Englishman who had presumed his mastery of the French language. A more obvious volte-face soon follows, which clarifies the initial prevarications and expedites the linguistically hobbled reader on an intensely fulfilling, sensually alert discovery of a text – which they access precisely *because* they lack the inborn, intellectual assurance of the native speaker:

> English – the ordinary daily English of which most books are made – [is] as colourless, as tasteless as water. French, even the French of daily use, has wine in it; it sparkles, it tingles; it has savour. Here and there, in Saint Simon for instance a curious word unknown and therefore uncoloured by habit, emerges, so that one can feel it, and see it apart from the text and wonder for a moment what sort of meaning we shall fill it with when we have looked it up in the dictionary. (Woolf 2009: 4)

In other words, behind the veil of respectful courtesy, there is also a gentle reminder to the French that native reading habits which rely on an innate sense of linguistic mastery tend to be complacent, content with face value, while the fortunate foreigner will be rewarded for slower, more tentative incursions into unfamiliar words and worlds glimmering beneath the surface.

My preoccupation here is very similar, offering a cross-Channel perspective on what can be gained, feared, lost and found *only* when texts, languages and cultural materiality are approached from outside *and* inside, and then side by side, crossing divides. Crossing from the localist geographies and mindscapes of little magazines to the globalist transpositions inherent in textual circulation,[3] I will consider one 'somewhat fuzzy concept' (Miao 2016: 193): the *almost* transparent, *near* homophonic, homographic word 'rhythm'. It soon turns out that behind the apparently modest cross-Channel transfer from 'rhythm' to 'rythme', there is 'an alternative history of an idea' (Boym 2010: 5–7) to be found, in which resonances are decidedly different, and less compatible. What might this imply in terms of a specifically Anglo-French perspective on modernism?

Who would deny that in 1910–11 'rhythmic expansion and vitality [were] in the air in this country' (Carter 1911a: 36), making 'rhythm' a watchword and slogan of all the material forms and modes of early twentieth-century anglophone modernism?[4] It was to France that those looking for rhythm tended to head; if drama critic Huntly Carter's columns in the *New Age* are to be believed, it was a land so totally saturated in rhythm, of a new, distinctly Bergsonian variety, that the Channel itself was transfigured once the shores of France hove into sight:[5]

> Crossing to Paris I was given a suitable reminder of what the new movement in art and the new *intuition* really are. From Newhaven to Dieppe the sea spread like a waveless plain saturated with vaporous air. Trailing *rhythmically* across this greenplain were soft amethyst columns of *vibrating* light that dipped far above and below into the sea-*dissolved* air and the air-dissolved sky, seeking infinity islanded by the vast world of *consciousness*. From Dieppe to Paris there were corresponding symbols of the *rhythm and continuity of life*. . . . in all these were signs of *creative evolution*. The new *intuition* is the apprehension of Reality underlying forms of *life*, of things *living and evolving*. (Carter 1911a: 82, emphasis added)

Once in Paris, the dazzled Englishman discovered a land where the pulse of life was more intense and where metropolitan rhythms promised a heady world of sensuous desire, urban grandeur and intellectual acuity:

> The intuitional philosophy of Bergson – a system of philosophy for elevating and making vision more penetratingly human – has so taken possession of Paris that the spirit of it seems to fill every place. I have heard it discussed when seated at the long glittering café that shoulders the perpetual mass of the magnificent Renaissance Opera House breasting the broad boulevards that flow away in leagues of rhythmical lustre. (Carter 1911a: 44)

Even discounting the dithyrambic raptures of youth and the exoticisation of the foreign, it is still hard not to concede Carter's point. Over the past two decades, Paris had attracted (to name but the best known examples) the Scottish Rhythmists and Fauvism, Isadora Duncan's neo-Hellenism, Jaques-Dalcroze's Eurhythmics, Stanislavski's Moscow Arts Theatre, the Ballets Russes, and a host of international political exiles dreaming of new world orders; the city harboured the Western world's best known salons, cosmopolitan cafes and jazz cabarets in three separate hubs of creative energy – Montmartre, Montparnasse and the Left Bank. The birthplace of Bergson, in other words, was synonymous with creative dynamics and protracted intellectual philosophising.

The lure of the capital inspired comparable enthusiasm and exuberance in John Middleton Murry and J. D. Fergusson, prompting them to launch the now iconic review *Rhythm*, in Paris, in summer 1911. With its bold visual pragmatics, confident cosmopolitan outlook and bright-eyed correlation of brutality, unbridled modernist energies and an aesthetically driven ideal state whose twin tutelary deities were Bergson and rhythm,[6] everything about the magazine denoted the effervescence of the era:

> The philosophy of Bergson has of late come to a tardy recognition in England. In France it is a living force. It is the open arrival of the supremacy of the intuition, of the superior vision of the artist in form, in words, in meaning. (Murry 1911a: 9)

Retrospectively, the review also stands as a visionary modernist prototype for a future that wasn't to be; it marks a heady cusp moment, midway between *fin de siècle* aestheticism and revolutionary iconoclasm, that was about to be shattered and entirely reconfigured by the First World War:

> Our intention is to provide art, be it drawing, literature or criticism, which shall be vigorous, determined, which shall have its roots below the surface and be the rhythmical echo of the life with which it is in touch. Both in its pity and its brutality it shall be real. (Murry 1911b: 36)

All this is, of course, perfectly familiar – so familiar, in fact, that the very self-evidence of a supposedly 'new rhythm' radiating from and in France ought to set alarm bells ringing. As Woolf gently reminds us in 'On Not Knowing French', one should beware when foreign words have too much power: 'When we are thus susceptible, when influences and suggestions of this kind have such power over us, who can say how insidiously our critical sense may not be seduced and the object of criticism transformed?' (Woolf 2009: 6). What if our critical sense had been seduced by rhythm? The potentially misleading weight of legacy when staking out the ambiguous territory of the 'new' has been fruitfully explored in recent years, transforming our understanding of the 'complex lines of connection and difference running between the final decades of the nineteenth century and the opening decades of the twentieth' (Binckes 2010: 42–6). My focus on 'rhythm' here explores exactly these complex lines, but is predicated less on chronological than on spatial, *bi-localist*, dynamics. How exchangeable, in other words, were French *rythmes* and philosophical concepts drawn from Bergson? It turns out that reservations on the grounds that the object of criticism had indeed been seduced or transformed were being expressed even as the dreams of modernist rhythmic bliss were first broadcast.[7] One of the earliest warnings in print came from a Mr Gustav Hübener from Göttingen, responding to Carter's *New Age* article the previous week:

> Sir, – I hope to correct the impression Mr. Huntly Carter had of the all-pervading influence of Bergson in Paris, when I state here my observation that the great intuitional philosopher is very popular among foreign artists and students in the Latin Quarter, but not at all among Frenchmen. I asked several students at the Sorbonne, and especially members of the Ecole Normale Supérieure, who represent fairly well the tendencies of the young French generation, for an explanation of this apparently queer fact. This was mostly the answer: 'You see, we Frenchmen are by tradition, education and temperament rationalists. We don't trust a man who puts at the end of his thinking, as the solution to all problems, the word 'intuition'. (Hübener 1911: 94)

After publishing John Middleton Murry's spirited rejoinder the following week, *New Age* let matters drop.

The authority with which Hübener states his case, however, and his sometimes discomfiting counter-arguments invite reflection. Reconstructing the brief polemic reveals that Hübener was a modern languages and philosophy student studying with Husserl; in other words, his agenda was clearly more complex than what might first be supposed. Such provisos notwithstanding, however, the underlying doubts remain: How reliable are these suspicions allegedly circulating at the Sorbonne? How did Paris feel to the French? What did the

French feel about Bergson? Were French artists 'primitively yawping' in time with the primeval or barbaric rhythms in the air, as Holbrook Jackson claimed in *Rhythm* (Jackson 1911: 9)?[8] A timely coincidence offers a revealing first answer: just months before *Rhythm* first came out, a new review, *Le Rythme – magazine militant*, was being announced in two French little magazines.[9] It sought to be affordable (30 centimes), eclectic both in readership (addressing the passionate rather than the specialised), and in coverage, accepting contributions only if they were unpublished and new.

With its head offices in the 7th arrondissement, and a monthly public reception hour (9 p.m. on the first Monday of the month) at 1, rue de Fleurus, in the 6th, the review would indeed seem to promise authentic insights into the arts of the Left Bank, in just the sector where Murry and Fergusson were talking *Rhythm*.[10] Despite its promising subtitle ('magazine militant'), however, a glance at the cover pages of *Rhythm* and *Le Rythme* side by side is a first indication of the different faces of 'militantisme' either side the Channel (see Figure 1.1).[11] *Rhythm*'s stark bold print, lino cuts and sweeping lines are all the harsher compared

Figure 1.1 Cover images for the first issues of (a) *Rhythm* and (b) *Le Rythme*, designed by J. D. Fergusson and Camille Schuwer respectively. *Rhythm* reproduced from the Modernist Journals Project (searchable database). Brown and Tulsa Universities, ongoing. http://www.modjourn. org. *Le Rythme*, private collection; available on Les Petites Revues (searchable database). http://petitesrevues.blogspot.com/

Figure 1.2 *Le Rythme*, cover page for regular issues from no. 2 onward, designed by G. Lecornu. *Le Rythme*, private collection; available on Les Petites Revues (searchable database). http://petitesrevues.blogspot.com/

to the classical proportion, symmetry, restraint and balance on *Le Rythme*'s first cover, or the 'Belle Époque' grace and sketchy handcraft of *Le Rythme* from the second issue onwards (Figure 1.2). Similarly, the gender politics of upfront nudity and sexual self-assuredness stand out all the more starkly in contrast with a suggestively half-draped allegorical or neoclassical 'Semeuse' type.[12] The contents pages, however, seem to indicate more insightful parallels in the pages to come. Like its Parisian-born anglophone counterpart *Rhythm*, *Le Rythme* announces: 'Features', 'Poetry', 'Short stories', 'Philosophy', 'Theatre Reviews' and a 'What's On' summary of art exhibitions. It thus appears a reliable source of information on what France had to say on matters of rhythm, and the contemporary art world.

The results come as something of a surprise. An impassioned 'Anatomy of Theatre' gives a rather less enticing view of Parisian artistic life than most modernist memoirs and literary histories suggest. According to 'Desforges', the columnist, contemporary audiences fall into the following categories:

> 'Foreign rastas[13] counting on free shows to learn the language'
> 'Pimps, horse traders, jewellery hawkers hoping to find trade outlets'
> 'Society women vaguely involved in literary and charitable works, side-line bartering and gallant brokering'

'competitors tensely fearing the show will be a success, and jovial whenever they see a flop'
'critics – a complex mixture of jealousy and priestly vocation'
'failed actors who haunt the auditoriums since they can't make it to the stage, rendered overwrought by their own dramas'.
('Desforges' 1911: 6)[14]

The creative writing sections are equally intriguing. In mood and style the dominant mode is languorously *fin de siècle*, with titles such as 'Je rêve d'amour', 'Invocation', 'Prière –poëme pour elle', 'L'Heure d'amour', 'Résignation'.[15] The tone is disabused, melancholy and retrospective; the pulse is alexandrine, the rhyming schemes are classical:

> Tu as raison, ma blonde amie. Je ne suis pas fait pour aimer. Mais pour souffrir
> [You are right, my blonde friend. I am not made for love, but for suffering] (Albert-Jean 1911: 14)

> Je rêve d'un amour couleur de feuilles mortes . . .
> et que nous sentirions près de s'éteindre en nous,
> tel un lys effeuillé que la rafale emporte ('E. M-R' 1911: 12)[16]

Of the various prose poems and short fiction, the longest is 'L'inventoriée', a wry, somewhat condescending cautionary tale by Banville d'Hostel on the woes and wiles of 'l'attraction féminine' and the mysteries of the female soul, much in the vein of Daudet's 'La chèvre de M. Séguin'. It depicts the downfall of Joella, a manicurist's daughter, who encounters a medium, a former disciple of Mesmer; lured from the safety of home, she finds her come-uppance (D'Hostel 1911: 5–7). The dated theme, narrator's voice, embedded narrative structure, tone and classic sexual politics recall the popular 'penny shockers' of mid- to late-nineteenth-century magazines, and frustrate the critic hunting for signs of modernist writing and 'rhythm' in any possible mode. The same, however, is true of the first fictional prose to appear in Murry's *Rhythm*, which was faulted, from the outset, for its inconsistent avant-garde stance and aesthetics, notably in terms of prose.[17] Issue 1's 'The Death of Devil' by Hall Ruffy, or Arthur Crossthwaite's 'Ennui' are as *fin de siècle* in character as 'L'inventoriée', for example. Similarly, the rather dated aesthetics of the prose pieces in *Rhythm* by the soon-to-be-labelled 'Fantaisiste' poet Francis Carco are easily camouflaged by their being in French

(Carco 1911a and 1911b: 20–1).[18] As Binckes observes, Carco's 'Aix en Provence' is 'markedly similar' to Banville d'Hostel's 'Midi' in *Le Rythme* (Binckes 2010: 87). Carco's short prose poem 'Les huit danseuses' (1911), meanwhile, with its neoclassical, Botticelli feel, would be perfectly in keeping with *fin de siècle* images of Isadora Duncan's 'Isadorables' or the figure on the cover of *Le Rythme*.

Print styles, page layout and juxtaposed or complementary iconography likewise mark stark differences in editorial policy and aesthetic creed between *Rhythm* and *Le Rythme*. *Le Rythme* favours impressionistic, suggestive sketches in harmony with the poetic voice, and inclining in favour of sentimentalism and empathy rather than outspokenness and contrast. *Rhythm*'s bolder linographs stand out in starker, more ironic relief, when viewed in parallel (see Figure 1.3).

Iconographic selection suggests postlapsarian desire and dismay on the one hand (*Rythme*), and a primitive, Edenic abundance on the other (*Rhythm*). Crestfallen or alluringly glimpsed female figures, with loosely dishevelled hair and half-veiled faces, alongside despairing artists, are the dominant visual motifs throughout the first four volumes of *Le Rythme*, where *Rhythm* favours starkly

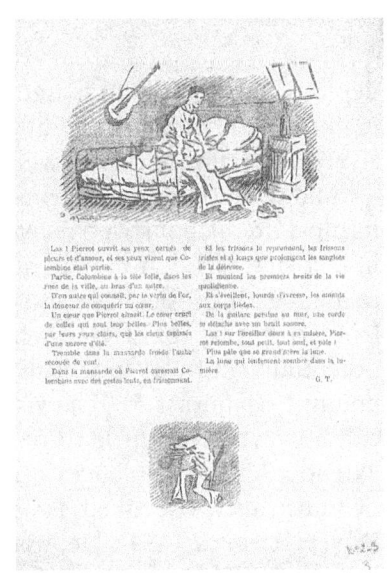

Figure 1.3 Page layout and visuals in (a) *Rhythm* 1.1, p. 12 and (b) *Le Rythme* 2, p. 7. *Rhythm* reproduced from the Modernist Journals Project (searchable database). Brown and Tulsa Universities, ongoing. http://www.modjourn.org. *Le Rythme*, private collection.

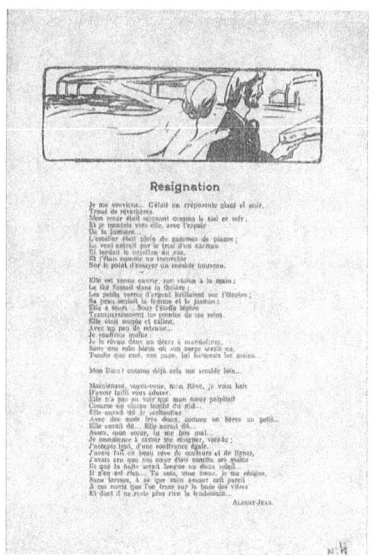

Figure 1.4 (a) André Derain's 'Creation' in *Rhythm* 1.3, p. 28. (b) G. Lecornu's 'Dessin' in *Le Rythme* 4.10. *Rhythm* reproduced from the Modernist Journals Project (searchable database). Brown and Tulsa Universities, ongoing. http://www.modjourn.org. *Le Rythme*, private collection.

depicted beasts and nude figures (Figure 1.4). The fact that *Rhythm* includes women artists, while *Le Rythme*'s contributors are exclusively male, undoubtedly weighs in the balance here.

And what of music, bearing in mind that, of all the arts, 'rhythm' is its most literal, constitutive feature? Musical coverage in both reviews in fact suggests that in neither language was a sense of 'rhythm' correlated with musical curiosity or knowledge. In *Le Rythme*, apart from one very brief summary of forthcoming concerts, the only potentially musical modernist resonances are in an etching, 'Clair de Lune' (Figure 1.5). The visual aesthetics are sketchy and whimsical, however, with little to recall the harmonic experimentalism and extended chord sequences associated with Debussy's 'impressionistic' musicality, as evoked, for example, by Rollo H. Myers in *Rhythm* (Myers 1911: 29–34). Debussy's name is cited by *Rhythm* contributors in a number of loose definitions of French modernism and rhythmic modernity,[19] and the article by Myers offers vibrant insights into pictographic and colour techniques in sound, but even these evocations of Debussy's rhythms are decidedly blurry: 'And his rhythms are marvellous. Rhythm in his hands is as expressive as harmony,

Figure 1.5 (a) Jessie Dismorr's 'Isadora' in *Rhythm* 1.2, p. 20. (b) Marcel Gromaire's 'Clair de Lune' in *Le Rythme* 2, p. 17. *Rhythm* reproduced from the Modernist Journals Project (searchable database). Brown and Tulsa Universities, ongoing. http://www.modjourn.org. *Le Rythme*, private collection.

and in welding the two he is without a rival' (Myers 1911: 33). Notwithstanding such vagaries in terms of rhythmic definitions, Myers's essay is ambitious and progressive in terms of musicology; it remains a one-off contribution, however, and music is hardly mentioned other than via a composer's name in subsequent issues of *Rhythm*.[20]

What about the vital rhythms flourishing in the cultural and intellectual milieu of Paris? These are best reflected in a regular column, a 'Review of Reviews', offering extended coverage of the contemporary print world, and a reader's questionnaire in the second issue, 'Que Faut-il penser de l'élément amateur dans toutes les branches de la production intellectuelle?'[21] with answers published in the fourth and fifth issues. To start with respondents to the questionnaire, Issue 4 includes seven readers' comments, and promises more in the months to come. Characteristic responses include the following:

> 'Long live the talented amateur' (Max Daireaux).
> 'There should be a law forbidding the sale or exhibition of works by amateurs. They are by and large useless and pretentious, the

worst enemies of true artists whom they pillage mercilessly' (J.-F. Louis Merlet).

'I sincerely believe amateurs should be guillotined, for if we do nothing more than lock them up, they might still go on with their industrious labours in the comfort of our republican prisons' (Gaston Derys).[22]

Even allowing for a touch of irony, the keynote remains a suspicion of novelty and newcomers, and a concern with staunchly traditional aesthetics.

By far the most illuminating section for any scholar looking in parallel at the little magazines world in Paris and London is the 'Review of Reviews' extending over four double pages.[23] It begins with a synopsis of the review market, before passing in detail over fifteen to twenty separate reviews, with comments on various contributors, events covered and editorial policy. The column gained in length from one issue to the next. Useful as it is as a reminder of the huge buoyancy of the market, however, the general tendency is towards caustic commentaries that deplore the decadence or philistinism of the present. These are quoted at some length here to provide a more convincing array of examples:

> [From the introduction]
> 'About Little Magazines'
> Our era of motor sports and 50-centime cinema is heartily indifferent to the intellectual efforts of the Left Bank. The alleys of the Luxembourg are overflowing with those left dejected after short-lived triumphs. This is because, despite appearances to the contrary, the skies are too restricted, and when the reputation of a mock-negro boxer crosses the oceans, there is not enough breathing space for the old sorts, the Miltons, Pascals and Schillers.
> If there is such a thing as decadence, this is it, and it comes straight from America. With just a touch of cerebral muscle.
>
> [On best-selling magazines]
> Good at calming panics of any sort, they alone attract readers other than a few luke-warm Voltaires: elderly ladies who were once cultivated, and retired professors – these are the only readers in France today.
>
> [On new reviews and little magazines]
> This is where you can find the sap rising, youth, audacity, the future. . . . if you can hunt through the half-baked whimpering of

babes who are but teething, little starchy maidens educated by old spinsters preoccupied only with scissors and sterility, and of course those hurling themselves headlong into the ring who risk emerging with a bulging black eye like second-rate suburban boxers who missed a punch.[24]

Discounting the carping tones, the wit and irony of which remain perfectly conventional, the column offers an extensive survey of Paris magazines, and indicates how a small group hoping to defend the arts and make their mark read their way through the production of the day.

So, what coverage was there of rhythm, Bergson, Parisian artworlds and vital new energies? The single most representative answer is in *Rhythm* and *Le Rythme*'s handling of 'the present Maeterlinck–Bergson cult' (Whitby 1911: 109), since, on both sides of the Channel, Maurice Maeterlinck's name was almost systematically coupled with rhythm.[25] *Le Rythme* devoted a special issue to the playwright in June 1911, subsequent to his being awarded the Nobel Prize in Literature. Here, extensive coverage is given to his biography, spiritual creed, stagecraft and aesthetics, with close focus on a contemporary production of *Blue Bird*, notable for a 'pursuit of truth', and its 'simplicity, humble beauty, gentle joy, love and truth' (Leblanc 1911: 8–10). However, the visual presentation of the review, the largely deferential, intimist tone (assured above all by contributions from his partner, Georgette Leblanc, a renowned operatic soprano, presented here, however, in her role as tenderly loving helpmate), and the series of first-hand testimonies suggest a more mainstream audience is being targeted (Figure 1.6); Maeterlinck's symbolism and spiritual heritage is broadly evoked, but there are no suggestions of any more contemporary, modernist resonances.

Maeterlinck appealed less to *Rhythm* contributors, however. In the article on Debussy, Myers insists on the aesthetic closeness between the composer and playwright ('no one can convey more perfectly the peculiar, poignant remoteness of Maeterlinckian romance than Claude Debussy'; Myers 1911: 34), and Georges Banks suggests a bold stage set for *Monna Vanna* in the third issue (Banks 1911: 21). The only other fleeting mentions are in contributions in French. In *New Age*, meanwhile, Huntly Carter was deeming Maeterlinck to be on 'a receding horizon' of writers 'who persistently sought words full of music and strange suggestions', while 'new and vital men' come to the front 'to cast overboard the word association' of the older generation (Carter 1911a: 44). Admittedly, the Parisian production

Figure 1.6 Cover page 'Special Issue – Maurice Maeterlinck', *Le Rythme*, June 1911. *Le Rythme*, private collection.

of Maeterlinck's 'third-rate' *Blue Bird* finds favour with Carter, on account of its 'Bergsonian' spirit which nourishes' and 'vitalises' (43) stagecraft in keeping with 'modern principles of continuity and rhythm' to create 'rhythm and vibrating atmosphere' (45). It could hardly count as 'Parisian', however: it was a Moscow Arts Theatre production, directed by Stanislavski. Meanwhile, in *Le Rythme*, there are no explicit evocations of Bergson; nor indeed is there of rhythm – unless 'rhythm' in the Reviews section implies taking the intellectual pulse of the capital. Even if this were the case, the pulse rate is decidedly slower than Carter's or Murry's when they perused the city.

Le Rythme magazine, in other words, fails to shed light on 'rythme' and how it equates with Bergsonism. The matter is further complicated by a brief detour via the 'more mainstream and powerful' *Nouvelle Revue française* (NRF) (Brooker et al. 2013: 33), the foremost review in France, founded in 1908, which, with the *Mercure de France*, were seen as solid, reliable indicators of France's intellectual avant-garde and cultural tradition, with sustained readerships both sides of the Channel. From 1910 to 1912, however, there are only fleeting allusions to Bergson in the NRF, all of which are in reviews or comments in passing; none of these express any great warmth. In fact, the only specific discussions of Bergson are in

1912 reviews of Julien Benda's much-applauded critique of Bergsonian theories of time. This comes as no surprise if we recall the rather reluctant reception of the philosopher in France, as Hübener had so rightly recalled. The Sorbonne, which delivered Bergson's doctorate in philosophy, proved reluctant to employ him, a disregard offset by his decidedly warmer reception in Britain.[26]

Nor is the NRF better situated to further any enquiry into rhythm of a new, Bergsonian, variety. No issue published between 1910 and 1911 yokes the two, in fact, although inevitably evocations of 'rythme' are widespread. Two detailed studies of 'rythme' however, are to be found: the first in an article entitled 'Une discipline du vers libre', championing rhythmic balance and unity in free verse (Ghéon 1910: 452–64); and the second in a review of an essay by Robert de Souza, 'Rythme en français', published in another, less ephemeral symbolist magazine *La Phalange*, and which faults the essayist for miscounting syllables in his assessments of poetic metre (Unsigned 1911: 635–7).

Since French reviews fail to provide insights into the yoking of Bergson and 'new' rhythm, we must turn to his own writings, as the best way to ascertain what rhythm meant when Bergson said 'rythme' or how he conceptualised those intuitional, primitive rhythms which the anglophone modernists equated with his name. His thesis, *Essai sur les données immédiates de la conscience*, published in 1889 and more prosaically translated as *Time and Free Will* in 1910, proves to be the ideal place to start. It is his founding text, laying down the groundwork for many of his later works; it is also, conveniently, the work where he draws most extensively on music. The basic thesis is familiar enough to require no introduction, and, to the contemporary mind, seems strangely self-evident: any understanding of consciousness must be predicated on a distinction between two distinct experiences of time: *le temps* (Time) which is spatialised, scientific, measurable, and *la durée* (Duration), perceived intuitively, a continuous, ongoing, spatially non-extensive vitality, a sense of life itself. From the opening sections, Bergson draws recurrently on *rythme* – rhythm – to illustrate how consciousness accesses such perceptions of fluidity. But then comes the hitch, as a close reading of the key passages soon makes clear. He establishes his point by observing a classical ballet dancer:

> Un troisième élément intervient quand les mouvements gracieux obéissent à un rythme, et la musique les accompagne *C'est le rythme et la mesure*, en nous permettant de prévoir encore mieux les mouvements

> de l'artiste, nous font croire cette fois que nous en sommes les maîtres. *Comme nous devinons presque l'attitude qu'il va prendre*, il paraît nous obéir quand il la prend en effet; *la régularité du rythme* établit entre lui et nous une espèce de communication, et les retours périodiques de la mesure sont comme autant de fils invisibles au moyen desquels nous faisons jouer *cette marionnette imaginaire*. Même, si elle s'arrête un instant, notre main impatientée ne peut s'empêcher de se mouvoir comme pour la remplacer au sein de ce mouvement dont *le rythme est devenu toute notre pensée et toute notre volonté.* (Bergson 2009a: 14, emphasis added)[27]

'Rythme', here, is anything *but* barbaric, yawping and brutal, as Holbrook Jackson in *Rhythm* had affirmed (Jackson 1911: 9). To the contrary, rhythm means a regular beat marking out time patterns that frame the dancer's docile movements. Rhythm is the mark of control, balance and accuracy which assure the dancer's gracefulness, grace alone being the final aim of the dance since in the predictability and continuousness of shape-forming movements lies the defeat of what is unshapely, harsh, irregular and unrestrained.[28] From the example of the dancer, Bergson turns to the well-known example of the chiming clock – where again rhythm is necessary, as the marker of Time (le temps), reassuring and mathematically measurable, as precisely as a metronome. The hypnotic lull of the regular (rhythmic) chime, he maintains, rocks and soothes the soul, inducing a state of self-forgetting. At which point, another perception of time becomes possible: 'la durée', where contours and divides merge and intertwine. No longer counting the beats as units in rhythm, the listener achieves another ongoing, drawn-out perception of time passing. Rhythm is none other than the structuring principle which, *once forgotten but instinctively felt,* allows melody to come to the fore, melody in Bergson's imagery being a flowing, ongoing, uninterrupted line of the ongoing present.

From the illustration of the bell, Bergson moves to the perception of music, and the recitation of poetry, again asserting that 'rhythm' is the regulating beat from which a slumbering consciousness will escape:

> Ainsi en musique, *le rythme et la mesure* suspendent la circulation normale de nos sensations et de nos idées en faisant osciller notre attention entre des points fixe ... une voix qui gémit suffira à nous remplir d'une *tristesse extrême*. [...] D'où vient le charme de la poésie? Le poète est celui chez qui les sentiments se développent *en images, et en images elles-mêmes en paroles, dociles en rythme, pour*

les traduire . . . mais ces images ne se réaliseraient pas aussi fortement pour nous sans les mouvements réguliers du rythme, par lequel notre âme, bercée et endormie, s'oublie comme en un rêve pour penser et voir avec le poète. (Bergson 2009a: 58)[29]

He then draws on classical architecture to extol the firm symmetries, measurement and balance of rhythm in granite and marble:

On retrouverait en architecture, au sein même de cette *immobilité saisissante, certains effets analogues à ceux du rythme. La symétrie des formes, la répétition indéfinie du même motif* architectural, font que notre faculté de percevoir oscille du même au même, et se déshabitue de *ces changements incessants qui, dans la vie journalière, nous ramène sans cesse à la conscience de notre personnalité* . . . (Bergson 2009a: 54)[30]

In Bergson's correspondence, meanwhile, the same ideas recur, notably in letters to his former classmate, the poet and musician André Suarès. The music Bergson cites most is that of Haydn and Schubert, while he admits having had to struggle to listen to Debussy, on account of the irregular, unfamiliar shapes of unrhythmical sound (Bergson 2002: 1558).

All his founding works and informal writings confirm Bergson's perception of rhythm as an instrument of organisation, discipline, distinction and domestication, ensuring rigidity, solidity and the mastery of instincts. He presents firmly structured rhythm as the founding principle of the arts, bestowing grace, symmetry, form, structured language and rational organisation. It thereby elevates art above the barbarities of nature: 'la nature procède par suggestion, comme l'art, mais ne dispose pas de rythme' (Bergson 2009a: 113)[31] – a far cry indeed from the sense of 'rhythm' that Murry and Carter and so many fellow early modernists attribute to Bergson, giving it the power to restore the primeval, barbaric, irrational impulses to the arts that convention, strict form and rationality smothered. In its anglophone variant, Bergsonian rhythm is an extremely rambunctious version of intuited *durée*, while in its French mode, intuition and duration are what fall outside rhythm. So, what does this mean? Are we on the verge of unveiling a terrible misunderstanding? Was Bergson wrong? Was anglophone modernism mistaken, and have we all been taken in?[32]

The answer is that of course we have, and of course we haven't. What we have is a riveting instance of intuitionism, when approached from two near-contemporaneous, intersecting localisms, and two sometimes misleadingly similar languages.[33] It exemplifies perfectly the admission made by German musicologist Curt Sachs in 1952, 'What is rhythm? The answer, I am afraid, is, so far, just – a word: a word without generally accepted meaning. Everybody believes himself entitled to usurp it for an arbitrary definition of his own. The confusion is terrifying indeed' (Sachs 1952: 12). Less perplexingly, it is also an example of exactly those changes in rhythm which occur when reading in a foreign language, as described by Woolf in 'On Not Knowing French':

> The sentence too takes a different curve. The old swing of the wrist, going up and down the page sowing phrases as mechanically as a man sowing seed, is altered. It takes a spirited, unusual pace which makes us wake and attend. (Woolf 2009: 4–5)

To return to the closing metaphor of her first paragraph, we are seeing a different body on the same head: the cultural history, etymological evolution, perception and conceptualisation of 'rhythm' in English, and 'rythme', in French, don't coincide, and this radically alters any feeling of what the 'pace' ought to be. While all sorts of linguistic theories and prosodic analyses can be evoked to explain this, there are certain key factors that come into play.

In terms of simple phonetics and language prosody, the mere sonorities of the long-drawn-out voiced fricatives [ðm] in the word 'rhythm' compared to the clipped consonant cluster [tm'] in 'rythme' are revealing first insights. The French language is essentially 'syllabic', sometimes referred to as 'the machine gun rhythm'.[34] Equally weighted syllables in succession explain why impassioned French accelerates but maintains a regular rhythm. English, meanwhile, is 'accentual' – also known as 'the Morse rhythm': the impassioned speaker increases the pace by eliding an ever-increasing number of vowels and weaker syllables, thereby accentuating the pattern of tonic accents, and creating an increasingly irregular rhythm. Such basic differences in how the ear and tongue perceive and produce meaningful sound and experience rhythm phenomenologically inflect on the cultural materiality of language, and accompanying codes of language etiquette, and the aesthetics of language – a phenomenon that Crystal refers to as 'rhythmical empathy' (Crystal 1995: 174–5). French tenets of stylistic perfection reflect the appeal of smooth syllabic regularity which ensures the alexandrine balance that Bergson deemed the pinnacle of poetic achievement, creating structure and harmony from twelve regular beats. Even French prose bears the legacy of the underlying pulse of the alexandrine, as evidenced, for example, in passing lines from the prose piece 'Aix-en-Provence' that Francis Carco contributed to the first issue of *Rhythm*: 'Et toujours sous le dome – or et vert amortis – des platanes, la statue du bon roi René'; 'Des roses de septembre s'effeuillent au corsage, des femmes et des arbres, atteints, eux aussi' (Carco 1911a: 20).[35] This classical form in turn inflects on how verse and elevated style should be performed; one need only think of the difference between the underlying flow and shapeliness of English blank verse and the hieratic regularity of the declamatory tradition of the Comédie française where regular rhythmicity, articulate control and precision were the measure of fine art.

It was precisely these 'rigid and puerile mechanisms of *rythme*' (Mallarmé 1945: 402) that precipitated Mallarmé's 1897 'crise de vers', his call to arms responding to the rebellion against rhythm's tyrannical structures which prompted many nineteenth-century French poets to champion prose. Baudelaire, for instance, frequently cited as a harbinger of modernism, and despite his extensive cultivation of the alexandrine in *Les Fleurs du mal*, claimed he became a poet of the city to escape rhythm, for which the prose poem becomes the prerequisite genre:

> Quel est celui de nous qui n'a pas, dans ses jours d'ambition, rêvé le miracle d'une prose poétique, musicale sans rythme et sans rime, assez souple et assez heurtée pour s'adapter aux mouvements lyriques de l'âme, aux ondulations de la rêverie, aux soubresauts de la conscience? (Baudelaire 1869: 2)[36]

Similarly, one of the most effective means French composers of the late nineteenth century found to escape the prescriptive, measured logic of 'rythme' (as prescribed in the classic 'solfège' class and musical manual) was precisely by shunning the vast orchestral works that required the centralising authority of a conductor beating counted time (Emmanuel 1981: 378–9). They favoured smaller musical ensembles, and the reduced scale of compositions which were more compatible with rubato, derhythmatised melodic patterns, 'nappes sonores' (layering of sound patterns), chromatism, or polyrhythmic, superimposed, syncopated patterns of melody, in more extreme cases even getting rid of bar lines.[37] An increased use of performance directions, in French rather than in Italian – the traditional language of musical annotation – likewise underlined the composer's concern that rhythmics should *not* be arithmetical (Goubault 2000: 194–5).

Such rebellions against prescriptively measured and rational understandings of rhythm in favour of intuitive and natural rhythms were of course not in themselves new, or specifically French: the philosophical debates extend back to Pythagoras and Plato, and forward into new neurological research in the twenty-first century. On the other side of Channel, however, there was an entirely different perception and intellectual model of rhythm – the English Romantics had been far more successful in breaking free of classical mathematical divisions, which, in the dramatic mode of blank verse, had only ever been a dominant rhythmic pulse, and certainly never a regular beat imposed throughout. The proto or early modernists could therefore embrace *notions* of rhythm they were perceiving in France as exciting means to break from strict tempo, or scientific, mechanical time, unaware that, to the knowing French ear, and to Bergson, *le rythme* was a strictly regular reassuring (or constraining) pulse.

Linguistic and cultural differences of these sorts, further complicated by metaphorical extensions and collocations, then expand exponentially in translation on either side of the Channel. The simple example of classic translations of musical terminology in early twentieth-century multilingual musicians' handbooks illustrates the point: apparently transparent words fail to coincide, again for reasons of rhythmical empathy, perception and cultural tradition:

Tempo [It] – Tempo [Eng] – **Rythme**, Le temps [Fr] (Wotton 1907: 196)

Misurato [It.] – **Rythmé** – Marked beat / measured / in strict time
   Stress the beat [Eng] – Marquer le **rythme**, accentuer la mesure / le pas [Fr] (Wotton 1907: 89–90)

Allegro giusto – **rythme** précis, exact, régulier – at a regular, precise, measured pace (Rougnon 1892: 8)

Tempo rubato – Interpretation désordonnée, sans mesure, sans **rythme** [fr.] – Free time values, slackened pace (Rougnon 1892: 128, emphasis added)

When compounded by the hazards of translation and usage, Bergson's musical analogies then presented obstacles in terms of translating, whether in the published translations at the time, or the translations the anglophone enthusiasts of 1911 established by themselves.³⁸ The issue is too vast to explore here, but three key terms illustrate the scale of the challenge, and its potential for misunderstanding. His notion of 'flux' is left unchanged as a lexical unit, although, like rythme/rhythm, it tugs semantically: the connotations of 'le flux' are not coterminous with English 'flux'. The same is true of 'Mélodie': although rendered as 'melody', it clearly overlaps, semantically, with English words such as song, tune, air: 'Un recueil de melodies populaires' would be translated 'Book of Popular Songs', and never 'Book of Popular Melodies'. 'Élan vital', meanwhile, is left untranslated as a foreign import as if the meaning were self-evident.

Philosophical tradition and scientific knowledge also played against Bergson's metaphors and analogies. Examples abound to underline the fact that, when Bergson sought a suitable means to express his dawning perception of an expansive, ongoing temporality within and outside the measured beat of clock time, and then alighted on musical metaphors, he underestimated their capricious slipperiness, perhaps 'not knowing music'. However difficult it may be to conceptualise time, it is considerably more complex to conceptualise rhythm, of which time and duration are but contributory factors.³⁹ Bergson himself appears to have realised the inadequacy of his own musically metaphorised conceptualisations, however, for after the *Essai*, he employs far fewer musical and poetical analogies (Corbier 2012: 298). When he continues to employ the term 'rythme', his usage changes: in *Matière et mémoire* (1896), for example, it shifts from a metaphorical to an ontological plane; he evokes the polyrhythms ('pluralités de rythmes') in duration (la durée) which 'for reasons of terminological precision' he henceforth refers to as 'flux' (Deleuze 2014: 90). In *Le Rire*, meanwhile, he refers to rhythm only in terms of its hypnotic sway. By 1922, in *Durée et simultanéité*, flux is no longer metaphorised by polyrhythms, but by 'mélodie', the closest musical analogy he reaches to illustrate constantly ongoing duration.

But is 'melody' a safer analogy than 'rythme'? Metaphorically, 'melody' might help suggest what *durée* is, but perceiving musical shape is not the same as the perception of ongoing sound. As neurologists have now proven scientifically, recognising melody or musical tunefulness relies on intense multilevel, neural circuitry in the brain, and requires emotional, motoric, linguistic and rational skills to be able to retrieve sequences and patterns that have already been heard, and anticipate the patterns and resolutions to come (Sacks 2008: xii). Marcel indeed intuitively understood as much in

À la recherche du temps perdu: 'la petite phrase de Vinteuil' is itself wholly polyrhythmic, gradually taking shape from a whole series of performances and memories of heard melody, which reconfigure in Swann's mind and punctuate his narrative as periodically echoing resonances, but which the reader can only grasp at intuitively – there is no external, independently accessible 'petite phrase de Vinteuil' outside Proust's text.

The heart of the matter, however, is that such misunderstandings and serendipitous misuses are quite immaterial. None of these desynchronised, mismatching labels undermines Bergson's essential exploration of time and consciousness, or the anglophone modernists' instinctive perception of how his philosophy could serve to apprehend the swiftly evolving dynamics of the era. Artists and philosopher alike had intuitively touched on the dawning challenge of modernity, but they were caught in the language strictures inherited from their own, cultural-defined nineteenth century, just as Darwin, as Gillian Beer demonstrated so persuasively, perceived a new world order but then had to verbalise it in the overdetermined, creationist, subject-empowering idiom of his era (Beer 2009: 32–7). Like Darwin in unknown South American forests, or like Woolf's Orlando discovering love with Sasha, Bergson *and* the early modernists were 'ransacking their language'[40] to find new means of expression. In many cases they opted for the language of music because it was the least pre-appropriated and semantically straitjacketed in their own cultural milieu; it was therefore best able to transmit a sense of some new, vital, ongoing living. Admittedly, they were shackled by their own limited familiarity with the languages of music, and the highly debateable issue of musical meaning.[41] But however mistaken, limited or incomplete their theorising, they had sensed what lay outside the domain of the familiar, and sensed that the answer might lie in switching media or languages, very literally crossing channels, to find forms of international connectivity and post-humanist expressivity that we have come to associate so directly with modernism.[42]

It is in this way that Mallarmé's charge that 'philosophically, verse makes up for what languages lack' (Mallarmé 1945: 364), or Pound's over-cited credo, 'It can't all be in one language' are no mere manifesto slogans in support of defamiliarised and exoticised form.[43] To champion multilingual cross-purposes, dislocated accents and foreign alternatives is a radically political act – and this still holds today, possibly more so than it did a hundred years ago. Here too is surely one of the deftly camouflaged cross-Channel points that Woolf's front-page article in the Sunday *Figaro* was making in 1929, and to which she would return, increasingly stridently, throughout the 1930s. There is a highly desirable, and subtly ethical, advantage to having our critical senses seduced and the objects of our criticism transformed. For it is then that we can grasp

> this, that, and the other – a sound, a colour, here a stress, there a pause . . . the words give out their scent and distil their flavour, and then, if at last we grasp the meaning, it is all the richer for having come to us sensually first, by way of the palate and the nostrils, like some queer odour. Foreigners, to whom the tongue is strange, have us at a disadvantage. (Woolf 2009: 202)

Notes

1. The Femina was the most prestigious literary prize in France, reserved at the time for works in foreign languages; the shortlist was drawn up by a French committee, but the annual winner was nominated by an English committee that met in Cambridge.
2. For a comprehensive study of Woolf's wide-ranging, aesthetic, rhetorical and political use of the discourse marker 'but', see Ryan and Bolaki (2012).
3. For rich conceptualisations of localist modernism and periodical culture, see White (2013).
4. My warmest thanks to Chris Mourant for the rewarding discussions we had during his year in Paris for doctoral research that prompted me to delve further into ideas explored here. Mourant offers a splendid reading of early twentieth-century periodical culture, including a (post) colonial perspective on *Rhythm*, as 'spaces of mediation, in which writers could negotiate conflicting positions and translate their experiences in one country into a new cultural context' (Mourant 2019: 15).
5. Carter's contribution to what we might call the era's 'rhythm fever' is yet to be fully explored, but it would appear sizeable, particularly considering his output and coverage in little magazines at the time. While the *New Age* reviews cited here imply Carter is giving a distinctly French flavour to 'rhythm', he was also charting the rhythm of a 'New Spirit' in thirteen cities across Europe, from London to Moscow; see Carter (1911c) and his *The New Spirit in Drama and Art* (1912), the frontispiece to which was a painting by John Fergusson. A host of recent scholars have charted the passion for rhythm in the years 1910–12, and thereby informed my own research – see in particular Rebecca Maclean in Beasley and Bullock 2013.
6. See, for example, the credo voiced in the first issue: '[Modernism] penetrates beneath the outward surface of the world, and disengages the

rhythms that lie at the heart of things, rhythms strange to the eye, unaccustomed to the ear, primitive harmonies of the world that is and lives' (Murry 1911a: 12).
7. T. E. Hulme's discussions of the challenge, as a philosopher and translator of Bergson, also illuminate the era's engagement with Bergson; see Hulme (1911a: 587–8; 1911b: 610–12).
8. See Jackson's 'Plea for a Revolt in Attitude': 'But the modernists of paint . . . join issue, not alone in their barbarism, with the rhythmical verbal utterance of the poet who sounded his barbaric yawp over the roof of the world' (Jackson 1911: 9).
9. Binckes refers briefly to the review, underlining a 'single degree of separation' between the two journals (2010: 87). See also Brooker et al. (2013: 314–26). For prior advertisements in the French press, see inside back covers of *Les Guêpes* (nos 19–20, December 1910) and *Chronique des Lettres françaises* (no. 28, December 1910).
10. Like its English counterpart, *Le Rythme* was 'ephemeral' (Arbour 1956: 7–8), as were at least two hundred magazines launched in Paris alone in the years 1900–14. *Le Rythme* ran from January 1911 until October 1912; it began as a monthly before quickly becoming bimestrial; publication became more erratic still after the first six months (Arbour 1956: 56). In terms of the review's general evolution, it is notable that after the fourth issue, short pieces by ad hoc contributors were abandoned in favour of fewer, longer articles in which the tone is more earnest, cultural and political coverage more explicit, and topical focus more biographical; after the second issue, each review came accompanied with short pamphlets or facsimiles by individual contributors. One of the review's founders, Banville d'Hostel, also the author of two free supplements, clearly had an influential role in the shift of focus. Never widely acknowledged as a poet and critic, D'Hostel was above all a militant anarchist who by December 1911 was transferring his allegiances from *Le Rythme* to the more explicitly militant reviews *L'Idée libre* and *Le Semeur de Normandie*. He was clearly the mind behind the last special issue of *Le Rythme*, devoted entirely to the life and ideas of Hans Ryner, a fellow anarchist, journalist and pacifist.
11. For the evolution of Fergusson's cover design, see Miao (2016: 194–7).
12. The figure recalls both the early Greek tunic-clad Isadora Duncan, and 'La Semeuse', the Marianne figure on French postage stamps introduced in 1903. Critics tended to overlook the progressive gender politics of *Rhythm* while debate focused on the decadent/pre-modernist stance of the magazine. See Binckes, in Churchill and McKible (2007: 29).
13. A Rastaquouère or 'rasta' in French was a pejorative literary term in circulation since the late 1880s, derived from Spanish, referring to suspicious-looking foreigners on the make (*Le Grand Robert de la langue française*).

14. Throughout this essay, translations from the French are my own.
15. 'I dream of love', 'Invocation', 'Prayer – poem for her', 'The hour of love', 'Resignation'.
16. The three lines are alexandrine. A non-scanned translation runs as follows: 'I dream of a love the colour of dead leaves / and which we would feel ebbing away inside / like a leafless lily borne away by the wind'.
17. See Binckes (2010: 42–6) for detailed coverage of the ambivalent reception of *Rhythm*, particularly in *New Age*.
18. Carco is referenced in Anglo-French modernism mainly as the soldier and lover who inspired Katherine Mansfield's 'An Indiscreet Journey' (1915) or as the novelist translated by Jean Rhys. His intermediary place in the circulation and coverage of little magazines across the Channel would nonetheless merit attention. Carco arrived in Paris in January 1910, determined to make his name as a poet and writer, notably via the network of literary reviews. One of the founders of the Fantaisiste poetry movement in 1911, and a key novelist of the Parisian 'Apaches', his favoured literary mode was 'plaintive romanticism' in which 'l'exotisme se mêle au merveilleux avec une nuance d'humour et désenchantement' [Plaintive romanticism, in which exoticism mingles with the fantastic, with a touch of humour and disenchantment] (Carco 1934: 72).
19. See also Murry's extremely impressionistic yoking of Debussy and Mahler when trying to define 'Modernism . . . when I use it': 'Debussy and Maehler [*sic*] in music; for Fantaisisme in Modern French literature, and generally if you like for "guts" and "bloodiness"' (Lea 1959: 52).
20. The article is one of Myers's earliest published essays on modern music; he went on to enjoy considerable success as a music journalist, translator and broadcaster with an unquenchable passion for modern, and particularly French, music.
21. 'What should we make of elements of amateurism in all branches of intellectual activity?'
22. See 'Quelques Réponses à notre enquête', *Le Rythme*, 4: 3–4.
23. Carco contributes a highly comparable but shorter 'Revue des revues' section to *Rhythm*, 2: 9.
24. See 'B and M', 'Revue des Revues', *Le Rythme*, 2: 21–3.
25. Both Miriam in *Pilgrimage* and Dorothy Richardson claimed to have learnt French, and rhythm, from Maeterlinck. See Bowler (2016: 74–5).
26. The year 1911 happens to be the year in which Bergson undertook his most extensive, to date, lecturing in Britain, following his first meeting with William James in London in 1908, and the first English-language translation of his *Essai* in 1910. The 1911 lectures took place in Oxford, Birmingham and London, and reflected two other key translations of his works (*Matter and Memory* and *Creative Evolution*). For extensive coverage of Bergson's reception in Britain, see Gillies (1996) and Ardoin et al. (2013).

27. 'A third element intervenes when *gracious movements obey a rhythm and music accompanies them*. It is the *rhythm and the beat [le rythme et la mesure]* which enable us to predict the artist's movements better, giving us the impression that we are in control. We can almost predict the dancer's moves; he seems to be obeying our will. *The regular beat of the rhythm* sets up a form of communication between him and us, and the to-and-fros of the beat are like invisible threads allowing us to play with this imaginary puppet. Should the puppet stop for a moment, our impatient hand will go on *marking out the same movement, the rhythm* of which has entirely taken over our thoughts and our will' (emphasis added).
28. See Bergson's ardent defence of grace over irregularity: 'nous finissons par trouver une aisance supérieure aux mouvements qui se faisaient prévoir, aux attitudes présents où sont indiquées et comme préformées les attitudes à venir. *Si les mouvements saccadés manquent de grâce*, c'est parce que *chacun d'eux se suffit à lui-même et n'annonce pas ceux qui vont* suivre. Si *la grâce préfère les courbes aux lignes brisées,* c'est que la ligne courbe change de direction' [We will end up finding greater ease in movements that could be sensed in advance, in poises in the presents that indicate and anticipate poises to come. If fitful movements lack grace, it is because each one is self-contained and doesn't lead anywhere. Grace prefers curved lines to broken lines, because the curved line is leading somewhere else] (Bergson 2009a: 52).
29. 'Likewise in music, *rhythm and beat* suspend the usual circulation of our sensations and our ideas by making our attention oscillate between fixed points . . . A plaintive voice can be enough to fill us with extreme sadness . . . Where does the charm of poetry come from? The poet is he whose feelings develop in images, images themselves translated into words, *which are docile in rhythm* . . . but these images would not have that strong impact without *the regular beat of the rhythm*, which lulls and soothes the slumbering soul, which by forgetting itself as if in a dream, thinks and sees with the poet' (emphasis added).
30. 'In architecture too, even within its striking immobility, we would find certain effects comparable *to rhythm. The symmetry of forms and the suggested repetition of the same architectural motif* mean that our perceptive faculties oscillate from own thing to its identical repetition, thereby shedding the habit of those incessant changes of daily life which constantly recall us to the consciousness of our personality' (emphasis added).
31. 'nature proceeds by suggestion as art does, but nature has no rhythm'.
32. See, for example, the aptly chosen title of a 2013 study of Bergson's reception in Britain, *Understanding Bergson, Understanding Modernism*, ed. Ardoin et al. See also Gillies (1996: 29–37).
33. As such, it would well deserve an entry in Barbara Cassin's *Le Vocabulaire européen des philosophies: Dictionnaire des Intraduisibles* (2004),

in which the philosopher critiques and wilfully 'complicates' long-established presumptions of universal transparency and equivalence. See also Dayan and Evans's more recent critical engagement with the slipperiness of the term, in relation to the French 'Crise du Vers' (Dayan and Evans 2010: 147–57).
34. In contemporary phonetics, the standard binary divide has been questioned, although the underlying principle remains accepted. See Crystal (1995: 174–9).
35. A literal, unrhythmical rendering reads as follows: 'Yet still beneath the dome – faded gold and green – of the plane trees, stands the statue of the good King René.'
36. 'Which of us has not, in his ambitious days, dreamt of the miracle of poetic prose, musical with no rhythm or rhyme, both loose and jolty enough to adapt to the lyrical shifts of the soul, to the undulations of daydreams, and the judders of consciousness?'
37. See Goubault (2000: 167–73) and Emmanuel (1981: 438–43). Emmanuel was a pioneering musicologist in France in the 1890s–1900s, who contested the conventional coupling of rhythm and a measured, metronome-type pulse. His writings on links between eurhythms, classical dance and Greek art would appear to have influenced, or at least been appreciated by, Jane Harrison, although this aspect of cross-Channel philosophical exchange is beyond the scope of the present chapter. For a close study of the extended critique by Bachelard of Bergson's use of musical motifs, see Corbier (2012: 302–9).
38. See the special issue 'Traduire le rythme' published in the translation studies review *Palimpsestes* for extended discussions of how rhythm proves a radically complicating factor in translation.
39. This complication was left largely unexplored until Henri Lefebvre established a method and lexicon of 'rythmanalyse' in the 1980s to explore the conventions, nature and ethics of rhythm, as applied to the body, the city and customs (see Lefebvre 1992).
40. Orlando's attempts to fix the fascination with Sasha in words leads the narrator to comment, 'Ransack the language as he might, words failed him. He wanted another landscape and another language. English was too frank, too candid, too honeyed a speech for Sasha' (Woolf 1998: 45).
41. For an enlightening study of difficulties encountered in critical and artists' discourse alike when thinking between modernist arts, and especially music, see Heckert (2010: 49–66).
42. Hübener, the Husserl student who first voiced reservations about what he considered to be Carter's excessively pro-French Bergsonism (see above), gave a deft indication of the trans-European identity of Bergson's training towards the end of his letter, linking it to why, to the French mind, 'Bergson is appreciated only by foreigners': 'it may be interesting to hear that Bergson's mother was English. So light

falls on the strange phenomenon of a French philosopher, who has a typically Germanic way of thinking, who is strongly influenced by the Anglo-Saxon James, Dewey and Schiller, and who has his only living equal in the German Husserl' (Hübener 1911: 94).
43. See Taylor-Batty (1913) for an insightful study into the multilingual dynamics of modernism.

Bibliography

Albert-Jean [Marie-Joseph-Albert-François Jean] (1911), 'Poëme pour elle'. *Le Rythme*, 2–3: 14.

Arbour, Roméo (1956), *Les Revues littéraires éphémères paraissant à Paris entre 1900 et 1914*, Paris: Corti.

Ardoin, Paul, S. E. Gontarski and Laci Mattison (2013), *Understanding Bergson, Understanding Modernism*, London: Bloomsbury.

Banks, Georges (1911), 'Stagecraft', *Rhythm*, I.3: 19–21.

Baudelaire, Charles (1869), *Oeuvres complètes*, Vol. 4: *Petits poèmes en prose*, Paris: Michel Levy.

Beasley, Rebecca and Philip Ross Bullock (2013), *Russia in Britain 1880–1940*, Oxford: Oxford University Press.

Beer, Gillian (2009), *Darwin's Plot: Evolutionary Plot in Darwin, George Eliot and Nineteenth-Century Fiction*, Cambridge: Cambridge University Press.

Benda, Julien (1912), *Le Bergsonisme, ou Une Philosophie de la mobilité*, Paris: Mercure.

Bergson, Henri (2002), *Correspondance*, ed. André Robinet, Paris: Presses universitaires de France.

Bergson, Henri (2009a), *Essai sur les données immédiates de la conscience* [1889], Paris: Presses universitaires de France.

Bergson, Henri (2009b), *Durée et simultanéité* [1922], Paris: Presses universitaires de France.

Bergson, Henri (2012), *Matière et mémoire* [1896], Paris: Presses universitaires de France.

Binckes, Faith (2010), *Modernism, Magazines, and the British Avant-Garde*, Oxford: Oxford University Press.

Bowler, Rebecca (2016), *Literary Impressionism: Vision and Memory in Dorothy Richardson, Ford Madox Ford, H.D. and May Sinclair*, London: Bloomsbury.

Boym, Svetlana (2010), *Another Freedom: The Alternative History of an Idea*, Chicago: University of Chicago Press.

Brooker, Peter, Sacha Bru, Andrew Thacker, and Christian Weikop, eds (2013), *The Oxford Critical and Cultural History of Modernist Magazines*, Vol. 111: *Europe 1880–1940*, Oxford: Oxford University Press.

Carco, Francis (1911a), 'Aix en Provence', *Rhythm*, 1.1: 20.
Carco, Francis (1911b), 'Les huit danseuses', *Rhythm*, 1.1: 21.
Carco, Francis (1934), *Souvenirs sur Katherine Mansfield*, Paris: Le Divan.
Carter, Huntly (1911a), 'The "Blue Bird" and Bergson in Paris', *New Age*, 9.2: 43–4.
Carter, Huntly (1911b), 'The Independents and the new intuition in Paris', *New Age*, 9.4: 82–3.
Carter, Huntly (1911c), 'Art and drama', *New Age*, 10.2: 36.
Carter, Huntly (1912), *The New Spirit in Drama and Art*, London: Palmer.
Cassin, Barbara (2004), *Le Vocabulaire européen des philosophies: Dictionnaire des Intraduisibles*, Paris: Le Seuil.
Churchill, Suzanne W. and Adam McKible (2007), *Little Magazines and Modernism*, Aldershot: Ashgate.
Corbier, Christophe (2012), 'Bachelard, Bergson, Emmanuel: mélodie, rythme et durée', *Archives de Philosophie*, 72.2: 291–310.
Crystal, David (1995), 'Documenting rhythmical change', *Studies in General and English Phonetics*, ed. J. Windsor Lewis, London: Routledge, pp. 174–9.
Dayan, Peter and David Evans (2010), 'Rhythm in literature and the crisis in verse', *Paragraph*, 33.2 : 147–57.
D'Hostel, Banville (1911), 'L'Inventoriée, *Le Rythme*, 4: 5–6.
Deleuze, Gilles (2014), *Le Bergsonisme* [1966], Paris: Presses universitaires de France.
'Desforges' (1911), 'Anatomie du théâtre', *Le Rythme*, 2–3: 6.
Emmanuel, Maurice (1981), *Histoire de la langue musicale* [1911], Paris: Laurens.
Ghéon, Henri (1910), 'Une discipline du vers libre', *Nouvelle Revue française*, XVI (April): 452–64.
Gillies, Mary Ann (1996), *Bergson and British Modernism*, Montreal: McGill-Queen's University Press.
Goubault, Christian (2000), *Vocabulaire de la musique à l'aube du XXe siècle*, Paris: Minerve.
Heckert, Deborah (2010), 'Schoenberg, Roger Fry and the emergence of a critical language for the reception of musical modernism in Britain 1912–1914', in *British Music and Modernism*, ed. Matthew Riley, Farnham: Ashgate.
Hübener, Gustav (1911), 'Letter to the editor', *New Age*, 9.4 (25 May): 94.
Hulme, T. E. (1911a), 'Notes on Bergson – I', *The New Age*, 9.25 (19 October): 587–8.
Hulme, T. E. (1911b), 'Notes on Bergson – II', *The New Age*, 9.26 (26 October): 610–11.
Jackson, Holbrook (1911), 'A plea for revolt in attitude', *Rhythm*, 1.3: 6–10.
Lea, F. A. (1959), *The Life of John Middleton Murry*, London: Methuen.

Leblanc, Georgette (1911), 'Maurice Maeterlinck', *Le Rythme – Maurice Maeterlinck et Georgette Leblanc à l'Abbaye de Saint-Wandrille* [unnumbered, special issue, June 1911].
Lefebvre, Henri (1992), *Elèments d'un rythmanalyse*, Paris: Syllapse.
'M-R, E.' (1911), 'Je rêve d'un amour', *Le Rythme*, 2–3: 20.
Mallarmé, Stéphane (1945), 'Crise de vers' [1897], *Oeuvres complètes*, Paris: Gallimard.
Miao, Tracy (2016), 'Artistic coalescence and synthetic performance: Katherine Mansfield and her 'rhythms', in *Katherine Mansfield's French Lives*, ed. Claire Davison and Gerri Kimber, Leiden and Boston: Brill–Rodopi, pp. 191–208.
Mourant, Chris (2019), *Katherine Mansfield and Periodical Culture*, Edinburgh: Edinburgh University Press.
Murphet, Julian, Helen Groth and Penelope Hone, eds (2017), *Sounding Modernism: Rhythm and Sonic Mediation in Modern Literature and Film*, Edinburgh: Edinburgh University Press.
Murry, John Middleton (1911a), 'Art and philosophy', *Rhythm*, 1.1: 9–12.
[Murry, John Middleton] Unsigned (1911b), 'Aims and ideals', *Rhythm*, 1.1: 9–12.
Myers, Rollo H. (1911), 'The art of Claude Debussy', *Rhythm*, 1.2: 29–34.
Myers, Rollo H. (1923), *Modern Music: Its Aims and Tendencies*, London: Kegan Paul.
Nicols, Roger (1997), 'The reception of Debussy's music in Britain up to 1914', in *Debussy Studies*, ed. R. L. Smith, Cambridge: Cambridge University Press.
Nouvelle revue française (1909–43), nos 12–42, January 1910–April 1912.
Palimpsestes – Traduire le rythme, ed. Maria Karsky, no. 27, Paris: Presses universitaires de la Sorbonne Nouvelle, 2014.
Proust, Marcel (2007), *A la recherche du temps perdu* [1906–1927], 7 vols, Paris: Gallimard.
Rougnon, Paul (1892), *Dictionnaire musical des locutions étrangères*, Paris: Dupont.
Ryan, Derek and Stella Bolaki, eds (2012), *Contradictory Woolf*, Clemson, SC: Clemson University Digital Press.
Sachs, Curt (1952), 'Rhythm and tempo: an introduction', *The Musical Quarterly*, 38.3: 384–98.
Sacks, Oliver (2008), *Musicophilia: Tales of Music and the Brain*, New York: Vintage.
Taylor-Batty, Juliette (2013), *Multilingualism in Modernist Fiction*, Basingstoke: Palgrave Macmillan.
Unsigned [Murry, John Middleton] (1911), 'Aims and ideals', *Rhythm*, 1.1: 9–12.
Unsigned (1911), 'Revues', *Nouvelle Revue française*, XXIX (May): 635–7.
Whitby, Charles J. (1911), 'Domesticity', *The Freewoman*, 1.6: 109.

White, Eric (2013), *Transatlantic Avant-Gardes: Little Magazines and Localist Modernism*, Edinburgh: Edinburgh University Press.

Woolf, Virginia (1929), 'Quand on ne sait pas le français', *Le Figaro*, 10 February 1929, pp. 1–2.

Woolf, Virginia (1998), *Orlando* [1928], Oxford: Oxford World's Classics.

Woolf, Virginia (2009), *The Essays of Virginia Woolf*, Vol. 5: 1929–32, ed. Stuart Clarke, New York: Houghton Mifflin Harcourt.

Wotton, Tom S. (1907), *A Dictionary of Foreign Musical Terms*, Leipzig: Breitkopf & Härtel.

Chapter 2

Impressions of Translation: Ford Madox Ford's Cosmopolitan Literary Crossings

Max Saunders

The Channel crossings in Ford Madox Ford's biography are complex. His grandfather, Ford Madox Brown, was born in France and studied in Belgium. Ford's father was a German who studied Provençale and emigrated to Britain. During the First World War, Ford wrote propaganda books triangulating English, French and German culture. After returning from the Western Front, he emigrated to France. A primary emphasis of this essay will be how his formative collaboration with Joseph Conrad reinforced an ideal of the conscious artistry of French fiction (exemplified by Stendhal, Flaubert and Maupassant). Ford was delighted when *The Good Soldier* was described by a publisher friend, John Rodker, as 'the finest French novel in the English language' (Ford 1927: 5). The essay will explore how Ford's own work bears out his injunction to translate English sentences into French and then back into English as a means of clarifying and purifying them. This reverberation of languages, people and texts across the Channel will be shown to be constitutive of Ford's version of Impressionism in literature. However, the essay will also argue that the *transmanche* is always doubled, for Ford, by the transatlantic. American writers living in Britain and Europe, from Henry James and Stephen Crane at the turn of the century, to Ezra Pound in Edwardian London, and Gertrude Stein and Ernest Hemingway in Paris in the 1920s, themselves mostly saturated with continental literature and art, continually contributed to the development of Ford's Impressionism and modernity. The conclusion will suggest that Ford's cultural internationalism – his belief in a 'Republic of Letters' – crosses all borders, foreshadowing recent discussions of global modernism and of world literature – nowhere more so than in his last, immense and inclusive comparative study *The March of Literature* (1938).

The cosmopolitanism of Ford's heritage has been dealt with often enough to require only brief rehearsing here. His father's family, the Hüffers, were well established in France, Italy and the Netherlands as well as Germany. One had gone into tobacco in the United States. Franz Hüffer, Ford's father, was a free-thinking Schopenhauerian who championed Wagner, and ended up as music critic for *The Times*. Their house was full of international musicians and singers visiting London. Ford's maternal aunt married William Michael Rossetti, the brother of Dante Gabriel and Christina Rossetti, the children of Italian immigrants. Ford's education was comparably cross-Channel. From the age of seven he was sent to a school on the coast at Folkestone, run by a German émigré couple, Elizabeth and Alfred Praetorius, where the conversation would be trilingual: in German and French as well as English. Ford left able to write fluently too in German and French, and said: 'For as long as I can remember, I have been accustomed to think indifferently in French, in German, or in English' (Hueffer 1915a: viii). By the turn of the century he had developed a strong sense of the superiority of French prose fiction over English, a view that was to remain the core of his criticism, even in late books such as *The English Novel* (1929), and *The March of Literature* (Saunders 2007, 2016).

Translation was important to Ford in different ways throughout his working life. He wrote a preface to his wife Elsie Martindale's translations of *Stories from De Maupassant* (1903) (Chambers 2016). He was close friends with Edward Garnett, whose wife Constance was the period's great translator of Russian literature. Ford considered translating Proust in 1920, telling Ezra Pound, who appears to have suggested the idea:

> It wd. amuse to me to *Chez S[wann]* – & I would do it if publishers wd. give me *plenty* of time, so that I cd. do a bit now & then when not in the mood for other work. It they wanted a complete Proust I wd. edit it: i.e. go through anyone else's translation to see that it was all right, & write an introduction: but I couldn't translate the whole: it wd. bore me to tears. (Ludwig 1965: 122)

He continued to write prefaces for others' translations of works he admired. In the 1920s he even began a translation of his own *The Good Soldier* (Stang and De Julio 1989). But translation is of most interest in his work as a way of thinking about writing, criticism, aesthetics and culture. Therefore, it is Ford's thoughts about translation, and his uses of the idea of translation – in short, his *impressions* of translation – that are the main subject of this essay.

Collaborating with Conrad

Ford had thus crossed between languages all his life, and moved in cosmopolitan, polyglot circles from his youth. But it was during the ten-year period of collaboration with Joseph Conrad, most intense while they were working on their major and most collaborative novel, *Romance*, between 1898 and 1903, that translation could be said to have become integral to his (as it was to Conrad's) writing mentality.

Ford later recalled Conrad's literary career as beginning with an act of homage, connecting his English first novel to a French masterpiece:

> This writer published his first, quite unnoticed, novel in 1893, and as far as it faintly went it was a piece of impressionism. Conrad published his first novel *Almayer's Folly* in England in 1895. But the book was begun, and the coincidence is one of the most curious in literary history, on the margins and end papers of *Madame Bovary* whilst his ship was moored to the dockside in Rouen harbour, and the portholes of his cabin there gave a view of the house which Flaubert described as being the meeting place of Emma Bovary and Rodolphe. (Ford 1939: 840)

What does it mean to write your novel into someone else's, in another language? That paper was scarce on shipboard, perhaps. That Flaubert's was the book he had just been reading on the last voyage, or during leisure while overseeing the ship when in dock. But also – and surely this is how Ford construes it – that Flaubert's writing inspired Conrad, eliciting a novel of his own; a novel in English, but with the spirit of Flaubert's French presiding over it.

One interpretation of their attraction to the French of Flaubert and Maupassant – perhaps the standard one in Ford studies – is that these writers represented the crusade for *le mot juste* – the exact word; referential exactitude and verisimilitude. In Ford's poignant memoir of their friendship, written in the months after Conrad's death in 1924, he remembered their conversation as a constant quest for precise lexis:

> For the days have been innumerable upon which, behind the amiable mare of Conrad's or a far less amiable Exmoor pony of the writer's, we drove – say between 1898 and 1905 – over a country of commonplace downlands and asked ourselves how we should render a field of ripe corn, a ten-acre patch of blue-purple cabbage. We would try the words in French: *sillonné, bleufoncé, bleu-du-roi*;[1] we would try back into English; cast around in the back of our minds for other French words to which to assimilate our English and thus continue for quiet hours. (Ford 1924a: 31)

According to the *mot juste* theory, you would try to find 'French words to which to assimilate our English' because you wanted your English words to be more precise. This is translating to write rather than translating to translate. There is no French original; rather, an ideal of French style. Thinking how a writer like Flaubert would have phrased it enables them to find better English words and phrases. For Conrad, also trilingual, between Polish, English and French, writing in English may have been more like translating, if thoughts came to him first in Polish or French. Ford's translational model of writing may have been in part an assimilation to his friend and collaborator. But equally it may have recalled his father's command of English as a foreign language; or indeed, as we shall see, his grandfather's. Translation became an *exercise* for writing better English:

> We remembered long passages of Flaubert; elaborated long passages in his spirit and with his cadences and then translated them into passages of English as simple as the subject under treatment would bear. We remembered short, staccato passages of Maupassant; invented short, staccato passages in his spirit and then translated them into English as simple as the subject would bear. (Ford 1924a: 195)

This emphasis on simplicity is, however, only part of the story, since the kind of simplicity they admire is a crystallisation of complexity; of condensed suggestion. Translation also provides Ford with a heuristic for reading and criticising, in order to bring out such complexity. In one bravura example, he devotes seven pages of the Epilogue to his wartime book, *Between St Dennis and St George*, to the question of how best to translate just one sentence – the opening one – of 'Félicité', the first of Flaubert's *Trois Contes*:

'Pendant un demi-siècle, les bourgeoises de Pont-l'Evêque envièrent à Mme. Aubain sa servante Félicité.'

This simple sentence is the beginning of the story which, at this moment, is of most significance to the world. It means that for fifty years the middle-class housewives of Pont-l'Evêque envied Mme. Aubain her servant Félicité. Nevertheless, exactly and rightly to translate that simple sentence is a task of almost unheard-of difficulty. Let us consider for a moment these verbal exactitudes. Let us take the words 'Pendant un demi-siècle.' If we say 'During half a century,' the words have not a quite English sound. If we say 'For fifty years,' the period is too exact in appearance. It would give the suggestion that Mme. Aubain was about to celebrate a golden jubilee. And the opening words of a story are of immense importance because they strike a note in the reader's mind, so that if we start the reader anticipating the celebration of a golden jubilee, and if no such celebration take place, the reader's mind will be a little confused. In the French the sentence suggests no event of any kind, not so much as the shadow of an event. The clear, cold sentence, with its cadence just sufficiently long to leave the reader wishing for the next syllables, dictatorially limits the mind to the consideration, firstly, of Mme. Aubain, and then, by the careful reservation of the servant's name to the last words, indicates with absolute precision that the main interest of the story will be the servant Félicité. The use of the word *bourgeoises* indicates that Pont-l'Evêque is a town, or a large village, of sufficient importance to contain several families in fairly comfortable circumstances. The note thus exactly struck in the reader's mind amounts to this: that the story will concern itself with an affair lasting fifty years, that the affair will not contain any memorable events, and that it will centre round the life of a faithful servant for Félicité was for fifty years in the service of her mistress, and the other housewives of the place envied Mme. Aubain. (Hueffer 1915b: 199–200)

Translation here requires matching the *mot juste* in French with as exact an English equivalent – but to the extent that, with characteristic Impressionist licence, Ford proposes altering the number of years mentioned, while claiming paradoxically that this will create a comparable effect of precision:

> Personally, if I were writing the story on these lines I should begin with an exact statement of the number of years, softening off the exactness with the qualitative 'more than.' 'For more than thirty-seven years,' I should say, and I think I should arrive at about the sense of Flaubert's phrase. (Hueffer 1915b: 200–1)

The choice of such a precise figure not in the original may seem eccentric; even perverse. But the translator's licence has a surprisingly distinguished pedigree. As Marina Warner explains: 'The history of translation has developed along two branches, one growing from Augustine, who endorsed precise adherence to the original, the other from Jerome, who believed in adaptation and, to some extent, invention, in order to put the meaning across more effectively' (Warner 2018: 22):

> The contest between Augustinian scrupulous faithfulness and Hieronymite wilful nudging was very helpfully glossed by Dryden when he identified three different levels of translation: the first, hewing close to the original, he confusingly called 'metaphrase'; the second 'translation with latitude', which he again confusingly called 'paraphrase'; and the third and most illuminating 'imitation, where the translator (if he has not now lost that name) assumes the liberty not only to vary from the words and sense, but to forsake them both as he sees occasion; and taking only some general hints from the original, to run division on the ground-work as he pleases. (Warner 2018: 22)

Despite his creative accounting with the numbers, Ford's Flaubert is 'translation with latitude' rather than this cross-Channel encounter of the third kind. But Dryden's category of 'imitation' is a good description of kinds of homage Ford's own fiction continually pays to his masters (and not just the French ones, but also writers like Turgenev and James, whose manner Ford frequently translates into his own idioms).

Ford's quest for the *mot juste* goes beyond descriptive accuracy in other ways too. Flaubert's opening sentence is not a visual description. Nor does it convey a particular impression, at a particular moment. Rather, it creates a social world and a set of relationships and attitudes. Certainly, it does that with precision and economy; and with a formal panache, sketching in the servant who will prove the central character of the story obliquely, through the attitudes to her of her employer's neighbours. What comes across most strongly in Ford's virtuoso unpacking, drawing a world of nuance out of a single sentence of just fourteen words, is both a celebration of Flaubert's power of concentration – his ability to condense proliferating suggestions into a phrase or a tone – and also an ethical injunction to writers, that unless they aspire to a Flaubertian concentration their work will lack clarity and value.

Another passage from the Conrad memoir indicates a further way in which it was not just his English *words* that Ford wanted to sound Flaubertian. Here is how he describes 'Seraphina', his original pirate romance which Conrad would help him recast as *Romance*:

> Every sentence had a dying fall and every paragraph faded out. The last sentences of that original draft ran: *Above our heads a nightingale* (did something; *poured out its soul*, as like as not, or *poured out its melody on the summer air*, the cadence calling there for eleven syllables). *As it was June it sang a trifle hoarsely*. . . . The reader will observe that the writer had then already read his *Trois Contes*, just as the first words of Conrad's first book were pencilled on the fly-leaves and margins of *Madame Bovary*. The last cadences, then, of Herodias run: 'Et tous trois, ayant pris la t[ê]te de Jokanaan s'en allaient vers Galilé. Comme elle était très lourde, ils la portaient alternativement.'[2] . . . As cadence the later sentences are an exact pastiche of the former. In each the first contains nineteen syllables; the concluding one commences with "As it was", and is distinguished by the *u* sounds of '*June*' and '*lourd*' and the *or* sounds of '*hoarse*' and '*portaient*.' It was in that way that, before the writer and Conrad met, they had studied their Flaubert. (Ford 1924a: 14–15)

This appears to go beyond referential accuracy in a different way. The referents are so far apart (the carrying of the decapitated head of John the Baptist; the quality of birdsong) that it is virtually impossible to see how invoking one would help us to visualise the other. There is perhaps a *rapport* in the sense that an enervated irony at the effects of passion is implied in both cases. But that is, as Ford says, a matter of 'cadence', or of tone, which, after all, is distinct from reference; from precise description.

Ford wrote paradoxically about cadence, as at once expressing the intimate personality of a writer, and also as crossing between writers. Commenting on an obscure work by Samuel Smiles, the *Life of a Scottish Naturalist*, which Ford calls 'the most beautiful book in the world', he says:

> I found this book by chance a year ago, bought it for sixpence and recognised at once that my intimate cadence, the typical sentence that I try all my life to create, that I hear all the while in my ear and only once in a blue moon am aided to write, is to be found always in the recorded speeches of Thomas Edward. (Ford 1924c: 504)

But then that ambiguous quality of 'cadence' itself chimes with the collaborative discussions:

> This was the one subject upon which we never came to any agreement. It was the writer's view that everyone has a natural cadence of his own from which in the end he cannot escape. Conrad held that a habit of good cadence could be acquired by the study of models. (Ford 1924a: 200)

You may not be able to escape your own cadence, but that does not mean you cannot hear it in the words of others. The echo of Flaubert's cadence in 'Seraphina' is not exactly an allusion either; or at least, if it works as a kind of 'in joke' for fellow-craftsmen, it isn't an allusion most readers could be expected to recognise. Most would be unlikely to recognise a conscious imitation of a specific French sentence. The English sentence doesn't even sound particularly like French. Its anti-romantic anti climax indicates Ford is ironising his lovers in the way a French writer like Flaubert or Maupassant would, but an English one like Dickens would not.

Finding 'French words to which to assimilate our English' is then, in part, a matter of making English fiction sound like French in its tones and attitudes: making it sound serious, adult, ironic, modern. But there is also another effect conjured up by that phrase, which is also important to Ford, an effect which takes the phrase more literally: making English passages sound as if it they were actually written in French. It was the mirror image of the way Madox Brown – and Ford himself – spoke a foreign language, foreignly:

> I speak French with a strong British accent and much too correctly. When I was a boy my grandfather who was French by birth and had a strong French tinge to his English used to say to me: 'Fordie, you must speak French with absolute correctness and without slang which would be an affectation. But with the strongest possible English accent to show that you are an English gentleman.' (Ford 1931: 23–4)

That was when he was speaking French. But his English was accented too, and punctuated with French words:

> [Madox Brown] had been born and educated and lived in France until comparatively well on in life. He spoke always with a slightly un-English accent, and supplied missing words and phrases in his conversation with French expressions, a little old-fashioned because he dated from the days of Brummel in Calais. ([Ford] 1903: 571–2)

Translation theory distinguishes between 'domesticating' and 'foreignising' translations (Venuti 1995). Domesticating versions seek to assimilate the passage's qualities to the target language; foreignising ones preserve more qualities of the source language. Ford's and Conrad's attempt to make their English sound French was foreignising, except that it wasn't translation. Or was it? Just as Ford recalled translating words for cabbage colours into French with Conrad, and then they 'would try back into English', so in later life he would advise younger writers like Jean Rhys, if they were having trouble with a passage, to translate it into French and then back again into English.[3] The implication is that the words will come back changed by their adventures abroad. (If you put the sentence 'Every sentence had a dying fall and every paragraph faded out' into 'Google Translate' and select French, you get: 'Chaque phrase avait une chute mourante et chaque paragraphe disparaissait'. If you paste that back in and retranslate into English, you don't quite get back to square one, but to this: 'Each sentence had a dying fall and each paragraph disappeared' – in which Ford's sentence's dying fall has itself disappeared, or died.) Again, at one level such advice is about bypassing English's putative imprecision, and using French as a filter to ensure that the resulting version achieves the clarity and logic that Ford admired in French writers like Anatole France. At another, though, it is about making English sound other to itself; making it sound cross-Channel.

Donald Davie described Pound as writing some passages in 'translatorese' – a sort of ironic or parodic rendering of how other translators approach the writers he admired (Davie 1965: 87). In *Homage to Sextus Propertius* (1917) the irony is at the expense of inept or anachronistic translations. In the early *Cantos*, Pound makes a montage of archaic and more modern versions of the classics, taking in Renaissance and late Victorian translators of the *Odyssey*. Ford's sounding of one language through another works differently. Call it 'translationese'. Poundian translatorese expresses a sensibility which realises the power of the classics through translators' failures to do so. Fordian translationese enhances the power of its English by letting us hear French in it. 'Three long parallelograms existed: pale glimmerings above, cut two-thirds of the way down by the serrations of chimney pot and roof-shadows!' (Ford 2010: 340). As Tietjens returns to his flat in the middle of the night, at the end of the first volume of *Parade's End*, having said goodbye to Valentine Wannop without sleeping with her, he becomes aware of the dawn beginning to break. The first light makes shapes through the high windows: parallelograms because they are at an angle to him; and registered by him as such because he is a mathematician. It is a fine and rapid notation in free indirect style (itself identified mainly as a French mid-nineteenth-century development, though pioneered by Jane Austen). But it is also not quite idiomatic English. It is not ungrammatical. It is just that an English writer would not normally tell you that things they are describing exist. The fact that they are describing them tells you they exist, so to say so explicitly should feel tautologous. If it doesn't quite feel that here, it is because it sounds more like a gesture towards a French construction: 'il existait trois longs parallélogrammes . . .'.

During the collaboration on *Romance*, a phrase of Ford's got taken up as a catch-phrase or running joke: 'Excellency. A few goats.' Conrad said it was 'genius' (Conrad and Hueffer 1903: 395; Ford 1924a: 147). A local farmer is being questioned by a judge, and when he is asked his occupation, gives this answer. It evidently mattered to Ford that Conrad described anything of his as the product of genius; though he may have been wary of the possibility Conrad was being ironic, and said he 'imagined' the words (rather than writing them) in 'a quite commonplace frame of mind' (Ford 1924a: 147). But one can see why it struck Conrad. It has the concision (as well as the disconnectedness) of Haiku. 'Excellency' pinpoints the abjection of the frightened local, as does his inability to complete his next sentence – which nonetheless gives in miniature his life, his poverty, his playing down of his worth so that authority will not think him important enough to interfere with. The notion of 'a few goats' being an 'occupation' is worthy of a Lady Bracknell epigram. But we might also notice that it is an impeccable example of translationese – in this case from the Spanish. 'Excellency' is foreignising (rather than 'Your Honour', say). Also, the slight obliqueness of the answer – not giving the name of a job, like 'farmer', but just mentioning the animals he works with – while it also contributes to his self-belittling (are the goats his, or is he hired to tend them?), also sounds a note of strangeness, the unidiomatic. The term the narrator John Kemp uses to describe the man is a clue to how the passage works. He is a *lugareño*, a word which doesn't denote a job, but a locality. A *lugareño* is a local or a native. But of course, the word is not native to Kemp's English, the language of *Romance*. Ford's lighting on a foreign word for someone not a foreigner is a *mise en abime* of translationese. 'Excellency. A few goats' is a miniature of free indirect style; but it is free indirect style (or *style indirect libre*) free of a single language, and existing between two of them.

Ford advocated cultural crossing and fusing in ways that make it sound like educational exchange:

> And, for my part, if I could have my way, I would introduce a conscription of the French language into this country and a conscription of the English language into France, so that every soul from County Galway to the Alpes Maritimes was transfused with the double civilisation. For it is only through language that comprehension and union can arise, and it is only by the careful and strained attention to the fine shades of language in common use that comprehension of language can be reached. (Hueffer 1915a: 205)

The French must attend to English, and the English to French. But one way of doing it is to enact the 'double civilisation' within a single sentence. That is why Flaubert's prose assumes such importance for Ford during wartime: as rendering the other with such precision as to enable comprehension, and thus peace.

Translation, then, whether from one language to another, or out of English and back again, is for Ford also a method of writing and criticising. Note that he does not quite say he would *translate* Flaubert's '*demi-siècle*' with 'more than thirty-seven years', but that that is how he'd put it 'if I were *writing* the story on these lines' (emphasis added). It would take a Borges to elaborate that hint of one writer writing another's fiction in a later era. It is an aspect of a broader tendency, in Ford's criticism, to illustrate his critical points with creative examples: nailing his objections to Yeats's romantic poses with a hilarious parody of 'The Lake Isle of Innisfree' (Saunders and Stang 2002: 163–7; see also Saunders 2004); or crystallising the differences between Victorian moralising and Impressionism by offering what he calls an 'imaginary', again parodic, passage from *Vanity Fair*, saying that it 'would not be impressionism', and then rewriting the same scene in an again parodically exaggerated register which this time is Impressionist (Ford 1939: 767–8).[4] The ability to recast ideas in different styles demonstrates what Ford means by the concept of 'Conscious Art': a saturation of writing by critical and technical considerations. It is not translation from one language to another, but does represent translation between different uses of the same language, different aesthetic norms: translating *fin de siècle* pastoralism or Victorianism into Impressionism.

Literary Impressionism

Soon after the analysis of 'Félicité', Ford recalls an episode from when he was living in Kent, near the Channel coast, and working with a handyman to break a window through the wall of a cottage:

> it was not until we had well squared out the space into which the window-frame would go that I stepped back into the room, much as an artist steps back from his canvas, to consider what might be the view that we had opened up. The room was lowish, coolish, and rather dark; the day was astonishingly bright. It was one of those days when the sun diffuses an almost painful light from a blue sky that is like polished metal, whilst underneath it ran a cruel east wind. And suddenly, in a square before the eye hung a most astonishing picture a belt of painfully vivid blue, a belt of painfully vivid pink, and above the pink another belt of blue. And, in the belt of pink, which was formed by the French cliffs, there were nacreous markings, for all the world like the little ruddled and bluish shadowings of pink mother-of-pearl – they were the Cathedral of Boulogne, the houses of Boulogne, and the column that Napoleon I erected to commemorate the invasion of Great Britain . . . times in which France, as it were, seems to come into England, are not unchronicled in history. (Hueffer 1915b: 209–10)

I have discussed this passage elsewhere, as an instance of the 'double civilisation' Ford advocates, wanting French and English to communicate with each other; and how his vision of the linguistic and the cultural is framed by the aesthetic (Saunders 1993). What I would add now, and in the present context, having worked more on Ford's relation to Impressionism, is that it is a profoundly *Impressionist* vision. Impressionist in palette, certainly; in its attention to light, colour and atmospheric perspective. It is a view of the kind of coastal scene beloved of the Impressionists, even if the French coast is seen from a greater distance. But it is also Impressionist in its abstraction (though also Post-Impressionist: the belts of painfully bright colours are more De Staël than Monet), in its heightening of effect, its exaggeration. The reference to Napoleon's column slyly acknowledges that, and doubly: first, because that was itself a distortion of history, a monument erected before the event – an event that in fact never happened; second, because of the implausibility of being able to see it (without a telescope) across the Channel. The sudden irruption of the vision of the French coast into the cottage room evokes an invasion – not a military invasion, however, but an aesthetic one. The point is not so much that France looks like an Impressionist canvas because it was the home of the Impressionists, as that Ford sees France impressionistically because he has assimilated Impressionist aesthetics – Impressionism being, at the turn of the century (the time he is writing about), France's most successful aesthetic export.

Ford's upbringing had been among Pre-Raphaelites rather than Impressionists. Madox Brown was a close friend of Dante Gabriel Rossetti. Pre-Raphaelism, with its narrative subjects from literature, myth and history, its sharp-focus photo-realist surfaces crowded with minute detail, could scarcely be further from Impressionism, with its rapid, sketch-like handling, its experiments with light, shadow and colour, and its subjects of the modern city and bourgeois leisure (Saunders 2009). It was later, while he was living on the Channel coast, that Ford's Impressionism took root. It was deepened by the collaborative work with Conrad. But, as he says, his immersion in the French stylists he described as Impressionist – Flaubert and Maupassant especially – had begun earlier; as had his acquaintance with the other writer in English he most admired, Henry James, living close by in Rye. Ford got to know Stephen Crane too, who was also living in the area, at Brede. He thought that this group of writers based around the Romney Marsh – James, Conrad, Crane and himself – who all discussed literary technique with a Gallic concentration, and were certainly preoccupied with 'the impression' and how to render it, constituted a group, which he consistently described as impressionist (Saunders 2008a). In his memoir of his pre-war literary life, *Return to Yesterday*, he has another friend, H. G. Wells, calling them 'a ring of foreign conspirators plotting against British letters' (Ford 1931: 29). Indeed, he saw Impressionism as the major literary movement of the modern age, and gave it a much broader definition than most anglophone theorists, stretching from Flaubert and other mid-nineteenth-century writers now usually described as realist or naturalist, through to the writing now described as modernist: work by Ford's contemporaries such as Joyce, and the younger generation he also championed, such as Pound, Hemingway and Rhys (Saunders 2008b).

Between St Dennis and St George was written in 1915, as a book for Ford's friend, the Liberal cabinet minister C. F. G. Masterman's 'Wellington House' wartime propaganda operation. It was during the previous two years, while publishing his *Collected Poems* and writing *The Good Soldier*, that Ford had written two major essays elaborating and announcing his Impressionist position. 'Impressionism – Some Speculations' was first published in the influential Chicago magazine *Poetry*, then revised into the Preface for the *Collected Poems* (Hueffer 1913). Then, in 1914, he published 'On Impressionism', probably his most widely read essay, and, along with the third section of his book on Conrad analysing their fictional techniques, the nearest thing he wrote to a literary credo. *Between St Dennis and St George* is like no orthodox work of propaganda. It is propaganda by Impressionism. One reason why Ford's vision of France coming into England is Impressionist – at a time, of course, when the British Expeditionary Force had come into France, not to invade Napoleonically, but to defend its ally – is that Ford had just made his stand for Impressionism.

It will have been noticed that it is not only his fiction that Ford wants to foreignise, but his criticism, and specifically his critical terminology, as well. He either uses French terms, like *mot juste*, or, when he uses English terms like cadence or 'time-shift', he uses them in unfamiliar ways or combinations. The implication is that English is still too unsophisticated to have developed such an analytic terminology:

> [W]ith Madame Bovary the novel really appeared as a complete work of art, having at once *progression d'effet, charpente façade, cadences, mots justes*, and all the other accoutrements and attributes of a work of art in its glory, for which the English language has no name. (Ford 1939: 498)

One attraction of the term 'Impressionism' may thus have been that it was first used in France. Ford describes the conversation among the cross-Channel Impressionists as taking place in French, and peppered with such French terms of art-speak:

> James always addressed Conrad as '*Mon cher confrère*,' Conrad almost bleated with the peculiar tone that the Marseillaise get into their compliments '*Mon cher Maître.*'. . . Every thirty seconds!

When James spoke of me to Conrad he always said: '*Votre ami, le jeune homme modeste*'.[5] They always spoke French together, James using an admirably pronounced, correct and rather stilted idiom such as prevailed in Paris of the 'seventies. Conrad spoke with extraordinary speed, fluency and some incomprehensibility, a meridional French with as strong a Southern accent as that of garlic in *aioli*. (Ford 1931: 23)

As we see here, however, Anglo-French crossings are only one aspect of Ford's cosmopolitan story. James – the other key figure in Ford's pantheon of writers in English alongside Conrad – was of course American, and as such, representative of how, as Chris GoGwilt has argued, for Ford the transmanche was always overlaid with the transatlantic (GoGwilt 2012). This is evident in the magazines he edited: the *English Review*, under his editorship from 1908 to 1910, which published Tolstoy, James and President Taft, and in which Conrad reviewed Anatole France; and the *transatlantic review* (1924), which was published in New York as well as London and Paris, and which increasingly gave space to the American expatriates in Paris, but also published work in French.

Ford's modernist magazines thus represent a further, exemplary, form of collaborative boundary crossing. Just as the group smuggling Impressionism across the Channel into Kent and Sussex, and into English literature before the war, included two Europeanised Americans (James and Crane), so the group Ford gathered around the *transatlantic review* in post-war Paris included numerous American expatriates, Europeanised to different degrees, alongside the British, Irish and European contributors. The *transatlantic* published Joyce, Rhys, Dorothy Richardson, Basil Bunting and Havelock Ellis; published work in French by writers and critics such as Philippe Soupault and Valery Larbaud; and illustrated visual art by Picasso, Juan Gris, Man Ray, Gwen John, Braque and Brancusi. But it was the American writers, including Stein, Pound, Hemingway, John Dos Passos, William Carlos Williams, H.D., Djuna Barnes and e. e. cummings, who began to dominate the magazine, and contributed to Ford's sense that the centre of gravity of serious modern experimental literature had shifted from Europe to the United States – or rather, to writers from the States who had shifted to Europe. Ford's own readership became increasingly American with the publication of *Parade's End*, his tetralogy about the war (1924–8), to the extent that he was to describe himself, by 1934, dividing his time between Paris, Provence and New York, as a 'modern Franco-American writer'.[6] He was rarely in Britain after leaving in 1922. After that, he was more often crossing the Atlantic than the Channel.

Ford's cultural internationalism – his belief in a 'Republic of Letters' – was long-standing; and a venture like the *transatlantic* was meant to consolidate it. Yet throughout the 1930s, as the international situation looked increasingly as if another world war was imminent, Ford devoted more of his energies to elaborating and advocating cosmopolitanism. He drafted *A History of Our Own Times*; wrote two volumes of memoirs detailing the international friendships and exchanges described here: *Return to Yesterday* (1931), about his life in pre-war England, and *It Was the Nightingale* (1933), about his decision to move to France after the war. He completed two out of a projected three volumes about travel and culture: *Provence* (1935), and *Great Trade Route* (1937), which takes the image of the silk road as an impressionist metaphor for a truly global flow of trade, culture and art. Such work foreshadows recent discussions of 'world literature' – nowhere more so than in his last and immense comparative study *The March of Literature: From Confucius' Day to Our Own* (1938). He had written in 1924: 'the problem – the really very great problem of the day – is precisely the evolution of a prose language that shall have a certain international validity' (Ford 1924b: 3). True, his vision of literary transnationalism is a pre-post-colonial one; and though certainly no imperialist in his political pronouncements – he supported both Irish Home Rule and the decolonisation of Africa – his exemplary literary works are representative of the period in coming mainly from the imperial powers rather than the colonies. But note that he says 'a prose language' rather than 'an English prose style'. What language is that prose language? It might be any language, or all languages. Or it might be a language which incorporates linguistic diversity, which assimilates other languages to itself: in short, 'translationese'.

Notes

1. Furrowed; deep or dark blue; royal blue.
2. 'And all three, having taken the head of Jokanaan, set off towards Galilee. As it was very heavy, they carried it in turn' (my translation). Ford was recounting this scene a quarter of a century later without recourse to the manuscript of 'Seraphina'. In fact, the sentence about the nightingale is quite different – 'suddenly from behind us rang out the voice of a nightingale' – and is not the conclusion. See Saunders (1996a: 113).

3. 'One of the tricks he taught me', Jean Rhys told Diana Athill about Ford: 'if you aren't sure of something you've written, translate it into French. If it doesn't seem right then, it's wrong.' Athill to Arthur Mizener, 28 March 1966: Cornell University Library; quoted in Saunders (1996b: 281).
4. See Saunders (2008c) for a more detailed discussion.
5. 'My dear fellow'; 'my dear Master'; 'Your friend, the modest young man' (my translations).
6. The phrase 'Franco-American' appears twice in the typescript at Cornell, but was deleted for the published version of 'Autocriticism' (Ford 1933: 249).

Bibliography

Chambers, Helen (2016), 'Le Traducteur E. M. (une Femme)': Conrad, the Hueffers and the 1903 Maupassant translations', in *Ford Madox Ford's Cosmopolis: Psycho-geography, Flânerie and the Cultures of Paris*, ed. Alexandra Becquet and Claire Davison-Pégon, Leiden: Brill, pp. 155–73.

Conrad, Joseph and Ford Madox Hueffer (1903), *Romance: A Novel*, London: Smith, Elder & Co.

Davie, Donald (1965), *Ezra Pound: Poet as Sculptor*, London, Routledge.

[Ford, Ford Madox] (1903), 'Nice People', *Temple Bar*, 128 (November): 564–78.

Ford, Ford Madox (1924a), *Joseph Conrad: A Personal Remembrance*, London: Duckworth.

Ford, Ford Madox (1924b), 'Literary causeries: VII: Pullus ad Margaritam . . .', *Chicago Tribune Sunday Magazine* (Paris) (30 March): 3, 11.

Ford, Ford Madox [as 'Daniel Chaucer'] (1924c), 'Stocktaking [. . .]', 'X', *transatlantic review*, 2/5 (November): 502–10.

Ford, Ford Madox (1927), 'Dedicatory letter to Stella Ford', in *The Good Soldier*, ed. Max Saunders, Oxford World's Classics, Oxford: Oxford University Press.

Ford, Ford Madox (1931), *Return to Yesterday*, London: Gollancz.

Ford, Ford Madox (1933), 'Autocriticism', *Week-End Review*, 8 (9 September 1933), 249.

Ford, Ford Madox (1939), *The March of Literature*, London: George Allen and Unwin.

Ford, Ford Madox (2010), *Some Do Not . . .*, ed. Max Saunders, Manchester: Carcanet Press.

GoGwilt, Christopher (2012), 'Ford Madox Ford as Queen Victoria: the English sovereignty of Impressionist memory in Ford's transatlantic modernism', in *Ford Madox Ford and America*, ed. Sara Haslam and Seamus

O'Malley, International Ford Madox Ford Studies, 11, Amsterdam and New York, pp. 85–95.

Hueffer, Ford Madox (1913), 'Impressionism – some speculations', *Poetry*, 2 (August and September): 177–87, 215–25.

Hueffer, Ford Madox (1915a), *When Blood is Their Argument*, London: Hodder and Stoughton.

Hueffer, Ford Madox (1915b), *Between St Dennis and St George: A Sketch of Three Civilisations*, London: Hodder and Stoughton.

Ludwig, Richard M. (1965), *Letters of Ford Madox Ford*, Princeton, NJ: Princeton University Press.

Saunders, Max (1993), 'Ford Madox Ford and European culture', in *English Studies in Transition*, ed. Robert Clark and Piero Boitani, London and New York: Routledge, pp. 208–16.

Saunders, Max (1996a), *Ford Madox Ford: A Dual Life*, vol. 1, Oxford: Oxford University Press.

Saunders, Max (1996b), *Ford Madox Ford: A Dual Life*, vol. 2, Oxford: Oxford University Press.

Saunders, Max (2004), 'Critical biography: rhetoric, tone and autobiography in Ford's critical essays', in *History and Representation in Ford Madox Ford's Writings*, ed. Joseph Wiesenfarth, International Ford Madox Ford Studies 3, Amsterdam: Rodopi, pp. 173–88.

Saunders, Max (2007), 'Tradition and the march of literature: T. S. Eliot and Ford Madox Ford', in *T. S. Eliot and the Concept of Tradition*, ed. Giovanni Cianci and Jason Harding, Cambridge: Cambridge University Press, pp. 185–200.

Saunders, Max (2008a), *Oxford DNB* Reference Group article on 'Literary Impressionists', Oxford: Oxford University Press.

Saunders, Max (2008b), 'Ford and Impressionism', in *Ford Madox Ford: Literary Networks and Cultural Transformations*, ed. Andrzej Gasiorek and Daniel Moore, International Ford Madox Ford Studies 7, Amsterdam: Rodopi, pp. 151–66.

Saunders (2008c), 'Impressionism, fiction, and the location of the ethical', in *Ethics in Culture: The Dissemination of Values through Literature and Other Media*, ed. Astrid Erll, Herbert Grabes and Ansgar Nünning, Berlin and New York: Walter de Gruyter, pp. 299–316.

Saunders, Max (2009), 'From Pre-Raphaelism to Impressionism', in *Ford Madox Ford and Visual Culture*, ed. Laura Colombino, International Ford Madox Ford Studies 8, Amsterdam: Rodopi, pp. 51–70.

Saunders, Max (2016), '"Adventures of the soul among master-pieces": Ford and France (Anatole)', in *Ford Madox Ford's Cosmopolis*, ed. Claire Davison and Alexandra Becquet, Leiden: Brill, pp. 129–54.

Saunders, Max and Richard Stang, eds (2002), *Ford Madox Ford: Critical Essays*, Manchester: Carcanet Press.

Stang, Sondra J. and Maryann De Julio (1989), 'The art of translation: Ford's "Le bon soldat"', in 'Ford Madox Ford and the Arts', ed. Joseph

Wiesenfarth (guest editor), special issue of *Contemporary Literature*, 30.2 (Summer): 163–334, 263–79.

Venuti, Lawrence (1995), *The Translator's Invisibility: A History of Translation*, New York: Routledge.

Warner, Marina (2018), 'The politics of translation', *London Review of Books*, 40.19 (11 October): 21–4.

Chapter 3

Sydney Schiff and Marcel Proust: Table-talk, Tribute, Translation

Emily Eells

On 18 May 1922, Sydney Schiff and his wife Violet hosted a late-night dinner at the Hôtel Majestic in Paris to celebrate the premiere of Stravinsky's *Renard*. Among the guests at the party honouring the artists who had created the work – the composer, the dancers of the Ballets Russes and their impresario Diaghilev – were Pablo Picasso, James Joyce and Marcel Proust. That 'great modernist dinner party' (Davenport-Hines 2006)[1] is without doubt the epitome of Sydney Schiff's activity as an international go-between and promoter of culture.

Schiff, the illegitimate son of a beautiful high society lady and a rich Jewish German banker, embodied cosmopolitanism. He was a British writer and patron of the arts with a complex identity: he published under the pen-name Stephen Hudson and created a double self-portrait in his autobiographical works where he was both the fictitious character Richard Kurt and the first-person narrative voice. His second wife, Violet Beddington (1874–1962), was his accomplice in matters social and literary; together they developed a wide, international friendship circle, as T. S. Eliot reports:

> In the 1920s the Schiffs' hospitality, generosity, and encouragement meant much to a number of young artists and writers of whom I was one. The Schiffs' acquaintance was cosmopolitan, and their interests embraced all the arts. At their house I met, for example, [Frederick] Delius and Arthur Symons, and the first Viscountess Rothermere, who founded *The Criterion* under my editorship. [John] Middleton Murry and Katherine Mansfield knew their house, and Wyndham Lewis and Charles Scott Moncrieff, and many others.[2]

Eliot defined the 'great point in the Schiffs' favour' as '[their capacity when entertaining] of bringing very diverse people together and making them combine well' (Eliot 1988: 411). In her presentation of the letters exchanged between Sydney Schiff and Aldous Huxley, Clémentine Robert stressed that Violet and her husband were at the heart of an intellectual and artistic 'plexus' (Huxley 1976: 16). They kept an open house favouring cross-Channel exchange which Robert described as the prefiguration of a cultural Common Market:

> Cet apolitisme du juger fait de [Schiff] un cosmopolite. L'art est sans frontières et la production littéraire est vue à l'échelle européenne. Autour de lui se crée un marché commun des lectures. . . . Sydney Schiff est lui-même une véritable 'circulating library', et le livre est la monnaie d'échange entre amis. (Huxley 1976: 16)[3]

The Schiffs were determined to foster artistic creation and were known to have welcomed Filippo Marinetti into their London home where he preached the aesthetics of Futurism to their guests (Grindea 1957: 8).

Sydney Schiff is best known for his self-appointed role as Proust's agent in England. In his first letter to Proust, discovered by Pyra Wise,[4] he used flattery as the opening gambit: 'Depuis la publication de votre délicieux ouvrage "Le cote de chez Swann", vous êtes considéré par tous ceux qui m'entourent comme un écrivain de premier rang.'[5] He succeeded in forging a friendship with Proust which was founded on mutual self-interest. Schiff not only wanted to claim Proust as his literary property in England, he also wanted Proust to help him get his own work published in France. Proust saw Schiff's community of friends as an asset which he hoped to exploit through the sale of the luxury edition of *Du côté de chez Swann*. Just a few months after receiving Schiff's first letter, Proust wrote to ask if he and his wife knew potential buyers (Proust 1970–93, vol. 18: 293). When the volume was ready for purchase a year later, he headed the list of contacts he sent to his publisher with the Schiffs' name and London address (Proust 1970–93, vol. 19: 355). In the intervening months, Proust had tried to curry favour with the Schiffs by dropping Sydney's name in a pre-published extract from *Albertine disparue*. He has his character M. de Norpois specify that the man he is talking about is an English Jew named Sydney, adding parenthetically '(aucun rapport avec le charmant Sydney Schiff)'.[6] Proust apologises that he had not asked Schiff for permission to cite his name albeit with a flattering epithet and attempted to ingratiate himself by calling the citation a 'petite carte de visite amicale' (Proust 1970–93, vol. 19: 418).[7]

Schiff had adopted a similar strategy when he dedicated his novel *Richard Kurt* to 'Mr M. P.'. The dedication was intended to be a token of admiration but, given that he had not yet met Proust when *Richard Kurt* was published in 1919, it comes across more as a boastful claim to the close relationship he hoped would ensue. Positioned on the threshold of the text in the space in between the intimacy of reading and writing on the one hand and publication and open circulation on the other, the dedication characterises the relationship between Proust and the Schiffs which conflated the public and the private. Schiff reiterated his obsequious esteem of Proust when he dedicated his novel *Prince Hempseed* 'To the Memory of my Beloved Friend, Marcel Proust, November 18 1922' (Hudson 1923c).

Proust and Schiff did not meet until August 1920, after both writers had proclaimed the other's name in their publications. The exchange that followed highlights how Schiff assured the reception of Proust's work both informally through table-talk and correspondence, and more conventionally as translator of the concluding volume of *À la recherche du temps perdu*. Schiff also authored a review of Proust's work covering the parts that had been published by 1919 and paid formal tribute to him on his death in 1922.

Background modernist music

The Schiffs' most ostentatious promotion of modernism was undoubtedly the dinner party at the Majestic celebrating Stravinsky's *Renard* staged by Diaghilev. The pulse of modernism was already palpable in Paris when it premiered in the spring of 1922: Joyce's *Ulysses* had been published a few months earlier and Proust's *Sodome et Gomorrhe II* went on sale at the end of April 1922. The scandal of the first performance of *The Rite of Spring* in 1913 had catapulted Stravinsky into the vanguard of modernism. Although *Renard* made much less of a mark than the riot provoked by *The Rite*, it is given pride of place by Daniel Albright who opens his study *Untwisting the Serpent: Modernism in Music, Literature and Other Arts* by citing *Renard* as an example of how 'Modernist art often assaults the concept of genre' (Albright 2000: 1). Stravinsky calls his composition a 'burlesque' but that term fails to take account of its original use of acrobatics and interchangeable vocal parts. Stravinsky was commissioned to compose *Renard* by Winnaretta Singer, the American heiress to the Singer sewing machine fortune who became Princesse de Polignac when she married Proust's friend Prince Edmond de Polignac, who was himself a composer. The fact that Stravinsky composed the work during the war necessarily had an impact on it: his brief was to produce a piece which could be performed in a domestic space, hence with a reduced orchestra. Despite the constraints, Stravinsky composed music that was innovative and marked a new stage in his work.[8] He satirises power by setting his burlesque in a barnyard with animals playing the parts of violent trickster oppressor (the fox), the proud, gullible victim (the cock) and admonishing advisers (the goat and the cat). Its energy results from the conflation of songs derived from traditional Russian folk music and acrobatic dancing inspired by the circus. It is noteworthy for its constantly changing time signature and syncopated rhythm which Sylvia Kahan describes as 'angular music, clangorous and vibrant' (Kahan 2009a: 228). It is emblematic of modernist creation because it cannot be labelled as belonging to a conventional genre: as Kahan explains, it 'ascribes no strong definition to the identity of its characters; the placement of the singers in the midst of the orchestra blurred the identification of a voice with its corresponding onstage character. Most importantly, the lines between sound and visual image are blurred' (Kahan 2009a: 228).[9] Theodor Adorno signalled *Renard*'s modernist destruction of all coherence of character in his *Philosophy of New Music*, interpreting it as the composer's defiant attempt to 'épater le bourgeois' (Adorno 1990: 155).[10]

Stravinsky's use of the octatonic scale accounts for the work's disconcerting sonic modernism. Built on eight notes alternating between intervals of a whole tone and a half tone, the octatonic scale undermines the reassurance guaranteed by conventional resolution on the tonic key. Stravinsky's recourse to the octatonic scale at key moments in the piece enhances their bizarreness: the instrumental ensemble accompanying the cock's 'leap of death' at rehearsal bar 20 plays all the notes comprising the octatonic scale; the duet of the two horns marking the arrival of the cat and goat on the scene (rehearsal bars 24–6) also uses all the notes of the octatonic scale; and the lament the cock sings when the fox begins to pluck its feathers is composed as a descending octatonic scale (rehearsal bar 57). The sense of unease in these passages is created by the unusual tonality of the octatonic scale which destroys familiarity and gives rise to discomfort. Stravinsky's use of the octatonic scale was an artistic stance as well as a sycophantic tribute to the Princess de Polignac's late husband who had claimed to have invented it.[11]

Renard was also inspired by Russian folk music which, according to Kahan, 'conformed perfectly to the ideals of 1920s modernism' (Kahan 2009a: 228). The libretto used nonsense syllables and neologisms which resist translation. Stravinsky cites it as an example of what cannot be translated without destroying cultural unity, though ironically the work premiered using a French libretto and not the original Russian. He points to the passage he calls a *'pribaoutki'* ('a droll song, sometimes to nonsense syllables, sometimes in part spoken'), affirming that 'no translation of this passage can translate what I have done musically with the language.' This untranslatability brands the work as modernist because, according to Stravinsky, semantic meaning is only a part of the composition, not its defining feature: he celebrates the rich culture of multilingualism dominated by the language of music, concluding that, 'musically speaking, Babel is a blessing' (Stravinsky and Craft 1959: 36).

The first performance of *Renard* was conducted by Ernest Ansermet, using a set and costumes designed by Michel Larinov and choreography by Bronislava Nijnska who also danced the title role. At the Paris Opera on 18 May 1922, Stravinsky's twenty-minute piece was part of a double bill following Tchaikovsky's *Le Mariage de la Belle au Bois Dormant*. The classicism of the first piece did not prepare the ground for a favourable reception of Stravinsky's *Renard* and reviews in the press the following days ranged from guarded, to bemused, to downright dismissive. André Messager conceded that the piece was amusing and ingeniously novel, despite its extremely strange musical effects.[12] Louis Schneider thought that the work defied classification in the way it confounded music and noise. He conceded that Stravinsky had great talent and recognised the experimental quality of *Renard*. For all its dissonance, *Renard* has a purer musical line than *The Rite of Spring*, though Schneider questioned where Stravinsky's perilous wanderings would lead him in the domain of music without music.[13]

Stravinsky's work might have served as a pretext for Schiff's dinner party, but it diminished into background music during the evening itself. Although Proust admired Stravinsky's 'genius' and the 'prodigious efflorescence of the Ballets russes' (Proust 1987–9, vol. 3: 140), he did not attend the premiere of *Renard*. Nor did the piece elicit much reaction from the other guests, judging from the fact that there is no record of what was said about it. Nevertheless, the party has become legendary because it was where Proust and Joyce met for the first and only time.

Table-talk across borders

The various accounts of the meeting of the quartet of modernist artists orchestrated by Schiff all agree that the 'great' event was in fact a non-event. Proust left no trace of the conversations he allegedly had with Stravinsky[14] and Joyce, though the latter recalls how inconclusive theirs was:

> Our talk consisted solely of the word 'No'. Proust asked me if I knew the duc de so-and-so. I said, 'No.' Our hostess asked Proust if he had read such and such a piece of *Ulysses*. Proust said, 'No.' And so on. Of course the situation was impossible. Proust's day was just beginning. Mine was at its end. (Budgen 1955: 11)

That version was corroborated by Violet Schiff who wrote, 'so far as I can tell not many words were exchanged between them. Naturally they knew of each other's fame, but neither of them had read the other's books' (Schiff 1957: 64).

Proust and Joyce left the party together, with the Schiffs, and found themselves literally face to face during the short ride back to Proust's apartment. The only words pronounced were to ask Joyce to extinguish his cigarette and to instruct him to close the carriage window. Joyce's wistful regret that their conversation remained so banal is expressed through aposiopesis: 'If we'd been allowed to meet and have a talk somewhere –' (quoted in Ellmann 1977: 524). He might be transposing that disappointment in *Finnegans Wake*, when he rewrites the English title of Proust's *Sodome et Gomorrhe – Cities of the Plain* – as 'pities of the plain' (Joyce 2000: 564). Joyce clearly associates Proust with homosexuality as he embeds that phrase in a passage replete with bawdy references to anal sex. Although the literary outcome of the Proust–Joyce meeting was so meagre, it gave rise to several first- and second-hand accounts – notably by Clive Bell, Ford Madox Ford and William Carlos Williams – which contributed to the circulation of Proust's name in the English-speaking world. The Schiffs' dinner party thus led to some indirect publicity for Proust's work.[15]

The Schiffs tackled their mandate of establishing Proust's reputation in England by mentioning his name as often as possible, boasting in a letter to him: 'Nous parlons de vous tout le temps.'[16] They introduced Katherine Mansfield to his work, as Sydney reports to Proust that during a luncheon with her, 'nous n'avons parlé que de vous'.[17] The Schiffs took credit for making Proust known in England: 'Tu es, si tu le veux ou non, bien nôtre découverte. Avant nous il n'y avait personne mais après nous tous ceux que tu veux. C'est nôtre partie à nous et personne au monde ne peut nous la voler.'[18] They were possessive of Proust, but their claim that they were the first to discuss him in England is overstated as *Du côté de chez Swann* had been reviewed in the *Times Literary Supplement* a couple of years before the Schiffs had even heard of its author.[19]

Literary criticism in action

Schiff's informal promotion of Proust in society was complemented by the articles he published as tributes to his work. He counts among Proust's earliest reviewers in England, publishing 'A Note on Marcel Proust' under his pseudonym Stephen Hudson in the autumn 1919 issue of *Art and Letters*. The journal was a channel for modernist work and published drawings by Modigliani, Wyndham Lewis, Paul Nash and Henri Gaudier-Brzeska; criticism by T. S. Eliot; prose by Katherine Mansfield; and poetry by Edith Sitwell and her brother Osbert. Schiff's article foregrounds Proust's modernism in its opening question: 'What is a novel?' He argues that new terminology is required to account for Proust's innovative writing as his work does not fit into existing categories. He praises Proust as 'the most distinguished living exponent' of a writer 'making a deliberate attempt to express vital experience' (Hudson 1919: 200). He illustrates his points through two long extracts, reproduced in French, both from *À l'ombre des jeunes filles en fleurs* which had prompted his article. The first passage[20] relates how the young narrator experiences place names through sensory associations. Those experiences are compared to the perception of music which varies according to transposition involving different harmonies or orchestration. Schiff questions the notion of significance in literature, contrasting Proust's work with contemporary English novels by H. G. Wells and Arnold Bennett:

> Now, after all, what is a 'trivial' subject? M. Proust's atmosphere is, it is true, unsordid. Are coal-miners or Welsh peasants less trivial than wealthy Parisians? Do 'Mr. Britling' and 'Clayhanger' rule fiction by divine right? In the commonwealth of letters has any set of characters more right than another set to lord it over their fellows? (Hudson 1919: 204)

Schiff suggests that literature should not be preoccupied with social hierarchy when he answers the question 'What is a "significant" subject for a novel?' by another question: 'In nature, is the life of a cart-horse more significant than the life of a bird of Paradise?' Schiff claims that Proust's portrayal of the higher social spheres was fortuitous and not a deliberate choice on his part: 'it so happens that M. Proust writes about people who are by fortune removed from activities which absorb the multitude' (Hudson 1919: 204).

The second passage Schiff quotes at length[21] illustrates the cultural differences between England and France, underscoring that the *grande bourgeoisie*'s social values were little known on the other side of the Channel. Schiff posits that the upper bourgeoisie in France 'is very exclusive in every sense and the exclusiveness is based upon a security, familial and moral, foreign to English habits' (Hudson 1919: 205). The Proust passage he chose to make his point relates the young narrator's devotion to his grandmother which Schiff thought would be considered ridiculous in an English context. He quotes extensively to let Proust's prose speak for itself, explaining that 'His is a delicate sensibility and to analyse it would be something of an outrage' (Hudson 1919: 205–6).

Schiff contributed to the volumes of official tribute published in both England and France in the wake of Proust's death. The first contribution, signed Stephen Hudson and edited by the *Nouvelle Revue française* (NRF) in January 1923, asserts Schiff's status as a writer in its title 'Témoignage d'un romancier'. He begins by describing his relationship with Proust as organic: 'Marcel Proust prit racine en moi en 1915' (Hudson 1923a: 254).[22] He defines Proust's method as one of assimilation and praises his audacity in mapping Sodom and Gomorrah (Hudson 1923a: 256), singling out his portrait of Charlus as the novel's greatest triumph. Schiff's tribute in the NRF's *Hommage à Marcel Proust* endows Proust's work with an international dimension, as he views it from the perspective of 'son legs à la civilisation européenne' (Hudson 1923a: 258).[23]

Schiff wrote the opening piece of *An English Tribute*, which was edited by Proust's first translator, Charles Scott Moncrieff. Entitled 'A Portrait', Schiff began by declaring that he knew of no better word than 'unique' to describe Proust's contribution to literature (Hudson 1923b: 5). He praised Proust as a master of alchemy who transforms the finest, apparently insignificant, detail into art:

> He possessed that rarest gift of touching everyday people, things, and concerns with gold, imparting to them a vital and abiding interest. Anything and everything served as a starting point, nothing was too minute to kindle an idea and provoke suggestive utterance. (Hudson 1923b: 6)

Schiff insisted that Proust was not an aesthete in search of 'an aesthetic disguise for the ugly, the sordid, or the base' (Hudson 1923b: 6). Schiff did not consider him to be egotistical, though he concedes that he was 'intensely concerned with his own consciousness' (Hudson 1923b: 7).

Schiff not only authored articles on Proust, he also ensured that his name was cited in English-language publications. As a patron of *The Tyro*, he endorsed the presence of Proust's name in the context of modernism and the editorialist's claim that it would be 'impossible to destroy' Marcel Proust (Lewis 1922: 6). Schiff also paid tribute to Proust in his fiction. His short story 'Céleste', published in the *Criterion* in April 1924,[24] narrates the last stages in the composition of Proust's novel from the point of view of his housekeeper, Céleste Albaret. Schiff invents an example of how Proust appreciates the transformative power of light playing on everyday objects which he presents as a series of still lifes:

> He never noticed things at all apart from some quality of interest or beauty he found in them. When, for instance, the sun, casting its rays into the corner of the room, illuminated it in some fashion that pleased him, or touched with fantastic colour an object – a jug or coffee-cup or a half-emptied glass of beer – then his eyes, falling on whatever object it was, would remain fixed upon it, even for an hour or more, and whether it was day or night, he would not allow it be moved. Sometimes he insisted on its remaining indefinitely because he wanted to renew the sensation it had given him, so it often happened that in different parts of the room there were articles left for days in quite unsuitable places in case the light or the atmosphere should again transmute them into something other than they were. (Hudson 1924: 20–1)

As well as a piece of literary criticism 'in action', to use Proust's term (Proust 1970–93, vol. 8: 61), this short story also recreates Proust's world: 'Céleste' is an amalgamation of fiction and biography which invited English-speaking readers into the intimacy of the bedroom where Proust composed his work. It is an important text in terms of the circulation of culture because it foregrounds the role played by the actors in the wings: Proust's housekeeper, the errand boy, his editor and Schiff himself cast as an amicable cultural attaché.

Schiff also authored several semi-autobiographical novels, casting himself in the role of Richard Kurt. *Richard, Myrtle and I*, published in 1926, is a curious allegory of literary creation which makes striking use of a first-person narrative voice. The eponymous 'I' is a disembodied voice which carries out a dialogue with Richard, persuading or dissuading him in his actions. The narrative revolves around Richard's desire to become a writer which is only fulfilled thanks to an encounter with Proust. Myrtle is the first to discover the French author and the narration of how she reacts to his work transposes Schiff's critical essay on Proust into a piece of creative writing. In his 'Témoignage d'un romancier', he had described the impact of reading Proust as a process of assimilation (Hudson 1923a: 255); in the narrative, he writes that 'the book ... entered into the fabric of her being' (Hudson 1962: 127). Proust cast a spell over Richard, Myrtle and 'I', fundamentally altering their outlook as well as fuelling their joint creativity by disclosing 'an unsuspected outlet for the force that was driving' them onwards (Hudson 1962: 128). In his narrative, Schiff reiterates his conviction that Proust had forged an original literary form which surpassed the conventional novel and transcended national boundaries:

> this epistolary wizard had not only created a new mould for literature, he had imposed upon the French mind a new standard of human values which must inevitably influence European thought and by which, as inevitably, the creative literature of the future must be judged. (Hudson 1962: 127)

Schiff's literary criticism in action is at the same time a fictionalised account of the French author's agency in Kurt's creativity and certainly his most original tribute to Proust.

In addition to publicising Proust in print, Schiff carried out an extensive correspondence constituting a largely unpublished record of how Schiff engineered Proust's reception in England.[25] It began with Schiff's request for an article he could publish in his journal *Art and Letters*. In keeping with his multiple identities, Schiff pretended he was writing on behalf of a friend, namely his literary persona Stephen Hudson:

> Un de mes amis intimes, Stephen Hudson, écrivain qui sortira sans doute bientôt d'une obscurité relative, va éditer une revue périodique trimestrielle reprise depuis la guerre, 'Art and Letters'. Il désire faire de ce journal dont la publication n'a d'autre objet que de servir l'art, un forum international pour des discussions d'intérêt artistique. Il vous serait infiniment reconnaissant si vous vouliez lui envoyer une courte contribution de caractère psychologique; un simple fragment suffirait. Il paraîtrait naturellement comme vous l'auriez écrit, en français.[26]

Schiff hoped his letter would set in motion the eddying currents of cross-Channel exchange which would characterise his 'international forum'. Schiff was not discouraged by Proust's initial negative response (Proust 1970–93, vol. 18: 165), and a couple of years later reiterated the request for an extract, this time for Eliot's *Criterion*, the journal which superseded *Art and Letters*. Schiff was quick to point out his decisive role as intermediary and even enabler on multiple fronts:

> T.S. Eliot (le poète et critique dont je vous ai souvent parlé et qui fait les articles sur la littérature anglaise dans la N.R.F.) est venu me voir. Il sollicita mon intermédiaire auprès de vous pour avoir quelquechose d'inédite pour la nouvelle revue trimestrielle (subventionnée par Lady Rothermere femme du frère de Lord Northcliffe) dont il est rédacteur. J'ai beaucoup à vous dire à ce sujet. Suffit-il maintenant que je vous dise que cette conjonction de Eliot et de Lady Rothermere s'est accomplie par mon entremise.[27]

Schiff added that Eliot's journal was designed to be a forum for modernism comparable to the *Nouvelle Revue française*: 'Cette revue sera, je crois, la meilleure et la plus moderne en Angleterre, un peu du genre N.R.F.'[28] Eliot's concern to assert his journal's status on the international scene prompted him to write to Ezra Pound: 'Do you recommend anybody in France for the *Criterion*? ... the only name worth getting is *Proust*, whom I'm fishing for' (Eliot 1988: 539). He told Schiff that he wanted to 'secure [Proust's] support before the appearance of the first number' (Eliot 1988: 543). Schiff jealously guarded his position as go-between and responded with irritation when he learnt that Eliot had written directly to Proust, advising the latter: 'Je préférerai pour beaucoup de raisons qu'en ce qui concerne cette question (i.e. vôtre [*sic*] contribution à la revue de Eliot) toute communication passe par moi.'[29]

Eliot flattered Schiff that he would make the best translator of Proust (Eliot 1988: 537), and yet it was Scott Moncrieff who produced the English version of the pre-published excerpt from *Albertine disparue*. Schiff did not participate directly in the final exchanges between Eliot and Proust's editor Jacques Rivière but can take credit for having initiated the proceedings which led to the publication of the 'The Death of Albertine' in the *Criterion* of July 1924. Although the publication was, in Eliot's mind, 'merely a necessary sensation' (Eliot 2009: 233) designed to ensure 'the making' (Eliot 2009: 369) of the next issue of the *Criterion*, it also partook in the reception of Proust's work across the Channel.

The empathy of translation

In the course of their ongoing correspondence, Proust turned to Schiff when the question of translating his novel into English arose: 'Savez-vous que beaucoup de journaux anglais sont très gentils pour moi et font allusion familièrement à de si minces détails de *Swann* que cela prouve une grande connaissance. Quel malheur que ce ne soit pas traduit' (Proust 1970–93, vol. 19: 436).[30] In his response, Schiff explained that the translation might not circulate widely in England as the few people there who appreciate good literature would probably prefer to read Proust's work in the original French. His concern about finding a competent translator could not have made his arrogance more evident: 'Je n'en connais aucun excepté moi-même qui en ferait une traduction convenable' (Proust 1970–93, vol. 19: 451).[31] Schiff repeatedly boasted that he shared Proust's sensibility and intelligence, claiming an affinity which set him above other critics and translators:

> il n'y a pas qui comprennent comme nous comprenons, qui apprécient comme nous toutes les nuances, qui sentent ce qui n'est pas dit autant que ce qui est dit, qui réagissent comme nous dans les fibres de notre être à vos pensées intimes. (Proust 1970–93, vol. 21: 303)[32]

Schiff literally imbibed Proust, as he said in his praise of *Le Côté de Guermantes* which he was savouring through slow reading: 'voulant saisir et posséder entièrement votre pensée aussi fugitive (évitante?) ou subtile qu'elle soit. Je goûte vos phrases comme on goûte le parfum d'un vieux Chambertin dont on roule une bouchée sur la langue avant de l'avaler' (Proust 1970–93, vol. 19: 592).[33] Schiff took possession of Proust's thoughts and feelings, incorporating them and making them his own. Proust returned the compliment by pointing out the similarity in the attitude of Schiff's mother-in-law during his wife's illness and that of the grandmother's sisters towards her in his novel, exclaiming 'quelle "Harmonie préétablie" entre nous' (Proust 1970–93, vol. 19: 602).

Schiff was caught between his sense that he was best placed to translate Proust thanks to their affinity and his apprehension that he would not be able to do justice to the original text. His disappointment at not being appointed translator was overshadowed by the jealousy he felt towards Scott Moncrieff, knowing that translation means penetrating the intimate workings of the mind of the author of the source text:

Au fond, je ne regrette pas de ne pas l'avoir faite parce que j'en aurais jamais été content et parce que j'aurais trop souffert. C'est vrai que j'ai été jaloux de l'intimité avec vôtre [sic] âme que Moncrieff a mérité si, comme il paraît, la traduction est bonne.[34]

Although the English translation was entrusted to Scott Moncrieff, Schiff wanted to take charge of it, explaining to Proust that he could act as go-between with his publisher:

Quant à la traduction tu n'as qu'à dire à Gallimard que tu veux que les éditeurs anglais se mettent d'accord avec moi. Je veillerai à ce que les titres soient au moins convenablement adéquats et si la traduction n'est pas passable je te le dirai. Mon temps et toute la capacité dont je dispose sont à toi.[35]

He had a predictably negative view of Scott Moncrieff's work, in particular his choice of titles. In his letter to Proust on the subject, he retranslated the English titles back into French, revealing that he had failed to recognise Scott Moncrieff's suggestive use of a line from one of Shakespeare's sonnets:

Les titres ne me plaisent pas. 'Souvenir de choses passées' et 'À la manière de Swann' ou 'La façon de Swann'. Je pense qu'on aurait pu trouver des titres plus près des tiens qui sont si admirablement choisis. Il y a dans *À la recherche du temps perdu* une nuance mélancolique, un je ne sais quoi de poignant et de suggestif – un double sens dans le mot perdu – est-ce que ce temps était perdu? Est-ce qu'il est regretté? Tant d'autres pensées. Et *Du côté de chez Swann* en contenant le double sens du point de vue de Swann et de la localité – un double sens miraculeusement bien trouvé, suggère un autre qui en son tour exprime la psychologie de ce garçon adorable qui vivait de l'autre côté, ses rêves et ses désirs, ses regrets et ses espoirs. (Proust 1970–93, vol. 21: 469)[36]

After this initial outburst of criticism, Schiff conceded that Scott Moncrieff's translation was better than he and his wife had expected and admits that it furthers the cause of the favourable reception of Proust's work in England: 'nous croyons que le traducteur a apprécié le livre et qu'il en a admiré et aimé l'auteur. En somme nous pensons que c'est une chose bien réussie et que tu peux t'en féliciter.'[37] Schiff confessed that he was devoured by jealousy ('la jalousie me mange'), going so far as to say that he never wanted to hear Scott Moncrieff's name again because 'chaque fois que j'en lis ou que j'en entends des louanges est comme un poignard fourré entre mes côtes'.[38] He had a similar visceral reaction when he heard praise for the translator despite his vicarious pleasure that Proust's book was receiving critical acclaim in England:

> Je ne peux pas me plaindre de la façon dont ton livre a été reçu par les critiques anglais dans son habit anglais. Les tailleurs anglais sont reconnus comme les meilleurs et c'est l'affaire des journaux de faire marcher le commerce. J'ai chaque fois un peu envie de vomir quand je lis de nouveau les éloges effusifs qu'on prodigue à ton traducteur mais je les avale avec la meilleure grâce que je puis me commander en pensant à l'effet avantageux pour toi dont je jouirai par substitution. (Proust 1970–93, vol. 21: 534–5)[39]

Schiff was also dissatisfied with the English critics' reaction to Proust: he said he would have undertaken a serious analysis of his novel himself had he not lacked the critical fibre to do so, repeating the same phrase he had used about translating Proust's text: 'Je ne pourrais pas me satisfaire moi-même' (Proust 1970–93, vol. 21: 303).[40] Despite his reservations about them, Schiff had the grace to recognise that the translation and its reception in the press were instrumental in making Proust's name known in England.

Sydney Schiff took over the translation of Proust's multi-volume novel when Scott Moncrieff's death left the task unfinished. Schiff's translation of the last volume of *À la recherche du temps perdu* was published in 1931, under his pen-name Stephen Hudson. His title *Time Regained* resonates with Miltonian overtones in harmony with the phrase from Proust's novel cited on the title page: 'les vrais paradis sont les paradis qu'on a perdus' (Proust 1987–9, vol. 4: 449).[41] The first sentence of Proust's *Le Temps retrouvé* provides a good illustration of how Schiff translated:

> Toute la journée, dans cette demeure de Tansonville un peu trop campagne, qui n'avait l'air que d'un lieu de sieste entre deux promenades ou pendant l'averse, une de ces demeures où chaque salon a l'air d'un cabinet de verdure, et où sur la tenture des chambres, les roses du jardin dans l'une, les oiseaux des arbres dans l'autre, vous ont rejoints et vous tiennent compagnie – isolés du moins – car c'étaient de vieilles tentures où chaque rose était assez séparée pour qu'on eût pu, si elle avait été vivante, la cueillir, chaque oiseau le mettre en cage et l'apprivoiser, sans rien de ces grandes décorations des chambres d'aujourd'hui où,

sur un fond d'argent, tous les pommiers de Normandie sont venus se profiler en style japonais, pour halluciner les heures que vous passez au lit, toute la journée je la passais dans ma chambre qui donnait sur les belles verdures du parc et les lilas de l'entrée, sur les feuilles vertes des grands arbres au bord de l'eau, étincelants de soleil, et sur la forêt de Méséglise.

Schiff translated as follows:

Tansonville seemed little more than a place to rest in between two walks or a refuge during a shower. Rather too countrified, it was one of those rural dwellings where every sitting-room is a cabinet of greenery, and where the roses and the birds out in the garden keep you company in the curtains; for they were old and each rose stood out so clearly that it might have been picked like a real one and each bird put in a cage, unlike those pretentious modern decorations in which, against a silver background, all the apple trees in Normandy are outlined in the Japanese manner, to trick the hours you lie in bed. I spent the whole day in my room, the windows of which opened upon the beautiful verdure of the park, upon the lilacs of the entrance, upon the green leaves of the great trees beside the water and in the forest of Méséglise. (Proust 1931: 1)

Schiff restructured the opening sentence into three, thereby failing to replicate Proust's inaugural reference to time which echoes back to the first sentence of the novel in *Du côté de chez Swann:* 'Longtemps je me suis couché de bonne heure.'[42] Schiff substituted time with place and deleted Proust's emphasis on duration achieved through the repetition of the phrase 'toute la journée' which is taken up again in the pronoun 'la'. There are several omissions in Schiff's translation: in the English version, the birds are not isolated, nor are they tamed and the trees do not shimmer in the sun. There is also an error in the interior decoration as the room Proust describes is wallpapered with a design featuring roses and birds, which the translator mistakes for curtains.

The translation was censured by Mina Curtiss as 'atrocious' (Curtiss 1978: 27) and as 'disastrous' by Joceyln Brooke, who condemned it further: 'Not only is the prose ... clumsy and unmusical, but the translation itself is either absurdly literal or downright inaccurate' (Brooke 1962: 76–80). She singled out a howler which is particularly egregious as it comes from a passage in which the narrator is reflecting on the interpretation of signs. It concerns the sentence: 'Mlle Swann me jetait de l'autre côté de la haie d'épines roses, un regard dont j'avais dû, d'ailleurs, rétrospectivement retoucher la signification, qui était du désir' (Proust 1987–9, vol. 4: 549). Schiff's translation reads, 'Mlle. Swann throwing some thorny roses to me from the other side of the hedge, with a look I had retrospectively attributed to desire' (Proust 1931: 341) and justifies Brooke's damning comment that 'one is tempted to suppose that Hudson simply didn't know French' (Brooke 1962: 79). In Schiff's defence, he was working from the first, faulty edition of *Le Temps retrouvé*: the phrase he so spectacularly mistranslated was missing the comma before 'de l'autre côté' which would have made the structure of the sentence clearer. Aldous Huxley, to whom Schiff turned for help in making sense of Proust's prose, agreed that it was a challenge to translate it: 'one has to be an Oedipus to solve the Proust enigma' (Huxley 1976: 71). Perhaps because he had been intimately involved with it, Huxley was complimentary about Schiff's translation: it 'seems to me to walk along Proust's devious tight rope of stretched words with all the grace and nimbleness that can be put into that all but impossible proceeding' (Huxley 1976: 73). Schiff openly acknowledged Huxley's contribution to the translation, expressing both gratitude and strategic name-dropping in the translator's note he added at the beginning of the volume. Huxley's part in the translation might have been limited to the interpretation of one sentence, but it is significant in that it adds another name to the group of English modernists encircling Proust.

Thanks to Schiff, Proust's name was linked with that 'excruciatingly irascible'[43] leader of the Vorticist movement, Wyndham Lewis. Lewis coupled their names together when he declared both of them exponents of what he called 'our present European movement' (Lewis 1922: 8), engaged in 'radical experimental work' (Lewis 1922: 3). Schiff shared Lewis's assessment of Proust's work which he felt had exhausted the possibilities of the novel: 'je pense qu'avec vous nous sommes arrivés à la fin de la forme du roman. Il ne reste plus rien que l'on puisse en faire, tout [ce] dont le roman est capable vous l'avez fait ou vous le ferez' (Proust 1970–93, vol. 21: 390).[44] Far from returning the compliment, Lewis insultingly classified Schiff as 'an ape of god' in his ferocious satire of the art world in post-war London, *The Apes of God* (1930). He alludes to Schiff as a 'pseudo-Proust' (Lewis 1981: 122)[45] and portrays him as Lionel Kein, scorning his artistic pretentions and deriding his hero-worship: 'At the name of Proust [Kein] ran up his state-flag. Proust, when he entered his soul, made him more self-confident than the Viking, even. He was ready for anything under that banner' (Lewis 1981: 246). Lewis mocked Schiff's obsession with Proust and his attempts to ensure his own literary celebrity through assimilation, scripting one character to pander to Kein when he calls him '*a perfect Proust-character!*' (Lewis 1981: 246). Proust himself was no less obsequious when he wrote to explain to Lewis that he would probably not be well enough to sit for the portrait Schiff had asked him to do: 'Et pourtant être dessiné par vous eût été ma seule chance de passer à la postérité!' (Proust 1970–93, vol. 21: 347).[46] Deleting the hyperbole, Proust's compliment indicates that he had been in contact with Lewis, through Schiff's intervention, and that he was aware of the latter's status in the contemporary art world.

Schiff was criticised for having many faults – snobbery, meddling, lionising – but he suppressed his self-interest when he ranked his translation of Proust above his other works: 'This is the only work of mine I know to be worth preserving because it is the interpretation of a masterpiece every word of which was and is precious to me' (quoted in Boll 1962: 39). Proust reciprocated by pressuring Rivière and Gallimard to publish Schiff's work. That came to fruition over ten years after his death, with the publication of Emmanuel Boudot-Lamotte's French rendition of *A True Story* by Stephen Hudson in 1935.[47] The French translations of Schiff's work illustrate how a major author enables the publication of a minor author's work while enhancing his own reputation. In his translator's note prefacing the text, Boudot-Lamotte explicitly points to Schiff's debt to Proust: 'S'il était d'usage de dédier les traductions, celle-ci le serait à la mémoire de Marcel Proust à qui elle doit d'exister' (Hudson 1935).[48]

Although Schiff's translation of *Le Temps retrouvé* was so full of errors that it was quickly superseded by a more accurate one, this networker par excellence played an appreciable part in introducing Proust to the London literary scene and transmitting his work in England. The way he idolised Proust might be derided by Lewis and yet, however negative, it was publicity for Proust across the Channel nonetheless.

Notes

1. *The Modernist Party* is the title of a volume of essays edited by Kate McLoughlin. In her introduction she stresses the 'huge significance' of the modernist parties in 'extending patronage, forging creative alliances (and *mésalliances*), sparking productive disagreements and enabling knowledge transfer' (McLoughlin 2013: 9). The Schiffs' dinner party

at the Hôtel Majestic heads the list of 'dazzling one-off set-pieces', but that is all that is said about it (McLoughlin 2013: 9).
2. From Eliot's note appended to the unsigned obituary of 'Mrs. Violet Schiff: All-Embracing Interest in the Arts'. See Eliot (1962: 18).
3. 'This apoliticism in Schiff's judgement made him a cosmopolitan. Art has no frontiers and literary production is seen on a European scale. A common market of reading emerges around him. Sydney Schiff is truly his own 'circulating library' and the book is the currency in which friends transact.'
4. Pyra Wise found forty-nine unpublished letters from Sydney and Violet Schiff to Marcel Proust at the Bibliothèque nationale de France (NAF 27352, fols 129–201). She presented this unpublished material in the paper she gave on the Schiffs at the 'Proust et ses amis' conference (Fondation Singer-Polignac, Paris, 2011) and published many of the extracts of the Schiffs' unpublished letters given in this paper (see Wise 2013: 209–23).
5. NAF 27352 (Abbreviated reference: MS). MS fol. 129, 20 March 1919. 'Since the publication of your delectable work "Swann's Way", everyone around me thinks you are a first-rate author.' In this, and subsequent transcriptions of his unpublished letters, Schiff's minor errors in French have been retained.
6. The excerpt was first published in *Le Matin*, 11 December 1919, and cited here from the illustrated version of the excerpt reprinted in Proust (1919: 6). Schiff's name is deleted from subsequent versions of the text.
7. 'a small, friendly calling card'.
8. For an in-depth study of the piece, see Taruskin (1996: 1237–92).
9. She derives these points from Albright (2000: 37–8).
10. 'To shock the middle class'. The phrase is in French in the original German text.
11. See his unpublished treatise 'Étude sur les successions alternantes de tons et demi-tons (Et sur la gamme dite majeure-mineure)', written circa 1879, transcribed and translated in Kahan (2009b: 143–334).
12. See Messager (1922: 5).
13. See Schneider (1922: 3).
14. For Stravinsky's version, see Stravinsky and Craft (1959: 99).
15. See, for example, Bell (1929: 12–14), Ford (1933: 293–4) and Williams (1951: 218).
16. See collection of letters in the Proust collection, *Bibliothèque nationale de France*, N.A.Fr. 27352. Abbreviated reference: MS fol. 176, 4 June 1922. 'We talk about you all the time.'
17. MS fol. 167, 21 May 1922. 'You were all we talked about.'
18. MS, fol. 184, 9 July 1922. 'Like it or not, you are indeed our discovery. No one knew about you before, but after us, you can take your pick. You are our prize catch and no one in the world can take that from us.'
19. See [Duclaux] 1913: 585.
20. Corresponding to Proust (1987–9, vol. 2: 22).
21. Corresponding to Proust (1987–9, vol. 2: 86–7).

22. 'Marcel Proust took root in me in 1915.'
23. 'his legacy to European civilisation'.
24. See Hudson (1924). The short story was reprinted in volume form by Blackamore Press, in 1930, embellished with a wood engraving by John Nash (Hudson 1930: 13–44).
25. Pyra Wise is preparing an edition of the complete correspondence between Proust and the Schiffs. See Wise (2013: 21n10).
26. MS fol.129, 20 March 1919. 'One of my closest friends, Stephen Hudson, a writer who will doubtless soon emerge from relative obscurity, is going to edit a quarterly review, "Art and Letters", whose publication has started up again after the war. His aim is to make the journal, whose sole objective is to serve art, into an international forum for discussions of an artistic interest. He would be extremely grateful if you would send him a short contribution of a psychological nature: a simple extract would suffice. It would of course appear as you wrote it, in French.'
27. MS fol. 178, 3 July 1922. 'T.S. Eliot (the poet and critic whom I have often mentioned to you, and author of the articles on English literature published in the N.R.F.) came to see me. He asked me to act as a go-between with you as he would like an original contribution for the new quarterly review he edits. It is subsidised by Lady Rothermere, the wife of Lord Northcliffe's brother and I have a lot to tell you about that. For the present let us just say that Eliot and Lady Rothermere have been brought together thanks to me.'
28. 'This periodical will, I believe, be the best and the most modern in England, a bit like the N.R.F.'
29. MS fol. 180, 5 July 1922. 'For various reasons, I would prefer that any communication relating to this question (i.e. your contribution to Eliot's periodical) should go through me.'
30. 'Did you know that many English journals are very favourably disposed towards me and refer to such small details in Swann so intimately that it proves how well they know it. What a pity it has not been translated.'
31. 'I don't know anyone except myself who could translate your work properly.'
32. 'There is no one who understands your work the way we do, who appreciates it in all its nuances as we do, who sense the unsaid as well as what is said, who react as we do to your intimate thoughts in the fibres of our being.'
33. 'wanting to grasp and to entirely possess your thought as elusive (evasive?) and subtle as it is. I delight in your sentences as if savouring the aroma of a vintage Chambertin wine, swilling a mouthful around on the tongue before swallowing it.'
34. MS fol. 189, 3 September 1922. 'Deep down, I have no regrets about not doing it because I would never have been happy with it and it would have cost me too much. It is true that I was jealous of the way Moncrieff communed intimately with your soul if, as it would seem, the translation is a good one.'

35. MS fol. 187, 18 September 1922. 'As for the translation, you could say to Gallimard that you want the English publishers to reach an agreement with me. I will see to it that the titles are at least decently rendered and if the translation is not acceptable, I will tell you. My time and the abilities I have at my disposal are yours.'
36. 'I do not like the titles. *Remembrance of Things Past* and *Swann's Way*. I think that something closer to your superbly chosen French titles could have been found. In *À la recherche du temp perdu* is there not a hint of the melancholic, a *je ne sais quoi* which is poignant and suggestive, a play on the word "lost" – was it wasted time? Or regret about time past? So many other thoughts. And the title *Du côté de chez Swann* contains the double meaning of Swann's point of view and the place – a double meaning which was miraculously well chosen. It suggests a further meaning which in turn expresses the psychology of this adorable boy who lived in a world of his own. In his dreams, his desires, his regrets and his hopes.'
37. MS fol. 188, 29 September 1922. 'We think that the translator appreciated the book and admired and liked its author. In short we think that it's a real success that you can be proud of.'
38. MS fol. 188, 29 September 1922. 'Whenever I read or hear praise of it, it feels like a dagger thrust between my ribs.'
39. 'I cannot complain about the way your book in its English attire has been received by English critics. English tailors are known to be the best and it is the business of newspapers to create turnover. Whenever I read some new effusive praise I feel slightly as if I'm going to vomit. The praise is addressed to your translator but I swallow it with the best grace I can muster thinking of the advantageous effect for you, in which I delight vicariously.'
40. 'I would not be able to satisfy myself.'
41. 'The epitome of paradise is paradise lost.'
42. 'For a long time I went to bed early.'
43. See Klaidman (2013).
44. 'I think that with you we've come to the end of the novel form. There's nothing more that can be done with it, everything that the novel is capable of you have done or will do.'
45. An extract containing this allusion to Schiff was printed in the *Criterion*, 2.7 (April 1924): 300–10. The phrase is on page 306.
46. 'And yet being drawn by you would have been my only chance of a place in posterity!'
47. Emmanuel Boudot-Lamotte's translations were all published by Gallimard: *Une histoire vraie I* (1935) contains the French versions of *The Prince of Hempseed* and *Elinor Colhouse*. *Une histoire vraie II* (1936) contains *Richard Kurt*. The translations of *Myrtle* were published in 1938 and *The Other Side* in 1950.
48. 'If it were the custom to dedicate translations, this one would be to the memory of Marcel Proust to whom it owes its existence.'

Bibliography

Adorno, Theodor W. (1990), *Gesammelte Schriften*, Vol. 12: *Philosophie der Neuen Musik*, ed. Rolf Tiedemann, Frankfurt: Suhrkamp.

Albright, Daniel (2000), *Untwisting the Serpent: Modernism in Music, Literature and Other Arts*, Chicago: University of Chicago Press.

Bell, Clive (1929), *Proust*, New York: Harcourt, Brace and Company.

Boll, Theophilus E. M. (1962), Biographical note and a critical essay on Stephen Hudson, in Stephen Hudson, *Richard, Myrtle and I*, Philadelphia: University of Pennsylvania Press, pp. 15–89.

Brooke, Jocelyn (1962), 'Translating Proust', *London Magazine*, 1.10: 76–80.

Budgen, Frank (1955), *Further Recollections of James Joyce*, London: Shenval Press.

Curtiss, Mina (1978), *Other People's Letters*, London: Macmillan.

Davenport-Hines, Richard (2006), *A Night at the Majestic: Proust and the Great Modernist Dinner Party of 1922*, London: Faber & Faber.

[Duclaux, Mary] (1913), 'Art or Life, "A Small Boy and Others"', *Times Literary Supplement*, 4 December, p. 585. The review is unsigned.

Eliot, T. S. (1962), Note appended to the unsigned obituary of 'Mrs. Violet Schiff: All-Embracing Interest in the Arts', *The Times*, 9 July, p. 18.

Eliot, T. S. (1988), *The Letters of T.S. Eliot*, vol. 1, ed. Valerie Eliot, London: Faber & Faber.

Eliot, T. S. (2009), *The Letters of T.S. Eliot*, vol. 2., ed. Valerie Eliot and Hugh Haughton, London: Faber & Faber.

Ellmann, Richard (1977), *James Joyce*, London: Oxford University Press.

Ford, Ford Madox (1933), *It Was the Nightingale*, London and Philadelphia: J. B. Lippincott.

Grindea, Miron (1957), 'In search of our Proust', *Adam International Review*, 260: 6–53.

Hudson, Stephen (1919), 'À la recherche du temps perdu', *Art and Letters*, 2.4 (Autumn): 200–6.

Hudson, Stephen (1923a), 'Témoignage d'un romancier', *Hommage à Marcel Proust, Nouvelle Revue* (January): 254–8.

Hudson, Stephen (1923b), 'A Portrait', in *Marcel Proust: An English Tribute*, ed. C. K. Scott Moncrieff, London: Chatto & Windus.

Hudson, Stephen (1923c), *Prince Hempseed*, London: M. Secker.

Hudson, Stephen (1924), 'Céleste', *The Criterion*, 2.7 (April): 332–48.

Hudson, Stephen (1930), *'Céleste' and other sketches*, with wood engravings by John Nash, London: Blackamore Press.

Hudson, Stephen (1935), *Une histoire vraie*, trans. Emmanuel Boudot-Lamotte, Paris: Gallimard.

Hudson, Stephen (1962), *Richard, Myrtle and I* [1926], with a biographical note and a critical essay by Theophilus E. M. Boll, Philadelphia: University of Pennsylvania Press.

Huxley, Aldous (1976), *Aldous Huxley, exhumations: correspondance inédite avec Sydney Schiff, 1925–1937*, ed. Clémentine Robert, Paris: Didier.
Joyce, James (2000), *Finnegans Wake* [1939], London: Penguin.
Kahan, Sylvia (2009a), *Music's Modern Muse: A Life of Winnaretta Singer, Princesse de Polignac*, Rochester, NY: University of Rochester Press.
Kahan, Sylvia (2009b), *In Search of New Scales: Prince Edmond de Polignac, Octatonic Explorer*, Rochester, NY: University of Rochester Press.
Klaidman, Stephen (2013), *Sydney and Violet: Their Life with T.S. Eliot, Proust, Joyce and the Excruciatingly Irascible Wyndham Lewis*, New York: Doubleday.
Lewis, Wyndham (1922). Editor's Introduction, *The Tyro*, 2: 3–10.
Lewis, Wyndham (1981), *Apes of God*, afterword by Paul Edwards, Santa Barbara, CA: Black Sparrow Press.
McLoughlin, Kate (2013), *The Modernist Party*, Edinburgh: Edinburgh University Press.
Messager, André (1922) '"Figaro-Théâtre; Les Premières": Théâtre national de l'Opéra (Saison de balles russes)', *Le Figaro*, 21 May 1922, p. 5.
Proust, Marcel (1919). 'À Venise', *Les Feuillets d'art*, 15 December 1919, pp. 1–14.
Proust, Marcel (1924), 'The death of Albertine', trans. Charles Scott Moncrieff, *The Criterion*, 2.8 (July): 376–94.
Proust, Marcel (1931), *Time Regained*, trans. Stephen Hudson, London: Chatto & Windus.
Proust, Marcel (1970–93), *Correspondance de Marcel Proust*, ed. Philip Kolb, 21 vols, Paris: Plon.
Proust, Marcel (1987–9), *À la recherche du temps perdu* [1913–27], ed. Jean-Yves Tadié, 4 vols, Paris: Gallimard, Bibliothèque de la Pléiade.
Schiff, Violet (1957), 'Proust meets Joyce', *Adam International Review*, 260: 64–5.
Schneider, Louis (1922), 'Les Premières: Opéra – Les ballets russes', *Le Gaulois*, 21 May, 64–5, 3.
Stravinsky, Igor and Robert Craft (1959), *Conversations with Igor Stravinsky*, New York: Doubleday.
Taruskin, Richard (1996), *Stravinsky and the Russian Traditions*, vol. 2, Oxford: Oxford University Press.
Williams, William Carlos (1951), *The Autobiography of William Carlos Williams*, New York: Random House.
Wise, Pyra (2013), 'Sydney et Violet Schiff', in *Le Cercle de Marcel Proust*, ed. Jean-Yves Tadié, Paris: Champion, pp. 209–23.

Interlude: Fashioning

Claire Davison

The language of fashion is a Channel-crossing adventure in itself, which begins in the life of words as they dart back and forth, ferrying new meanings en route, losing part of the etymological body they started out with, and picking up new accoutrements along the way. Think of the word 'fashion' derived from the old French 'façon' meaning craft, workmanship, especially in the field or workshop. The sense lingers on in the English verb 'to fashion' and in its French counterpart 'façonner'; the noun 'fashion', like the adjective 'fashionable', on the other hand, are translated 'mode', 'à la mode' – indeed the idiom also works well in English, so long as it is pronounced with a slight French accent. The same is true of the term 'haute couture' – the guarantee of style, taste and expertise either side of the Channel; in French, however, the word still flaunts its temporal inflections in a way it doesn't in English – 'couture' ('sewing') bespeaks the essential craftsmanship of the garment; it exposes the seams and threads with which those first seamstresses ('couturières') at the Court of Versailles first earned their own guild in 1675 (see Levron 1965: 162–5; Steele 1998: 17). The French 'mode', meanwhile, provides the etymological blueprint of the English 'model', the cat-walking, style-displaying, time-crafted (since the aesthetics of the body is a matter of fashion) body; the French for 'model', however, is 'mannequin', a word which, left untouched on the other side of the Channel, serves merely to denote the dressmaker's dummy, that straw-filled torso upon which fabric is pinned and trimmed, and selvedges are tacked. 'Selvedges' is another word that tells a story, but a Germanic one this time, while the French term for seams and selvedge is 'ourlet', derived from the Latin 'orulare', or border – terms that never really crossed the Channel at all. Meanwhile, by betraying philological truth and ceding to the temptation of etymological fantasy, it is tempting to hear a complex plural of 'self' echoing in the

English 'selvedges', as if performing the very plurality of selves and surfaces which the world of fashion, and the ever-reflecting ricochet of mirror images that fuel it, holds up to the consumer. Might there be some subtler truth lurking beneath the surface of the Italian dictum 'traduttore, traditore' ('translator, traitor')? – as if some radical betrayal were an essential but serendipitous prize bestowed midway in the ramification of words?

There is little wonder, in other words, that in recent years the union of modernism and fashion has proved considerably more than a 'mariage à la mode'. As Kurt Back argued as long ago as 1985, fashion was a central concern of modernist aesthetics, displaying those parts of a garment that are usually kept hidden (Back 2007: 403–4). Nor was its signifying force limited to the foregrounding of significant forms and constituent parts; 'fashioning' has also proved an operative mode of critical debate. In the words of Sheehan, 'fashion is not only a system as a list of objects; it also operates as a contingent, contextual mode of perception that foregrounds how form and meaning shift across space and time' (Sheehan 2018: 2). This central metaphor of fashion, shifting, shuffling and shuttling, shaping constellations of new-fashioned selves along the way, is what runs through the chapters brought together here. The literal, however, precedes the metaphorical: the here-and-nowness of seams, textile and fashioner that says, 'This is clothing' (Back 2007: 401), and the embodied creativity of cross-dressing bodies which weave the cloth from which masks and costumes are made. Vassiliki Kolocotroni explores Jean Rhys's wardrobe of disguises as ghostwriter, translator, poseuse and vagabonde; Jane Goldman shows us Nina Hamnett in both 'fancy dress' and a 'radically prismatic', outlandish robe, designing herself to fit the fashions of Paris; Naomi Toth identifies a form of modernist *agon* as hero and protagonist of *A Portrait of the Artist* struggle to break free from the fetters of both nation and the 'body that is the Church . . . that seamless shirt of the Lord', and manage to do so only by urging the reader 'to don the robes of the priest'.

This series of chapters, in other words, marks the intersection, the crossroads, of real bodies and textual bodies, where gestural modernism, translational poetics and anachronistic, outlandish modes overlap (see Levenson 2011: 247–8).[1] It assembles scenes of escapade and extravagance which hover midway between mythologising and demystification, in which tessellated selves pose as models for a self fashioned through reading, rewriting and translation. In many ways, the repertoire of figures parading on a highly spectral, speculative backcloth of France read as exercises in modernist biography, merging the granite of sculpture and the rainbow of light on water in novel, Channel-crossing ways. Take Kolocotroni's portrait of Rhys, for instance. Her literary apprenticeship takes shape as an escape into foreignness as she is dragged over to Paris, dragged into writing, and named and styled by the partners who took her up and dropped her. It also shows her using the divide of water, land and language to channel a modernist voice of her own, a voice that grew first from translation in answer to the imperatives of survival, thereby turning the conventional idiom of displacement into a subtly crafted emplacement, comfortably, conveniently out of place (especially when the author she translated was writing from gaol; Taylor-Batty 2013: 90–4).

Goldman, meanwhile, gives the 'mannequin' (in the French and English senses of the term) – that faceless, nameless 'laughing torso'– her own story of shifting and shuttling from London to Paris via lives, lies, stories and body parts. Nina Hamnett proves as operative a model for the disruptive forces of modernist fashioning as she does a disruptive model in the artist's studio, in Goldman's terms 'sitting awkwardly' in the narratives of women artists and models, and just as awkwardly in the smoother historiographies of modernism. Like Rhys, she is fashioned out of others' words, and others' chisels – the difference being that in Hamnett's case, the chisel is literal, not figurative; she foregrounds the blunt truth that if fashion is about clothing, it is also about the bodies that wear the clothes and the fashion-making bodies that wear no clothes at all. Hamnett in the flesh and in the coldly crafted marble of Gaudier-Brzeska's *Torso* emerges as an Orlando figure, a complexly gendered and engendering model supporting the view that 'it is clothes that wear us and not we them; we may make them take the mould of arm or breast, but they mould our hearts, our brains, our tongues to their liking' (Woolf 2011: 110–11).

While Hamnett plays the part of the shadowy, marginal figure 'sitting awkwardly' and yet laughing a little too caustically in the channels of others' stories, and quite literally baring the devices that went into the making of modernist history, Toth turns our attention to that most central of modernist heroes, Stephen Dedalus, and the various portraits of the artist's self that he acts out, 'the figure of the writer-to-be' who, like Hamnett and Rhys, re-emplaces displacement. His multiple acts of departure and severance, wilfully blending 'exile and cunning' in the act – and art – of self-authorship, thereby leave him always in part hovering, 'suspended, over the Channel's waves'.

All three chapters immerse us in the complex spatio-temporal grid of cross-Channel modernist fashioning. We are always suspended midway between the realness of the waterway that is called the Channel, and 'la Manche', suggesting the sleeve of some other garment of continental European manufacture; between the feel and pulse of France, specious anachronisms and mirages of mimetic desire, and crafted retrospection – like Joyce's Stephen, creating the author, the author who will make and unmake him. Outmoded reinventions of Parisian Bohemia stand facing geological reality and imaginary geography (especially if we recall that one of the fondest sobriquets for England, in French, is 'la perfide Albion', 'perfidious Albion', on account of the alluringly white cliffs irrespective of how white the cliffs of Dieppe look when seen from the ferry). Both are part of the treacherous dislocative spirit speaking two tongues in mutually infecting idioms that cross-cut at will. Benjamin's angel of history thus flutters overhead, but so too does the Benjaminian angel of fashion, misleading, misunderstanding, brashly new yet recurrent, backward-referring and flaunted in the new arcades that take us from Brighton pier to Paris via Calais: 'Misunderstanding as [sic] constitutive element in the development of fashion. No sooner is the new fashion at a slight remove from its point of departure that it is turned about and misunderstood' (Benjamin 1999: 73–5).

Note

1. 'Outlands' and 'outlandishness' as modernist modes of conceptualisation are theorised in Davison and Smith-Di Biasio (2015).

Bibliography

Back, Kurt (2007), 'Modernism and fashion: a social psychological interpretation' [1985], in *Fashion Theory*, ed. Malcolm Barnard, London: Routledge, pp. 398–407.
Barnard, Malcolm, ed. (2007), *Fashion Theory*, London: Routledge.
Benjamin, Walter (1999), *The Arcades Project* [1982], trans. and ed. Howard Eiland and Kevin McLaughlin, Cambridge, MA: The Belknap Press.
Davison, Claire and Anne-Marie Smith-Di Biasio, eds (2015), *Outlanding Woolf: Etudes britanniques contemporaines*, no. 48, Montpellier: Presses Universitaires de la Méditerranée.

Levenson, Michael (2011), *Modernism*, New Haven, CT: Yale University Press.
Levron, Jacques (1965), *La Vie quotidienne à la Cour de Versailles au XVII–XVIIIe siècles*, Paris: Hachette.
Sheehan, Elizabeth M. (2018), *Modernism à la Mode: Fashion and the Ends of Literature*, Ithaca, NY: Cornell University Press.
Steele, Valerie (1998), *Paris Fashion: A Cultural History*, London: Bloomsbury.
Taylor-Batty, Juliette (2013), *Multilingualism in Modernist Fiction*, Basingstoke: Palgrave Macmillan.
Woolf, Virginia (2011), *Orlando* [1928], Oxford: Oxford University Press.

Chapter 4

Cross-Channel Modernisms and the Vicissitudes of a Laughing Torso: Nina Hamnett, Artist, Bohemian and Writer in London and Paris

Jane Goldman

This chapter is the fruit of my own cross-Channel scholarly activities, beginning with a lecture in June 2010 to the conference titled '"No Hawkers: No Models": The Vicissitudes of the Modernist Muse', held at the University of Westminster, London. I developed this work in April 2015 for presentation to the 'Cross-Channel Modernisms Symposium' at Reid Hall in Paris (the University of Kent's Paris Campus). The latter version was in fact delivered twice within the space of a few days, first on the University of Kent's home campus and then in Paris. Shuttling between England and France via the Channel tunnel, I was already reworking my text on a remarkable modernist cross-Channel figure who had shuttled a little less speedily but with greater sartorial panache by boat-train a century earlier.

Laughing Torso (1932), the 'reminiscences' of Nina Hamnett (1890–1956), recounts her notorious cross-Channel vicissitudes as a struggling artist in the 1910s and 1920s in bohemian London and Paris. It opens up all kinds of interdisciplinary modernist crossings and channels. Hamnett's was an astonishing career not only as a visual artist (whose reputation has only recently been recovered) and as a muse, model and self-fashioning bohemian (whose excesses in the bars of Fitzrovia, Soho and Montparnasse, for many of her critics, eclipsed her other talents), but also as a writer. Reappraisal of Hamnett opens fascinating conduits to numerous modernist circles and to many pressing as well as entrenched critical and theoretical questions on modernism, including its international, transnational and geopolitical, trans-temporal and interdisciplinary, and its (trans-)performative, lived and embodied, and cross-gender framings. Hamnett, in her cross-Channel person as well as in her art and writing, may be productively considered in response to Virginia Woolf's question 'who shall measure the heat and violence of the poet's heart when caught and tangled in a woman's body?' (Woolf 1929: 73) .

Critics tend to focus either on Hamnett's early identification with the acclaimed modernist marble *Torso* (1914), the sculpture made by the French artist Henri Gaudier-Brzeska in response to a segment of her supple body as a fragment of classical statuary, or on her reputation as 'Queen of Bohemia' in both Soho and Montparnasse over many decades in the company of luminary modernist artists, writers and critics. These include Walter Sickert, Augustus John, Aleister Crowley, Roger Fry, Virginia Woolf, Vanessa Bell, Olivia Shakespear, Ezra Pound, Amadeo Modigliani, Pablo Picasso, Serge Diaghilev, Jean Cocteau, Dylan Thomas and Francis Bacon. Yet Hamnett, highly regarded by Sickert and a key participant in early Bloomsbury's Omega Workshop phase, and later widely regarded in the 1920s as one of the most talented young artists in Paris, died in poverty and obscurity. Her reputation as an artist was ditched, overshadowed by her lengthy fall into drunken dereliction, and her presiding over the younger generations of artists in the bars of Soho during the 1940s and 1950s, as a barely surviving muse of old Bohemia.

Like Hamnett's visual art, *Laughing Torso* is a neglected, misunderstood modernist masterpiece. It should be read alongside Gertrude Stein's *Autobiography of Alice B. Toklas* (1933). This highly sophisticated document situates Hamnett precisely at the margins between the hegemony of Art (painting, sculpture and literature) and the emergent para-categories of 'gestural modernism' (Levenson 2011: 247), that is, 'experimental social aesthetics, or self-fashioning which vied with bourgeois norms' (Brooker 2007: 8). Distinguishing between textual modernism and gestural modernism, Levenson defines the latter with reference to 'all those events that live beyond the artefacts ... a question of the physical disposition of artists and their audiences – a question of personal style, of dress and costume, men in capes, women on bicycles, workers in the square, suffragettes on the street' and the 'increased visibility, not only of modernist art works but of modernist bodies', engaging in 'unrepeatable event and evanescent gesture' – happenings and spectacles that barely survive in 'half-reliable newspaper reports or memoirs' but 'were crucial to oppositional culture' (Levenson 2011: 247). *Laughing Torso* addresses the vicissitudes of Hamnett's experiences as an ambitious artist who is also positioned by herself and others as a muse and a model, a bohemian poser/poseuse, dancer and *flâneuse*, in both London and Paris. But it is also testament to her talent as a writer. Her writing relates the lives and intersecting circles of cross-Channel modernists. But it is itself an interdisciplinary form of modernist cross-channelling.

In 1914 Hamnett wore, to a fancy-dress dance in Paris, a radically prismatic, colourist blouse 'of a large cubist design in blue, orange and black'. It is depicted in monochrome in *Laughing Torso* in the black-and-white photograph 'Myself: A Fancy Dress Dance in Avenue Maine 1914', in which Hamnett is at the centre of the crowd 'where Modigliani is standing in the background' (Hamnett 1932: 67; see Koppen 2011: 20). This stunning blouse was designed in London's Omega Workshops, a truly cross-Channel modernist garment, and an ephemeral prop of the gestural that survives only in the black-and-white photograph illustrating her memoir: 'No one in Paris had seen anything like it and although Sonia Delaunay was already designing scarves, this was more startling' (Hamnett 1932: 66–7). The London Omega blouse she wore in Paris, Hamnett seems to suggest here, may have helped spur Sonia Delaunay to translate her avant-garde experimental colourism from scarves to other more ambitious wardrobe items. Yet Diaghilev's Ballets Russes was surely a common catalyst in 1910 and 1911 for both cities' fashion revolutions well before the Great War. By 1917, Delaunay herself was designing costumes for Diaghilev. Her later simultanist blouse design (1928) on the cover of the present volume nevertheless closely resembles Hamnett's 1914 cross-Channel oppositional colourist blouse.

But it is the marble sculpture *Torso* (1914), made in the same year as the blouse, in a collaboration between the French artist Gaudier-Brzeska and the British artist/model Hamnett, that is the focus of the present chapter. *Torso* is cross-Channel in its conception and in its translation eighteen years later from visual to verbal realm in and by *Laughing Torso*. If the sculpture *Torso* is understood as Levenson's more monumental textual modernism – a kind of corpse – is *Laughing Torso* announcing itself as gestural? Is this memoir a fleeting paroxysm of affect that revivifies the sculpture corpse in attempting to record some of the evanescent gestural performances that were vital to the material realisation of *Torso*? Yet *Laughing Torso* is no mere ephemeral footnote to the limbless, headless *Torso*. Perhaps the book may be understood to cross channels and turn the sculpture itself into an ephemeral illustration and record of the evanescent gestural performances vital to the material realisation of *Laughing Torso*, an indisputable instance of Levenson's monumental textual modernism. Who's laughing now?

Models and artists and bohemians

In undertaking to speak at the Kent/Paris Cross-Channel Modernisms events on both sides of the Channel, I was bodily following Hamnett's own crossings. But I have other experiences in common with her too, as an artist's model.

In fact, E—, my former colleague in my former profession, is now an artist, but she has many stories about her first career as an artist's model. I will restrict myself to just one. In a typical 'double life' class, E— was once posed seated with our colleague G— standing at her side in front of a large wall mirror. This was to be for two weeks. In the session after lunch a few days into the pose, G— suddenly burst into tears, put on her gown and ran sobbing from the set. E— went after her to the rest room where a very unhappy G— was eventually coaxed into explaining: 'E—, I'm so embarrassed! I just farted and I'm sure I've steamed up the mirror!' As it happens, her farts were not that powerful, but G—'s flight from the pose exposes the great paradoxical taboo of traditional life class – the fact of the living body of the model. In traditional life class, we must conspire to conceal the fact that the nude model in all their nakedness is an historically situated, embodied, living human being and that their body is always and already speaking, signifying, making marks and inscriptions and as such is co-shaping the art attributed to the artists on the other side of the easel who are themselves historically situated, embodied, living human beings and not divinely inspired, culturally transcendent geniuses.

This is certainly one thing we might learn from *Laughing Torso*. This book puts forward an avant-garde model of embodied creativity, a transformative modernist multiple artist's muse figure, shaped by and shaping a radical gender politics, and one that may stand with and productively speak to feminist modernism's more famous anti-muse, the messianic Shakespeare's sister of Woolf's *A Room of One's Own*, who is waiting to 'put on that body she has so often laid down' (Woolf 1929: 172).

My project to reclaim *Laughing Torso* is in conflict with itself. On the one hand, I want to endorse the very making visible and validating of Hamnett's 'gestural modernism' as a set of self-fashioning performances made available to us in retrospect through her own writings and artworks and those of the numerous sculptors, painters, writers, memoirists and even critics and cultural historians for whom she has been a topic and an inspiration. But on the other hand, I want to tear down this 'gestural modernist' that I know Hamnett, along with so many other women artists, has in any case always been (for a majority of what remains of her public), albeit in more derogatory terms, and usually to her detriment; and I want to make a possibly more conservative claim for due recognition of her talent, not only as a visual artist (which was not in dispute in her youth and has always retained a quiet following) but also as a *writer*. Lois Oliver, in her helpful essay 'Bodies of Work: Models as Artists' in Jill Berk Jiminez's *Dictionary of Artists' Models* (2013), cites Hamnett, along with Gwen John, as exemplars of models who 'were trained first as artists but posed for colleagues and friends as a means of supplementing their income. In most instances, the artist's reputation as a model has subsequently greatly overshadowed his or her work as an artist' (Oliver 2013: 20). Hamnett's artistic achievements, furthermore, as Katherine Mellor has rightly noted, 'have virtually been eclipsed by her "bohemian" reputation, as attested by her own memoirs and those of her contemporaries' (Mellor 2013: 260). Her oeuvre, not so slender or mediocre as some would have it, has certainly been overshadowed by accounts of Hamnett's later dereliction and her eventual and possibly suicidal end impaled on railings after a fall from her window. And the end of her life is most often encapsulated for commentators by the photograph of her seated on her bed in a shabby room surrounded by bottles. Less often shown is the photograph, from the same period, of her standing in dignified authority in her studio. The very title of Hamnett's memoir, *Laughing Torso*, of course already in 1932 recognises and further torques such tensions or vicissitudes inherent in her career and reputation.

Very soon after his death in the Great War in 1915, Gaudier-Brzeska's famous marble sculpture of Hamnett, *Torso* (1914), was acquired by the Victoria and Albert Museum (and since 1983 has been in the Tate). In fact, there are a number of such torsos by Gaudier-Brzeska made before and after his death:

> Gaudier made at least two other torsos of which he listed one, namely a torso in Seravezzo marble purchased by Olivia Shakespear, the mother-in-law of Ezra Pound . . . The other torso was made in clay and cast in plaster . . . Two plaster casts were made from the aforementioned plaster . . . An unrecorded number of bronze casts have been made posthumously from these plasters. (The Tate 1986: 174)

Likewise proliferating in number are the personae attributed to *Torso*'s model, Nina Hamnett. Gaudier-Brzeska also made a counterpoint sculpture of Hamnett, untruncated, entitled *Dancer* (1913), which is also in the Tate (The Tate 1986: 168–9). *Laughing Torso* appeared in standard and de luxe editions when it was first published in 1932, and was republished as a Virago paperback in 1984 (just after the *Torso* itself transferred to the Tate). Hamnett published a sequel, entitled *Is She a Lady?*, in 1955, the year before she died. If the title of her first volume of reminiscences indicates Hamnett's proud willingness to lock her reputation to her role as muse and model for one of the most renowned works of modern sculpture, so too does the much circulated anecdote from later life that, when she had become a notorious drunken and derelict fixture of Soho's bars and clubs, she would introduce herself, as she did once to Ruthven Todd in the company of Dylan Thomas: 'You know me m'dear . . . I'm in the V&A with me left tit knocked off!' – referring to a slight fracture in the marble (Hooker 1986: 213, citing Todd 1973). Another much repeated quip to an admirer was: 'Don't forget I'm a museum piece, darling' (Hooker 1986: 236, quoting conversation with John Heath-Stubbs 1982). And thus she appears in part 2 of Basil Bunting's poem *Briggflatts* (1966): The 'half-pint / left breast of a girl who bared it in Kleinfeldt's' (*Briggflatts* 2.18–19, Bunting 1966: 17). And there may be a further salutary nod to Hamnett, who introduced Bunting to Pound's poetry, in part 3: 'to hug glib shoulders, mingle herpetic / limbs with stumps and cosset the mad. / Some the Laughing Stone disables / whom giggle and snicker waste / till fun suffocates them.' (*Briggflatts* 3.56–9, Bunting 1966: 26).

Self-identification with and reification as the marble *Torso*, limbless and decapitated, may have been a cynical strategy to ensure her celebrity status, but of course the term 'torso' also speaks volumes about the status of women in art where the transition from muse to model to artist is not as simple as some cultural historians would have it. But we must also attend to the term 'laughing', which may at least suggest artistic agency and locates affect, expression and pleasure, whether voluntary or involuntary, as somatic rather than cerebral and, in the manner of surrealism, synthesises facial and genital organs. The epithet *Laughing* reanimates the petrified marble body of the *Torso*. Compare too the *Laughing Torso* with the singing head of Orpheus, the classical god of poetry, torn limb from limb by the frenzied Maenads (Graves 1955, vol. 1: 115). His singing head represents the transcendence of art (always and already masculine) over embodied, material life (always and already feminine). Or perhaps the headless and laughing *Torso* was once capped by the petrifying head of the Gorgon, Medusa, who was decapitated by Perseus and represents the monstrous feminine inverse of the Orphic. In death, her head could still turn onlookers to stone and it hangs as a trophy on the girdle of the patriarchal goddess Athena, who was born, motherless, from the head of Zeus (Price and Kearns 2003: 2).

My focus is both the *Torso* sculpture itself, and Hamnett's text *Laughing Torso*, mainly as it relates to the production of the *Torso* sculpture in that crucial cross-Channel period of her life between London and Paris, and the various accounts of either or both by artists, critics and historians. I am seeking to understand these accounts in relation to emergent modern theories and accounts of the changing status of women artists, which tend to posit an – in the main – optimistic historical trajectory from muse to model to artist, and to recently explored critical frames for reading 'gestural modernism' and modernist self-fashioning – such as the Bohemian and the Celebrity. Hamnett was later crowned 'Queen of Bohemia' and her name has become a byword for bohemian, but aside from mentioning how she met, around 1908, Arthur Ransome 'who had written a book called *Bohemia in London*' (Hamnett 1932: 22), she does not make use of the terms 'Bohemia' or 'bohemian' in *Laughing Torso*. She does, however, have a chapter entitled 'Back to Paris and to Celebrities'. Given Hamnett's haute bohemian credentials, it is no surprise that she features in Peter Brooker's excellent book, *Bohemia in London: The Social Scene of Early Modernism* (2007), which defines the bohemian as 'the figure in whom aesthetic and cultural style, artistic strategy and personal bearing, male and female, come together' (Brooker 2007: viii). Brooker seeks to explore 'the coordinated relations between self-fashioning personae and symbolic places, in modernism as an emerging aesthetic and art of life, and in the accompanying, inescapable fictions of the cultural record' (Brooker 2007: ix).

Unshackled from the *Torso* and even from her own record as an artist, Hamnett might have emerged in Brooker's book as an inspiring quixotic series of virtuoso, self-fashioning bohemian personae, given, for example, her accounts in *Laughing Torso* of her spirited campaigns from earliest childhood of resistance to interpellation by dominant gender ideology. On the opening page, Hamnett says of her own birth: 'Everyone was furious, especially my Father, who still is. As soon as I was conscious of anything I was furious too, at having been born a girl; I have since discovered that it has certain advantages.' She describes the savage beatings she took in girlhood from her father and how

> [a] large doll was brought for me with a view to instilling some feminine feeling into me, but being of imitative disposition I placed its head in the fire-place with its legs sticking over the nursery fender, stole one of my father's bamboo canes, turned up its skirts, and beat it so that its head was battered on the grate; it was mended but as this occurred again and again the family gave it up. (Hamnett 1932: 5)

In Paris during Bastille Day celebrations, 1913, Hamnett has her hair cut 'like a Russian peasant' by the sculptor Zadkine:

> I went to the Avenue du Maine and bought a pair of French workmen's peg-top trousers, I borrowed a blue jersey and corduroy coat from Modigliani and a check cap. I also bought a large butcher's knife made of cardboard and silver paper at the Bon Marché. This I put in the long pocket which was meant either for knives – as Apaches wear them too – or rulers. I dressed myself and went out alone. I met Modigliani at the corner of the Rue Delambre and the Boulevard Montparnasse. He did not recognize me and when I produced the knife he ran away. I went to the Rotunde, where the waiters did not know me, and to a fair outside the Closerie des Lilas. I returned to the Rotunde and we danced in the streets all night and kept it up for three days. (Hamnett 1932: 53)

In this rich account of cross-Channel, cross-gendered masquerade, Hamnett positions two famous male artists, Zadkine and Modigliani, as muses to her self-fashioning and revels in deceiving Modigliani with the disguise he helped create with his own clothes, and in the seizing of phallic power by brandishing a stage knife. Dressed as an Apache on another occasion, Hamnett moves away from the auspices of her male assistants, as she recalls how she was accompanied by a woman friend dressed as 'a female Apache, with a black shawl and a red rose in her ear. She painted her face very much and we went round Montparnasse arm-in-arm. We looked so realistic that no one suspected we were in fancy dress. (Hamnett 1932: 54)

Hamnett delights not only in gender-passing but in the autonomy of this couple of women conspiring to undo the boundary between masquerade and reality. But the creation of such personae in the medium of social aesthetics is represented in a continuum with her creation of other personae for herself in the more conventional medium of paint, as for example, when she describes her earlier attempt at a self-portrait (1913) while under the spell of Aleister Crowley:

> I now began to feel that having finished with Art Schools I must leave the student stage and become an artist. This I realized was a difficult thing to do as many students at the Art School – and they were of all ages – seemed to have remained students all their lives. I painted a life-size portrait of myself in the looking-glass. The colour was very dull but it was well drawn. I painted a pale-faced and half-starved woman in black, holding a yellow tulip. She was one of Crowley's poetesses and he called her the 'Dead Soul'; it was a very good description. (Hamnett 1932: 35)

Two paintings are elliptically described here ('I painted ... I painted') – a picture of herself, presumably *Self Portrait* (1913; Hooker 1986: 29) and *Dead Soul* (1913), a portrait of Crowley's associate, the poet and novelist Ethel Archer (188?–1961), but the juxtaposing of descriptions allows the reader to understand they could be one – a self-portrait *as* 'a pale-faced and half-starved woman in black'. Pay attention to Hamnett's artful syntax and use of personal pronouns here too. The transition from 'I' to 'she' while differentiating between herself and Archer, is nevertheless telling, and the implication may be, if she were still referring to her self-portrait *as* a dead soul, that this painted persona was stillborn. Crowley 'later referred to Nina as one of his students' (Hooker 1986: 35), so perhaps she is opportunely announcing the demise of the *painter* persona who was briefly under the sway of Crowley when she made this picture named by him in a gesture that also therefore anointed her as his follower. She certainly very soon took a different path after her 'brush with him', and Crowley later lost a libel suit he brought against Hamnett for some of her darker anecdotes about him in *Laughing Torso* (Hooker 1986: 35, 197–206). Compare her account of meeting Gaudier-Brzeska for the first time, four pages later where she identifies herself as the painter of the 'picture of a "Dead Soul"' he had seen in the Albert Hall, and he replies: '"Yes, of course, I remember it, you are the young girl who sat with my statues; my sister and I called you 'La Fillette'"' (Hamnett 1932: 39). In this dialogue Hamnett has herself anointed anew by Gaudier-Brzeska.

In the pages between these moments, Hamnett drops the story of the 'Dead Soul' to relate her Pound-like experience of spotting and pursuing a girl on the Tube with 'a most wonderful face, like the portrait of the girl in the National Gallery by Ghirlandaio; she was rather fatter and I decided that at all costs I must paint her portrait'. Eventually Hamnett gets her way with Dilys, 'and I painted a life-size portrait which delighted us both. I gave it to a second-rate woman novelist who, I believe, put it in the dustbin' (Hamnett 1932: 36). And soon Hamnett is telling us of her first encounters and meetings with Dora Carrington, Mark Gertler, Walter Sickert, Lucien Pissarro, Wyndham Lewis, T. E. Hulme, and Jacob Epstein and then Gaudier-Brzeska, all in a matter of three pages. The rapid-fire pursuit and creation of personae on and off canvas is the mode of the entire book.

Brooker's account of Hamnett tends to read the exuberant gestural modernism of her youth through the jaded lens of her later prolonged, derelict existence, and to downplay at all points her talent and her achievement as a painter. Commenting on her class status in comparison with other women bohemian-artists, such as Helen Saunders, Jessica Dismorr, Iris Tree and Dora Carrington, he notes that Hamnett, 'by contrast, though she plunged into the bohemian life of London and Paris, was an average artist who came from Tenby in South Wales and struggled financially all her life' (Brooker 2007: 126). I find it rather harsh to call her 'an average artist'! The fact is that Hamnett enjoys the reputation of having been identified as one of the most talented, successful, well-known and respected young artists in Paris in the 1920s, and it is her fall from this early pinnacle of promise that sets her apart from the average Soho alcoholic falling off the bar stool next to her. Brooker is no less harsh about Hamnett's talent for bohemian self-fashioning in foregrounding her launching gestures as cynical and perfunctory. Like Virginia Woolf, who in her diaries and letters glimpses 'in the midst of a chattering crowd (Nina Hamnet drunk)' and in parentheses (Woolf 1977–84, vol. 4: 51), Brooker has throughout his book knocked one of the Ts off Hamnett's surname – perhaps in silent homage to the damaged left breast of the *Torso*. At any rate, from Hamnett's heady and sparkling prose Brooker fishes out a somewhat tarnished and diminished younger persona kitted out to meet the dominant derelict persona of latter days with whom he travels with hindsight to greet her. Brooker's 'Hamnet[t]' serves a grim and cautionary function in his account of the stakes of bohemian self-fashioning in all its delights and perils. Hamnett is Brooker's prominent example of the bohemian career path more often designated to *women*: 'Once embarked upon, this life meant the role of minor artist or co-worker, editor or sponsor of others' art.' And he has Hamnett, with other women, complicit in disavowing her own status as artist in favour of self-fashioning in

> a life of masquerade in which their leading art exhibit was their own public image . . . The Bohemian option for women was to be first an artist-in-life and only secondly an artist in words or paint, and . . . this testing role could bring dissipation and a raggedly tragic end. (Brooker 2007: 108)

Brooker rightly identifies the treacherous risks women run in oscillating between 'artistic vocation and public image', but he seems only too willing to collude in positioning Hamnett as all image and little or no vocation. Meanwhile, Hamnett, in *Laughing Torso*, is at pains to present herself as an artist first and always foremost before she becomes bohemian or muse or model. And at numerous places in the text she distances herself as a serious and ambitious artist from the bohemians, dilettantes, collectors, patrons, muses *and* professional models who populate her narrative. *Laughing Torso* is, for Brooker,

> a series of endless encounters [sic] and adventures. Parties, affairs, bursts of spontaneous naked dancing and some painting and drawing pass by like entries in a day-by-day diary. Her beguilingly simple prose manages to hold off the deleterious effects of drink and age, but from the late 1920s, when she teamed up with Augustus John and Tommy Earp, the frazzled pub life of Fitzrovia began to take its toll. (Brooker 2007: 108)

However much drink affected her, Hamnett was in fact only forty years old when she wrote *Laughing Torso*, so it is gratuitous to suggest she was holding off 'the deleterious effects of . . . age'. Brooker renders Hamnett's 'raggedly tragic end' twenty-five years later thus:

> She was remembered in the 1930s and post-war years as a pathetic figure, obviously drunk and bemoaning the loss of a new beautiful young man or singing lewd ditties for a drink; a tramp on the cadge. The price of Bohemia was that her work was neglected and little regarded by herself or others . . . In December 1956, after a period in hospital, Nina Hamnet [sic] fell from her small second-floor flat in Westbourne Terrace, Paddington and impaled herself on railings below. (Brooker 2007: 109)

Brooker, whose main sources aside from Hamnett are Elizabeth Wilson's *Bohemians: The Glamorous Outcasts* (2000) and Hugh David's *The Fitzrovians: A Portrait of Bohemian Society 1900–55* (1988), at no point goes to Hamnett's biographer, Denise Hooker, whose excellent book, *Nina Hamnett: Queen of Bohemia* (1986) is a richly detailed and impressively argued 'attempt to recreate the myth' of Hamnett the bohemian personality and 'legend in her own lifetime', 'and to suggest the real talent for art and for life that lay behind it.' (Hooker 1986: 13). If only Brooker had read Hooker.

Elizabeth Bronfen, in *Over Her Dead Body* (1992), argues that our culture's self-representation is bound up with 'articulation as effacement of the unencompassable body of materiality-maternity-mortality' (Bronfen 1992: 434) and reflects in her closing chapter, 'From Muse to Creatrix', on the strategies of modern women writers and artists for intervening in the pervasive scene of Woman and Death. Here, she points out Woolf's strategy in *A Room of One's Own* of a 'double dialogue' with the fictional dead Shakespeare's sister and her present and living audience of women: 'Woolf's model also grounds writing in the death of a woman, yet the paradox that emerges in her anecdote is that, having inspired the writing of other women, the dead woman poet as muse will come into being again, for the first time' (Bronfen 1992: 398). Hamnett's revival and reanimation of the *Torso* as *Laughing Torso* is a similar gesture of messianic resurrection. Woolf's creative androgyny is also relevant: 'Some collaboration has to take place in the mind between the woman and the man before the art of creation can be accomplished. Some marriage of opposites has to be consummated' (Woolf 1929: 157). Celebrating these 'nuptials in darkness' (Woolf 1929: 157), Woolf posits refiguring the '*hierarchized* binary opposition' (Cixous 1981: 91) of male poet and female muse where the fatal opposition of body and mind may be undone by artists of any gender. Hamnett's *Laughing Torso* extends to and exposes in Gaudier-Brzeska's *Torso* feminist messianic resurrection and androgynous nuptials.

There are numerous studies of women artist/models, in which Hamnett sits awkwardly. Clearly, she does not quite fit with the kind of narrative related in Ruth Butler's *Hidden in the Shadow of the Master: The Model-Wives of Cezanne, Monet, & Rodin* (2008), nor with that of Karen L. Kleinfelder's *The Artist, His Model, Her Image, His Gaze: Picasso's Pursuit of the Model* (1993). Both of these works rely on familiar feminist analysis of the politics of the gendered gaze and of artist–model–muse relations. But it is refreshing to find Hamnett represented in both roles in Martin Postle and

William Vaughan's *The Artist's Model from Etty to Spencer* (1999), a book accompanying an exhibition. The book and exhibition are in four phases: 'From Academy to Art School'; 'Behind the Screen: The Studio Model'; 'Models and Muses'; 'The Naked and the Nude'. 'By the 1920s,' they conclude, 'the myth of the "muse" model was exploited largely by society and Academy artists. The most progressive artists no longer had much interest in it' (Postle and Vaughan 1999: 85).

Hamnett is first encountered in Postle and Vaughan's work as an academic tutor setting the pose at Westminster Technical Institute and joining her class in drawing from the life model. See her pen-and-ink *Life Class at the Westminster Technical Institute* (1919). This drawing by Hamnett appears in the first section (Postle and Vaughan 1999: cat. 37: 47), 'From Academy to Art School', which

> traces the development of the use of the model in art education from the study of the figure in the Royal Academy Schools to its use in the Government Schools of Design, private art schools and institutions such as the Slade School of Art where aspects of the French atelier system were introduced. (Postle and Vaughan 1999: 7)

And in this section Postle and Vaughan point up issues such as 'the propriety of using the naked model in state-funded institutions; the rights of women to study the model; and the status of models themselves within the *status quo*' (Postle and Vaughan 1999: 7). The note for the sketch explains how Hamnett got the post as tutor on the recommendation of Walter Sickert when he retired from it in 1918. She taught at Westminster for the next two years, three evenings a week, until she returned to Paris in 1920.

In Hamnett's own account of this experience in *Laughing Torso* she mentions that Augustus John joined Sickert in recommending her,

> and I got the job. The class consisted of five students when I arrived. They were as much frightened of me as I was of them. I wore a large grey hat pulled over my eyes which I never took off. I had to engage the models. A small girl and her brother came and sat for me and also a large and very fat woman. After several weeks I had thirty students, including five tough Australian soldiers, who were very serious and always kept cigarettes behind their ears. I used to ask them to tea, two at a time. They were very simple-minded and unspoilt. (Hamnett 1932: 111)

She also mentions that at her art class she 'generally drew with the students. I taught three evenings a week and for two nights a week I joined the St. Martin's Art School and drew from the nude' (Hamnett 1932: 115). Postle and Vaughan paraphrase Hamnett, but they also add Sickert's words of encouragement to her: 'I am convinced that once the students have had a fortnight's experience of you, you will create an enthusiastic following, because, firstly you have been through so much, and secondly because you have so much intellectual vitality and students quickly feel that' (Postle and Vaughan 1999: 47; Lilly 1971: 87). They observe the influence of Gaudier-Brzeska in Hamnett's 'fine outline technique' and emphasise that, in keeping with her own ethos when sketching in other contexts outside life class, 'it is the total situation she is recording rather than making a particular study of the model. The study does show, however, that Hamnett had no scruples about posing the male nude for female students' (Postle and Vaughan 1999: 47, citing Hooker 120–2, 124). Our first encounter with Hamnett courtesy of Postle and Vaughan, then, is heartening in its acknowledgement of her talent as a teacher and an artist, despite that niggling deference to Gaudier-Brzeska as dominant rather than mutual influence. And this sighting of Hamnett is dated 1918. But it is an *earlier* Hamnett whom they exhibit in the final phase and section of their show, 'The Naked and the Nude'. She is named as the model for cat. 109, Roger Fry's *Nude on a Sofa* (1917), and for cat. 111, Gaudier-Brzeska's *Torso* (1914). Postle and Vaughan explain:

> As in previous generations, it remained common practice for young student artists to act as models for themselves and each other, as when . . . Nina Hamnett posed for Gaudier-Brzeska. This was partly a process of self-discovery and partly an economic necessity. Few aspirant artists could afford to pay for substantial use of a professional model. With the change in social status of the model, it also became more common for artists to act professionally as models. This was, inevitably, more the case for female than male artists. For not only were female models in greater demand by this time, but women artists were also likely to be in greater financial need than males. (Postle and Vaughan 1999: 83)

This seems a fair comment, in some respects. But Fry and Hamnett, it is explained, had an affair between 1916 and 1918, and Fry's picture 'in which Nina's naked form is set against the bright colours of the Omega rug, reveals the casual intimacy of the relationship, and Fry's admiration for her "queer satyr-like oddity and grace"' (Postle and Vaughan 1999: cat. 109: 130; Hooker 1986: 91). But their reciprocal artistic relationship is also noted: 'Nina, in turn, made a number of pencil sketches of Fry naked, very much in the manner Henri Gaudier-Brzeska, whom she had also sketched naked, and for whom she had also posed as model (cat. 111)' (Postle and Vaughan 1999: 130). Hooker includes a fine sketch by Hamnett of Fry nude in 1918 (Hooker 1986: 113) – which might equally be, I suggest, very much in the manner of Nina Hamnett.

Torso and *Laughing Torso*

So now we come to the *Torso* itself (or *Torso*s themselves). The main source for Gaudier-Brzeska's documented conception of *Torso* remains H. S. Ede's *Savage Messiah* (1931), which precedes Hamnett's *Laughing Torso* by a year and makes extensive use of Ede's archive of Sophie Gaudier-Brzeska's diaries and Henri Gaudier-Brzeska's letters. For example, the Tate catalogue sees it 'both as an answer to Gaudier's critics who disliked his primitive, modernistic approach to sculpture and as the culmination of an ambition to make a sculpture in the classical style' (The Tate 1986: 74). They cite the artist's letter to Sophie Brzeska: 'I long to make a statue of a single body, and absolute, truthful copy – something so true it will live when it is made even as the model *himself* lives' (The Tate 1986: 174; see Ede 2011: 73, my emphasis), and his description of it to Major Smythies as 'a marble statue of a *girl* in a natural way, in order to show my accomplishment as a sculptor' (The Tate 1986: 174; Ede 2011: 187, emphasis added). So, if these refer to the same project, the artist himself refers to the model as masculine and the statue as feminine. The first citation is from a letter of 3 June 1911, which is years earlier than the second, and which actually continues: 'The statue has nothing to say – it should only have planes in the right place – no more' (Ede 2011: 73).

The Tate catalogue also cites Hamnett's much quoted account of posing for Gaudier-Brzeska and of helping him to steal the marble for *Torso* from a stonemason's yard. But it makes the point that as well as referring to a living model, Gaudier-Brzeska made the *Torso* with antique models from classical statuary in mind. *Torso* is, as the art historian Richard Cork remarks, '"a polished imitation of a Greek original – extended even to the broken arms and neck"', but the Tate, invested in the narrative of a naturalist project, adds:

Figure 4.1 Torsos: Henri Gaudier-Brzeska, letter 3 November 1912 (Ede 2011: 134).

'although he probably does not intend to imply by this that Gaudier actually copied a particular sculpture' (The Tate 1986: 174; Cork 1976: 1: 167). Postle and Vaughan draw on similar statements from Ede's archive, and also address the modernist conceit of the *Torso* as faux classical fragment. (It stands comparison to Pound's poem 'Papyrus' in this respect.) It is worth interjecting here that it was part of formal training for art students to 'draw from the antique', as Hamnett herself recounts (Hamnett 1932: 18). Gaudier-Brzeska, in a letter of 3 November 1912, illustrates it with a rhythmical sketch of four pairs of twisting torsos of indecipherable gender (Figure 4.1); he claimed inspiration in Beethoven's Fifth Symphony, which 'gives the impression of a very beautiful young woman's torso, firm but soft, seen at first by rarefied lights and then with strong light and shade' (Ede 2011: 133–4). The *Torso* is then also a distillation of music into line into flesh into marble.

Postle and Vaughan do acknowledge reciprocal posing of model and artist (which I will come to shortly). Yet in their summation of Hamnett's career in 'The Naked and the Nude', the final section of *The Artist's Model*, they have Gaudier-Brzeska after *Torso* going on to make more art before his untimely death in the Great War (the significance of which is *not* mentioned here and yet which surely has some bearing on why the *Torso* was acquired by the V&A), whereas they have Hamnett, 'soon to make full use of her newfound awareness of her body, dancing naked at parties in Montmartre. She also remained immensely proud of having been the model for this work, which had early won recognition for its exquisite beauty and which had been acquired by the Victoria and Albert Museum' (Postle and Vaughan 1999: 131). They close with the reproduction of Hamnett's much cited quips about being a museum piece with her 'left tit off'. Yet according to the opening section of this catalogue, Hamnett was also 'soon' (in 1918 at any rate) to take over Walter Sickert's teaching post at Westminster Technical Institute and continue her career as a serious artist. But having played fast and loose with chronology, Postle and Vaughan allow the impression to arise that in using Hamnett as the fleshly model for his marble *Torso*, Gaudier-Brzeska also simultaneously awoke in her a new bodily self-awareness and set her on her true vocation, not as an artist, but a bohemian poseuse and danseuse, presumably channelling in some necromantic fashion Beethoven's Fifth Symphony which they have given as the sculptor's originary inspiration. 'All too often,' Lois Oliver concludes, 'history has focused on the artist-model's personal life at the expense of his or her art' (Oliver 2013: 25).

Postle and Vaughan here contribute to entrenching further a dominant art-historical narrative of *Torso*, in which this work is created solely by Gaudier-Brzeska using Hamnett as his subordinate model. The piece is furthermore considered an exercise in naturalism by which the sculptor could demonstrate his virtuosity in classicism in the teeth of critical hostility to his apparently more avant-garde primitive works, and his correspondence with Smythies is cited where Gaudier-Brzeska claims making 'a marble statue of a girl in a natural way, in order to show my accomplishment as a sculptor' (Postle and Vaughan 1999: 131; Ede 2011: 187). Pound, too, makes the point that Gaudier-Brzeska wrote to him what amounts to 'the "renunciation" so vaunted by our enemies', from the trenches: 'If I ever come back I shall do more "Mlles. G...." in marble.' This, he explains, was 'the nickname of a naturalistic torse, plumper and not so fine as the one reproduced' which the artist 'had repeatedly stigmatised ... as insincere' (Pound 1916: 75). Presumably this is the second marble of Hamnett bought by his mother-in-law, apparently 'not so fine', in Seravezzo marble (The Tate 1986: 172). Is this actually a renunciation of his avant-gardism in either of these marble torsos? Gaudier-Brzeska had also written to Smythies: 'We are of different opinions about naturalism. I treat it as hollow accomplishment, the artificial is full of metaphysical meaning which is all important' (Ede 2011: 186). So, can we really understand *Torso* as a one-off cynical exercise in naturalism? And here, in any case, the sculpture may nevertheless cross gender channels and come retrospectively to commemorate the dead artist himself and other war dead whose mutilated corpses were strewn on the battlefields across the Channel but are now somehow transcended by this faux classical marble. The same narrative, keeping artist and model each to their own channel, also has Hamnett not only denied the status of artistic collaborator on this particular piece (as we will come to below) but also recast by it and thereafter stripped of her own calling as an artist, having somehow now become called back from aesthetic transcendence to her own living and mortal body free to cross and re-cross the Channel in a downward spiral towards drunken dereliction, cracking jokes about her mutilation by proxy as model for the statue. Demoted to life model, not collaborating artist, she is made to stand as guarantor of Gaudier-Brzeska's fabled sudden turn to naturalism in making the silent *Torso*. *Laughing Torso* offers an alternative account of *Torso*'s conception as radically cross-gendered and collaborative, opening to creative channels between artist and model.

Ede offers a key point of reference ignored by Postle and Vaughan and the Tate in the formative experience they claim for the creator of the *Torso*. This charming drawing depicts Henri and Sophie Gaudier-Brzeska as dancing and embracing nude lovers, their bodies symmetrically posed, with matching hairy legs, puckered lips, parallel pubic parts, and parallel torsos (Figure 4.2) (Ede 2011: 136). Closing

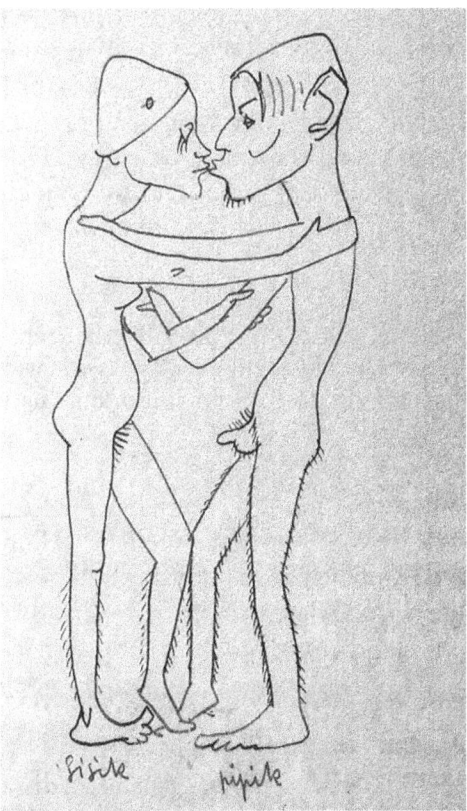

Figure 4.2 Henri and Sophie Gaudier-Brzeska dancing: Henri Gaudier-Brzeska, letter 3 November 1912 (Ede 2011: 136).

the same letter illustrated with the turning torsos, this seems the very image of Woolf's model of creative androgyny, the 'collaboration [that takes] place in the mind between the woman and the man before the art of creation can be accomplished', the consummation of the 'marriage of opposites', the 'nuptials in darkness' (Woolf 1929: 157). And it speaks to a sense of cross-gender collaboration available in Hamnett's account of the making of *Torso*. There is also, to complicate matters further, the closely related bronze, a later cast known as *Torso of a Woman* (1930), and taken from one of two plaster casts of an original clay made in 1913 at the same time as the marble *Torsos*. One breast was broken on the second plaster cast (hence presumably Hamnett's much cited 'left tit off' quip), and from it three bronze casts were made in 1930, one of which is now in the Tate (see Chamot et al. 1964: 207–8).

The entire memoir *Laughing Torso* constitutes Hamnett's own necromantic mythologised account of the collaborative creation of *Torso* and of its artistic, social and political confluences and influences. The more immediate circumstances of its creation are related in six pages (Hamnett 1932: 37–43). She begins with the 'Independents' exhibition in the Albert Hall where five of her works were shown, including the 'Dead Soul' and her portrait of Dilys. Finding Gaudier-Brzeska's sculptures also on show (and having seen his drawings in *Rhythm* magazine), she 'sat down on chair in the midst of his statues' and surmises that the young foreign man who was looking at her

> in an amused kind of way . . . was probably the sculptor, but was to [sic] shy to tell him how much I like his works. He walked away and afterwards . . . to my delight [I] found him standing in front of my pictures (Hamnett 1932: 38)

Later he anoints her: '"you are the young girl who sat with my statues; my sister and I called you 'La Fillette'"' (Hamnett 1932: 39). Posing for him, she emphasises his poverty and his respect for her as a fellow artist:

> I went one day to his studio in the Fulham Road and took off all my clothes. I turned round slowly and he did drawings of me. When he had finished he said, 'Now it is your turn to work.' He took off all his clothes, took a large piece of marble and made me draw, and I had to. I did three drawings and he said, 'Now we will have some tea.' From the drawings he did two torsos. The other day Harold

Nicolson published one of the drawings in the *Evening Standard* and said that the torso was of myself. Henri was very poor and lived with an elderly woman who, he told me, was his sister. We used to wander round Putney and look at stonemason's yards, where tombstones were exhibited, in the hopes of finding odd bits of stone in reach of the railings. (Hamnett 1932: 39)

There is a delicate ambiguity at work in Hamnett's exquisitely carved prose here allowing us to understand that 'the drawings' from which Gaudier-Brzeska worked to create the marble *Torso* were *hers* as well as his, and to read a teasing tone into her account of Nicolson's identification of herself as the model. Should Nicolson be so sure? Is the implication that Hamnett drew directly onto the 'large piece of marble'? We cannot ever know for certain whether or not Gaudier-Brzeska did create the androgynous morphology of his *Torso* out of drawings of himself as well as of Hamnett, but we might nevertheless acknowledge Hamnett's opening of this radical possibility in her own *Laughing Torso*, a gesture that seems to mirror Gaudier-Brzeska's original conception, in the letter that documents his inspiration, encompassing both his rhythmical series of (fe)male torsos *and* his mutually supporting, collaborative courting couple. Perhaps the two artist-models were playing a version of the game Hamnett later describes playing every Sunday afternoon during the war with fellow artists and her father, when

> we all played 'heads, bodies, and legs.' That is where everyone draws a head and leaves two lines indicating where the next person should begin the body. The pieces of paper were then passed to the next person and then again until the legs were done. The drawings were very funny and some of them very good. (Hamnett 1932: 85)

There is something eerie in her dwelling on the marble's tombstone provenance, given Gaudier-Brzeska's imminent death in the Great War and the subsequent cultural reception of his sculptures as a kind of Poundian 'Ode Pour L'Election De Son Sepulchre'. Indeed, it was exhibited at the memorial exhibition to Gaudier-Brzeska held at the Leicester Galleries in May–June 1918. It is not Hamnett's live body but the artist's own once living body and now mangled corpse that the *Torso* comes to elegise. Yet pages later in her memoir Hamnett records her own narrow escape from Zeppelin bombs, near the Gaiety Theatre in London in 1915, a grim reminder that there were war dead on both sides of the Channel, including civilians: 'The people in the 'bus that I should have taken, if I had not had another cigarette and a drink, were sitting in the 'bus with their heads blown off, as a bomb had dropped outside' (Hamnett 1932: 86). In describing this brush with death in London, she also relates re-meeting, five years later, a fellow survivor across the Channel in Paris:

> I took a 'bus to the Café Royal by the Savoy Hotel. In it were two Japanese. The evening cloak of one was torn to bits. He had been inside the Gaiety Theatre, but fortunately, his cloak had been hanging up in the cloak room. We all talked together of what had happened. In Paris in 1920 I met him. I said, 'I have met you in London.' He did not remember me but did when I reminded him of the air raid. The café was in uproar and everyone drank to celebrate their escape. Edgar and I saw the daylight air raid from our attic windows. (Hamnett 1932: 86–7)

Hamnett's sentences cross-cut between London and Paris, war and post-war, so quickly and cleanly that the drink celebrating survival may be happening in both places and both times at once. When she immediately cuts to the scene of her and her lover watching the daylight raid with artists' eyes, there is a startling turn from a sense of visceral danger to one of surreally detached spectacle: 'It was a fine sight, and they were in wonderful formation, like a flock of birds surrounded by the little white puffs of smoke of the British guns' (Hamnett 1932: 87). In the very next paragraph, Hamnett recounts wakening from a dream when staying with her parents in Acton and seeing from her window 'what I thought were fireworks, a big golden pencil diving to earth' and then with her father in the garden they 'saw it break in half and come down in a rain of golden showers. This was the Cuffley Zeppelin' (Hamnett 1932: 87). This was the first German Zeppelin to be shot down, and it happened in 1916. Just as much as Gaudier-Brzeska's fate in the trenches, these vignettes of Hamnett's experiences of the war zone in London may be understood as a kind of retrospective cultural patina accreting on *Torso*.

Returning to Hamnett's account of *Torso*, she continues with details of the domestic life, the poverty and austerity and sexual tensions of the Gaudier-Brzeska ménage, his avant-garde dress, his anarchist politics, and of another significant sculpture he made around the same time. It is not, as one might expect, the limbed companion piece, *Dancer*, that becomes Hamnett's focus here, but Gaudier-

Brzeska's notorious Hieratic Head of Ezra Pound: 'Ezra said, "You must make me look like a sexual organ." So Henri got to work with a piece of charcoal and drew on the stone. He chipped and he chipped and it was magnificent and it has been offered to and refused by many museums' (Hamnett 1932: 41).

I wonder if it is entirely modelled from Pound, or is there an element of self-portraiture here too? Whose priapic cock did the artist use as model for this head? In including this story Hamnett is surely offering comment on the equally radical status of *Torso*, which in her account at least confronts us with the inescapable presence of the body of the *artist* as well as the body of the model at the scene of its making. Yet in Hamnett's account of *Torso* its creation does represent a watershed of sorts in her own career. After all, this important period of artistic and sexual intimacy with Gaudier-Brzeska forms the conclusion to her chapter 'I Come of Age', and her coda certainly mixes up sexual and artistic imagery already at play in the Pound anecdote: 'Henri came to my room sometimes. He arrived one day and took out of his pocket a large statue. I could see it sticking out as it was about a foot long.' The reader could be forgiven for expecting, after this possible double-entendre, the protruding statue to be the *Hieratic Head of Ezra Pound*, but,

> It was 'The Singing Woman' and is now in the Tate Gallery. We put it on the table and admired it. Henri talked about art and said, 'Painting is an art for women, Literature is an art for old people, but Sculpture is the art for strong men.' (Hamnett 1932: 42)

This is probably *Singer* (1913), the stone statue Gaudier-Brzeska first titled *Chanteuse*, and, according to the Tate, was first referred to as 'La Chanteuse Triste' by Pound in 1916 (see Pound 1916: 159), who wrote of it in 1918: 'In the Singer we have what may seem an influence from archaic Greek, we have the crossed arms motif . . . also an elongation possibly ascribable to a temporary admiration of the Gothic' (Chamot et al. 1964: 203; see Pound 1980: 250). The elongation of this female form of course also lends to it the phallic qualities Hamnett plays upon in her memoir. And how pointed is its unsheathing there in her room along with Gaudier-Brzeska's macho declaration of gender divisions for artistic media. Whatever part Hamnett did play in the making of *Torso*, and whatever she may have thought of Gaudier-Brzeska's ruling, it was certainly to painting and other arts (and then to literature) that she turned. And she cuts from this preposterous macho ruling subtly to undercut it by explaining how she came next to work in Roger Fry's Omega Workshops, and then co-opted Gaudier-Brzeska:

> Feeling brave one morning I went to Fitzroy Square and asked to see Mr. Fry. He was a charming man with grey hair, and said that I could come round the next day and start work. I went round and was shown how to do Batiks. I was paid by the hour. I made two or three pounds a week and felt like a millionaire. I brought Henri round one day and he did a design for a tray which was eventually carried out in inlaid woods. (Hamnett 1932: 42–3)

The Omega Workshops was an avant-garde site where the (gender) channels of artistic production rashly endorsed by Gaudier-Brzeska were certainly being crossed and breached, where collective and anonymous production was not uncommon, and the boundaries blurred between art, craft and design. Indeed, the heroic classical tradition of individual statuary seems to come crashing down as Hamnett poignantly signs off her chapter with that modest domestic tray. The vicissitudes of her career after *Torso*, and of her subsequent reputation in art history and cultural criticism, for all that she and the modern art world were apparently moving away from forms dependent on the fraught gendered politics of artist and model, nevertheless demonstrate how entrenched arrière-garde views persist. That the body of the model might also be that of the artist still shocks.

Bibliography

Bronfen, Elizabeth (1992), *Over Her Dead Body: Death, Femininity and the Aesthetic*, Manchester: Manchester University Press.

Brooker, Peter (2007), *Bohemia in London: The Social Scene of Early Modernism*, Basingstoke: Palgrave Macmillan.

Bunting, Basil (1966), *Briggflatts*, London: Fulcrum Press.

Chamot, Mary, Dennis Farr and Martin Butlin (1964), *The Modern British Paintings, Drawings and Sculpture*, 2 vols, London: Oldbourne Press.

Cixous, Hélène (1981), 'Sorties', trans. Ann Liddle, in *New French Feminisms*, ed. Elaine Marks and Isabelle de Courtivron, Hemel Hempstead: Harvester Wheatsheaf.

Cork, Richard (1976), *Vorticism and Abstract Art*, 2 vols, London: Gordon Fraser.

David, Hugh (1988), *The Fitzrovians: A Portrait of Bohemian Society 1900–55*, London: Michael Joseph.

Ede, H. S. (2011), *Savage Messiah: A Biography of the Sculptor Henri Gaudier-Brzeska* [1931], with new texts by Sebastiano Barassi, Evelyn Silber and John Wood, Cambridge: Kettle's Yard.

Gaudier-Brzeska, Henri, *Dancer* (1913) The Tate no. 6092. https://www.tate.org.uk/art/artworks/gaudier-brzeska-the-dancer-t03726.
Gaudier-Brzeska, *Singer* (1913), The Tate no. 4514. https://www.tate.org.uk/art/artworks/gaudier-brzeska-singer-n04514.
Gaudier-Brzeska, *Torso* (1914), The Tate no. 3731. https://www.tate.org.uk/art/artworks/gaudier-brzeska-torso-t03731.
Gaudier-Brzeska, *Torso of a Woman* (1930), The Tate no. 4534. https://www.tate.org.uk/art/artworks/gaudier-brzeska-torso-of-a-woman-n04534.
Graves, Robert (1955), *The Greek Myths*, 2 vols, London: Penguin.
Hamnett, Nina (1932), *Laughing Torso: Reminiscences of Nina Hamnett*, London: Macmillan.
Hooker, Denise (1986), *Nina Hamnett: Queen of Bohemia*, London: Constable.
Jiminez, Jill Berk (2013), *Dictionary of Artists' Models*, London: Routledge.
Koppen, Randi S. (2011), *Virginia Woolf, Fashion and Literary Modernity*, Edinburgh: Edinburgh University Press.
Levenson, Michael (2011), *Modernism*, London and New Haven, CT: Yale University Press.
Lilly, Marjorie (1971), *Sickert: The Painter and his Circle*, London: Elek.
Mellor, Katherine (2013), 'Nina Hamnett', in *Dictionary of Artists' Models*, ed. Jill Berk Jiminez, London: Routledge.
Oliver, Lois (2013), 'Bodies of Work: Models as Artists', in *Dictionary of Artists' Models*, ed. Jill Berk Jiminez, London: Routledge.
Postle, Martin and William Vaughan (1999), *The Artist's Model from Etty to Spencer*, London: Merrell Holberton.
Pound, Ezra (1916), *Gaudier-Brzeska: A Memoir*, London and New York: John Lane.
Pound, Ezra (1980), *Ezra Pound and the Visual Arts*, ed. Harriet Zinnes, New York: New Directions.
Price, Simon and Emily Kearns, eds (2003), *The Oxford Dictionary of Classical Myth and Religion*, Oxford: Oxford University Press.
Ransome, Arthur (1907), *Bohemia in London*, London: Chapman and Hall.
The Tate (1986), *The Tate Gallery 1982–84: Illustrated Catalogue of Acquisitions*, London: The Tate.
Todd, Ruthven (1973), *Fitzrovia and the Road to the York Minster*, London: Parkin Gallery.
Wilson, Elizabeth (2000), *Bohemians: The Glamorous Outcasts*, London: I. B. Tauris
Woolf, Virginia (1929), *A Room of One's Own*, London: The Hogarth Press.
Woolf, Virginia (1977–84), *The Diary of Virginia Woolf*, ed. Anne Olivier Bell and Andrew McNeillie, 5 vols, London: The Hogarth Press.

Chapter 5

Jean Rhys's *comédie anglaise*

Vassiliki Kolocotroni

Jean Rhys crossed the Channel (in 1919) and channelled what we now call modernism, and what she called writing, by accident; as she wrote to her friend Peggy Kirkaldy on 6 December 1949:

> Now I'm really hanging on to my belief in fate – I never wanted to write. I wished to be happy and peaceful and obscure. I was *dragged* into writing by a series of coincidences – Mrs Adam, Ford, Paris – need for money. I tried to stop – again I've been dragged back. (Rhys 1984: 65)

Modernist *malgré elle*, artist mostly *manqué*, out of place, out of sync, out of sight for long decades of (self-imposed) obscurity, out of which she was 'dragged back' with the unexpected success of *Wide Sargasso Sea* in the 1960s, Rhys was always unprepared for the limelight, which, as she later intoned, came too late. Little did she know at the time that both the backward look and the use of the passive voice ('I was *dragged* into writing') would go on to become a signature style, proposed by her scholarly readers as key attributes of her unique blend of modernism.

Ella Gwendolyn Rees Williams was taken to Paris by her first husband, the Dutch writer and journalist Willem Johan Marie (called Jean) Lenglet. According to Martien Kappers-den Hollander,

> Lenglet wrote, and sometimes travelled, under the name of Edouard de Nève, a combination of his elder brother's Christian name and the surname he had once seen linked up with his own (as Lenglet de Nève) in Northern France. When his wife in turn needed a literary pseudonym, she concocted it out of her husband's nickname and that of her Welsh-born father: Jean Rhys. (Kappers-den Hollander 1984: 159)

But it was to help *Jean* make a name for himself that Jean was first dragged into writing. Before she met Ford Madox Ford, Rhys was matronised by Mrs H. Pearl Adam, a journalist she had met in London years before. Mrs Adam was eight years older than Jean and married to George Adam, the *Times* correspondent in Paris. She stayed with her for a while in 1922 just after the birth of her daughter, whom she eventually gave up for adoption. Rhys showed Lenglet's stories to Mrs Adam, which Adam didn't rate, but also left with her her own diary – and according to Lilian Pizzichini in a recent biography:

> Mrs Adam was excited. She divided Jean's diary into chapters, each headed with a man's name, and called the whole thing *Suzy Tells*. Pernod Suzy Fine was the name of a drink the English expats had invented: imitation absinthe, gentian and brandy. It was very strong. Mrs Adam decided that the tone of this new novel was bold and yet its style was 'naïve', and that Ford Madox Ford would like it too . . . In December 1924 the twelfth and last issue of *transatlantic review* included six pages of 'Vienne' from a novel called *Triple Sec* by Jean Rhys. Ford had changed her name, deciding that 'Jean Rhys' was more modern than Ella Lenglet. He had also changed the name Mrs Adam had given her novel, *Suzy Tells*. *Triple Sec* is another reference to absinthe. (Pizzichini 2010: 176, 168)

Rhys doesn't settle the matter of who christened her into modernity in her own unfinished, and highly controlled, elliptical autobiography, *Smile Please*,[1] but she does write about that time with pointed emotion in letters to Francis Wyndham, *Sunday Times* editor and her literary executor:

> Meanwhile I'd like to tell you about a book I read which helped me when I was very down. It is by a man who was a poet manqué and who knew me well – I would like to send it to you for I think that however unflattering his idea of me, it would show you that for a long time, for years, I escaped from an exclusively Anglo Saxon influence and have never returned to it.
> Of course *why* I was thought a doll when I was young by *everyone*, even by him, I do not know. Now of course I am no longer a doll, but a kind of ghost. Never to be taken very seriously anyway. It's just like that and one of those things. And who cares? ([27 May 1964] Rhys 1984: 281)

The 'poet manqué' is Lenglet/ Edward de Nève and the book *Les Verrous*, a novel that treated the same events as she described in *Quartet*, but from the (her) husband's point of view. Jean translated it from the French (as *Barred*), working at it 'with rage, fury and devotion' and tried hard to publish it – eventually placing it with Desmond Harmsworth in 1932.[2] As an account of that formative time for her as a writer in her own right and, chronologically speaking, the time of her most modernist affiliations, the reference to her translation of Lenglet's work is telling. Between two languages and two men, as she had embarked on an affair with Ford while her husband was serving a short stint in a Paris prison, and while clearly making amends on a personal level, Rhys positions herself in an ambiguous space between agency and objectification, between her own and another's experience and emotional truth (and literary fantasy). That she was so keen to 'work at' and disseminate a book that wrote her life, however 'unflattering[ly]', and to sanction it as setting the record straight, may be simply explained by the compulsions of retrospection that so pervade her later years, but may also be seen as an indirect gloss on her own formation as a writer and add important nuances to her signature style as a modernist. Somewhere between the 'doll' and the 'ghost' stands (or rather, lies) not 'the Rhys woman', as the critical shorthand has it,[3] but Rhys as a woman reader, ghostwriter and translator of her own and others' tales.

This essay focuses on that experience of fashioning through reading, rewriting and translating others, which speaks to the resonance of Rhys's cross-Channel encounters and complicates her current reception as proto-postcolonial modernist ingénue, or geographer of places of 'non-place' prone to *flânerie* and unwitting surrealist artistry.[4] While I would not disagree with Deborah Parsons that 'Rhys is a "stranger" in the city, rather than a "cosmopolitan"' (Parsons 2000: 136), I would argue that Rhys is not a *flâneuse*, not even a 'negative' one, as in Rachel Bowlby's rather tentative formulation (Bowlby 1992: 54); the slippage between 'Rhys', the 'Rhys woman' and Rhys's protagonists is partly the difficulty here, but my argument has more to do with the tendency to save Rhys from herself – or in other words, to insulate her from the perceived injustice or humiliation of a minor position, mainly associated with the brief episode of Ford Madox Ford's emotional and literary patronage, but not only.[5] As Lorna Sage was right to point out, Rhys was 'far more radically displaced than any of the literary figures imagination now obligingly supplies to surround her' (Sage 1992: 48), but her 'displacement' was very much emplaced and it was conscious and oppositional. The *vagabondage* of Rhys's writing, and all its cognate postures – streetwalking, café frequenting, people watching, drifting, slumming, rooming, sex with strangers – have been read by most critics as symptoms of a psycho-political condition (in terms of both gender and race), as aspects of a state of vaga-*bondage* to be partly redeemed (and to a degree sanitised) by the salutary superimposition of Benjaminian and related terminology (*flânerie*, surrealist walking, psychogeography), but they are, importantly, too simply that: postures, poses, sometimes parody, others pastiche, never original, always pointing to a pre-existing version. Rather than a *flâneuse*, then, I would propose Rhys in her earlier work as a *poseuse* – with a pretty broad repertoire of figures: debutante, chorus girl, courtesan/kept woman/'amateur', 'demi-mon-daine', mannequin, shop girl, doll, hunger artist, *cérébrale*, woman on a 'downward path',[6] '*la vieille*', ghost.[7] Rhys's posing channels cliché and cites familiar tropes of the literary and cultural kind. It is eclectic, sourced from high and low, often translated and always targeted. Before crossing the Channel, of course, Rhys was a poser in a different sense: in 1914, in Bloomsbury, according to Pizzichini, 'she posed in the nude for Sir Edward Poynter, the academician', who publicly defended the Englishness of his style by 'dr[awing] a firm distinction between his classical nudes and the disgraceful *baigneuses* of modern French painters' in a letter to *The Times* (Pizzichini 2010: 120). Rhys also posed 'in a slip' for the Irish painter Sir William Orpen, RA, and 'part of a younger generation of painters who preferred the boudoir nude of Degas, Renoir and Manet. In his basement-cellar room at 21 Fitzroy Street, a house that had formerly been a brothel, he painted "the English nude"' (Pizzichini 2010: 121). And in 1922, in Paris, she became an artist's model again, this time for the English sculptress Violet Dreschfeld, 'a classic British gentlewoman, competent and stoical' (Pizzichini 2010: 164). My version of Rhys's literary 'pose' incorporates this literal association, as I would argue that the visual and embodied aspect of representation of certain tropes, in painting and not only, is crucial to Rhys's scene setting.

Rhys's Paris abounds in clichés,[8] most already anachronistic by the time she arrives there. In a way, all cliché is by definition anachronistic, always already *passé* and nostalgically recreated or sought in remnants, what early twentieth-century anthropology would call 'survivals'. Rhys revels in them; as Christina Britzolakis astutely observes:

> Rhys's fiction claims an anachronistic affinity with the French bohemian tradition, symbolically organized around the bourgeois artist's attraction towards the city's liminal spaces, and identification with those excluded by its power centres. Bohemianism maps the city in terms of a strategic revaluation of urban 'waste,' drawing on an image repertoire including the sewer, the nomad, the prostitute and the carnivalesque. What Sasha [in *Good Morning, Midnight*] calls the 'nostalgie de la boue' – the bohemian 'craving for the gutter' – represents, at one level, a doomed, nostalgic attempt to pit an alternative, revitalizing modernity of dirt against bourgeois economic rationality. (Britzolakis 2007: 468)

Rhys's Left Bank is an appropriate stage for the performance of this longing that, as Susan Stewart would put it, 'of necessity is inauthentic because it does not take part in lived experience'. Nostalgia, for Stewart, 'is always ideological: the past it seeks has never existed except as narrative, and hence, always absent, that past continually threatens to reproduce itself as a felt lack' (Stewart 1993: 23).

In her early Paris-set work, Rhys exposes this ideological component by tracking its appeal for the naïve and undiscerning. In 'Tout Montparnasse and a Lady', a story from *The Left Bank* (1927) that did not survive the cut for the selection she prepared for *Tigers Are Better-Looking* (1968), Rhys writes of 'a very romantic lady, an American fashion artist, who was there to be thrilled, after having read the *Trilby* of du Maurier, and the novels of Francis Carco, which tell of the lives of the apaches of to-day' (Rhys 1927: 55). The 'there' is 'the little Bal Musette in the rue St. Jacques' (53), just vacated by the 'ordinary clients', 'the men in caps and the hatless girls' (53), to make room for the 'Anglo-Saxon section of Tout Montparnasse':

> In half an hour's time the fenced-off dancing floor is filled by couples dancing with the slightly strained expressions characteristic of the Anglo-Saxon who, though wishing to enjoy himself, is not yet sufficiently primed to let himself become animated. So even the best dancers look tense and grim though they sway and glide with great skill and have the concentrated air of people engaged in some difficult but extremely important gymnastic exercise. (Rhys 1927: 53)

The scene, a cheeky reconstruction of the famous 'Ford's nights',[9] couldn't be further from the expectations set up by a fascination with the 'apaches'. Severely let down by the tame spectacle ('"I don't get any kick out of Anglo-Saxons", she said out loud. "They don't ... They *don't* stimulate my imagination!"'; Rhys 1927: 56), the romantic lady finishes 'her sixth lemonade' and approaches the credibly bohemian-looking young man in the corner:

> She had been told that this was a successful and respectable portrait-painter as she was a successful and respectable fashion artist. . . . He like herself must now despise his success and must mourn for the higher ideals of his youth. . . . Though he was very young! . . . She drifted across the room, put a hand on his melancholy shoulder and murmured: 'You are sad! I am so sorry! I understand!' . . . 'I!' he exclaimed indignantly. 'I'm as happy as a sandboy!' . . . The tragic lady sighed and made ready to depart. (Rhys 1927: 57–8)

The narrative's correction of her delusion is pitiless and her fall from romanticism to tragedy a cautionary one. Armed with cliché about the bohemian life, the American lady is defenceless against the illusion of tragedy, one of the key motifs of the Left Bank; as the unnamed narrator wryly informs the reader in 'The Blue Bird', another of the stories not included in Rhys's later selection:

> Montparnasse is full of tragedy – all sorts – blatant, hidden, silent, voluble, quick, slow – even lucrative – A tragedy can be lucrative, I assure you.
>   On any day of the week you may catch sight of the Sufferers, white-faced and tragic of eye – having a drink in the intervals of expressing themselves – pouring out their souls and exposing them hopefully for sale, that is to say. (Rhys 1927: 132)

In the scenes Rhys sets up, failing to read the tragic pose correctly is as predictable as the pose itself. Her own pose is 'realness' – and I'm borrowing from the drag vocabulary here. As she put it in another of those retrospective letters, this time to Diana Athill, on 24 May 1964:

> I struck a book yesterday written about the nineteen twenties in Montparnasse. Not an Englishman. Very good. Very. Especially as he stressed something that no one here realises at all. The 'Paris' all these people write about, Henry Miller, even Hemingway etc was

not 'Paris' at all – it was 'America in Paris' or 'England in Paris.' The real Paris had nothing to do with that lot – As soon as the tourists came the *real* Montparnos packed up and left. . . . And if I saw something of the other Paris – it's only left me with a great longing which I'll never satisfy again. You see – I have never liked England or most English people much – or let's say I am terrified of them. (Rhys 1984: 280)

For the 'other Paris' is as real as Rhys's desire to inhabit it in a 'real', that is, non-Anglo-Saxon way. The true poetry of Paris is always a receding image, and its 'real' poverty a far cry from Ford's hired, ersatz Bal Musette.

In *The Left Bank* and the novel that immediately followed it, *Quartet* (1928), Rhys writes out that 'great longing' in real time. Both works are tainted by what Alice Gambrell has called the 'mimetic desire' of the 'insider-outsider' woman artist:

Prized in their own time – though in troubling and paradoxical ways – for the experiential immediacy that they would supposedly contribute to a series of cultural practices within which the pure value of 'experience' was itself being regarded with increasing skepticism, all of these women engaged in difficult, charged intellectual exchanges. (Gambrell 1997: 2)

And Ford's comments in 'Rive Gauche', his preface to the first publication of *The Left Bank*, amply make this case:

Setting aside for a moment the matter of her very remarkable technical gifts, I should like to call attention to her profound knowledge of the life of the Left Bank – of many of the Left Banks of the world. For something mournful – and certainly hard up! – attaches to almost all uses of the word *left*. The left has not the cunning of the right: and every great city has its left bank. London has, round Bloomsbury, New York has, about Greenwich Village, so has Vienna . . . Miss Rhys does not, I believe, know Greenwich Village, but so many of its products are to be found in the Left Bank of Paris that she may be said to know its products. And coming from the Antilles, with a terrifying insight and a terrific – an almost lurid! – passion for stating the case of the underdog, she has let her pen loose on the Left Banks of the Old World – on its gaols, its studios, its salons, its cafés, its criminals, its midinetttes – with a bias of admiration for its midinettes and a sympathy for its law-breakers. (Ford 1927: 23–4)

Following Gambrell (though not included in her test cases), Rhys's position as an agent for her and her husband's 'other Paris' experiences, including that of her being between two men, might be seen to manifest what she calls a 'mimetic desire':

> [W]hile the work of the insider-outsider intellectual tended to be valued as a result of a hegemonic *desire for mimesis* – embodied in her perceived ability to faithfully represent ranges of experience unfamiliar to her colleagues, but intimately familiar to herself – we might also do well to attend to the ways in which her work was also the object of an institutional form of *mimetic desire*: the desire – which is of course central to Rubin's . . . analysis of the 'traffic in women' – of one man for what another man has. One of the clearest markers of this condition is the regular appearance in texts by interwar women insider-outsiders of the figure of the exchanged woman – the prostitute, the courtesan, the debutante. (Gambrell 1997: 30)[10]

Rhys's procurement of underdog intelligence for Ford was conducted in 'real' spaces, but was also an informed, previously enjoyed practice. Ford may have 'made her read Anatole France and Colette and translate her own writing into French if she wasn't sure a passage was working' (Pizzichini 2010: 170), but Rhys was already and remained through her life a reader. As Marya Zelli – one of her later aliases – puts it: 'Not that she objected to solitude. Quite the contrary. She had books, thank Heaven, quantities of books. All sorts of books' (Rhys 1982: 10).

As a girl, Rhys wrote in her autobiography, she 'liked books about prostitutes' (Rhys 1979b: 63),[11] and in the 1920s she read Maupassant (whose story 'Mademoiselle Fifi' she turned into 'La Grosse Fifi' for *The Left Bank*), Mérimée, Zola, Flaubert, Bernanos, Rimbaud, Mallarmé, Daudet and Carco. As Helen Carr notes,

> she learnt from Maupassant about how to write about madness [and] from Rimbaud about the use of fantastic imagery. But it [was] not only for her a question of style, but also of a French tradition of anti-bourgeois, anti-establishment alignment of the writer with those despised by respectable society, almost an 1890s, Yellow Bookish admiration of the demi-monde. (Carr 1996: 44)

Her 'left-bankness', then, is as much a reworking of literary constructs as an authentic, lived experience – in that sense a remodelling, as the striking of a pose à la mode. Rhys worked hard at it. In 1928, she translated Francis Carco's *Perversité*, a 1925 novel treating in his famous and highly popular style the pathetic fortunes of Irma, a Paris prostitute. French-colonial Carco (born in New Caledonia) was known as the 'romancier des apaches' and was a key member of the early bohemian scene (and, back in 1915, a lover of Katherine Mansfield).[12] Less lovingly mentioned in Rhys's letters than her translation of her first husband's novel (perhaps because the publisher of *Perversity* mistakenly attributed the translation to Ford – something Rhys never forgave), that work saw Rhys immersed in two of her favourite subjects, poverty and prostitution. It also helped forge and finesse what Juliette Taylor-Batty has called the 'bilingual, translational style [of] her early fiction' (Taylor-Batty 2013: 80–1):[13]

> In her representation of a cosmopolitan Paris, Rhys uses French to unsettle English, to create a 'feeling' within the language that is appropriate to her displaced, peripatetic and often polyglot characters. Such bilingualism is closely intertwined with Rhys's own work as a translator to such an extent that, in her earliest work, translation becomes part of the compositional process, and at times shades imperceptibly into fiction, challenging the very boundaries between translation, adaptation and original composition. . . . Rhys's style is characterised not only by an effective creolisation of French and English, but by a frequent and disquieting sense of being 'already translated,' of being derived from some absent 'original' source text and language. (Taylor-Batty 2013: 81)

While that particular 'escapade' was not successful, Rhys's persistent use of French speech and writing in her work is integral to her style and works at many levels: in italicised form, French words authenticate speech acts and environments, but also function as pivots for twists in narrative perspective, as in cases when her character is singled out for unwelcome attention (the recurrent references to '*l'Anglaise*', or the moments when she falsely claims '*je ne parle pas français*'). In the latter mode, Rhys's French aids the poseuse to strike the appropriate pose – as world-weary ingénue or target of others' ill-considered, hostile associations, as well as her own 'self-directed irony', as Dolores Martínez Reventós has argued in her account of Rhys's sentimental and 'counter-sentimental' discourse (Martínez Reventós 1997: 105). Less noticed, however, is another Rhysian mode, namely the appropriation of highly crafted literary allusions deployed in a subtle but targeted way to 'other' Anglo-Saxony. In a brilliant example, unspotted by Rhys scholars, she recycles an unacknowledged phrase from Balzac's *La Comédie humaine* to strike a blow at the personal and political enemy. At the opening of *Quartet,* Marya is accosted by Miss Esther De Solla, 'a painter and ascetic to the point of fanaticism' (Rhys 1982: 8), who is amazed that Marya doesn't already know Heidler, the English picture-dealer, alias of Ford in the novel. She offers the following view:

> 'I do think that one ought to make an effort to get away from the Anglo-Saxons in Paris, or what on earth is the good of being here at all? And it isn't an easy thing to do, either. Not easy for a woman, anyhow. But, of course, your husband's French, isn't he?'
> 'No,' said Marya. 'He's a Pole.'
> The other looked across at her and thought: 'Is she really married to the Zelli man, I wonder? She's a decorative little person – decorative but strangely pathetic. I must get her to sit for me.'
> She began to argue that there was something unreal about most English people.
> 'They touch life with gloves on. They're pretending about something all the time. Pretending quite nice and decent things, of course. But still . . .' (Rhys 1982: 8–9)

The throwaway remark, 'they touch life with gloves on', conjures up a hilarious exchange in Balzac's *Splendeurs et misères des courtisanes* (1838–47) between the protagonist Esther van Gobseck and fellow courtesan Madame du Val-Noble on the insufferable manner of the (pretending-to-be) English baron that the latter is serving – rendered here in Rayner Heppenstall's English translation (published as *A Harlot High and Low*):

> 'But even you wouldn't dare ask him for two farthings. He would listen to you solemnly, and then he would say, in that British manner which makes you feel you'd rather have your face slapped, that he pays you quite enough for the *trifling thing love is in his poor life.*'
> 'To think that in our condition, we can meet men like that! cried Esther . . .
> 'Don't you lose your temper,' said Esther, 'and tell him a few home truths from time to time?'
> 'You'd try, I know, and you're clever, . . . but, well, however nice you were to him, he'd kill you with his frozen smiles. He'd say to you: 'You know, I am anti-slavery, and you are free . . .' You'd tell him the most amusing things, he'd look at you and say: 'Very good!' and you'd see that, in his eyes, you were nothing but a punch-and-judy show.'

'And when you're angry?'

'Just the same! It's a spectacle to him. You can operate on his left side, under the breast, and it won't produce the slightest effect; his insides must be made of tin . . . And always polite. His very soul wears gloves, my dear . . .' [*Ma chère, il a l'âme gantée* . . .] (Balzac 1970: 251–2)

The echo in the first name of Balzac's innocent courtesan and Rhys's ascetic painter may be serendipitous, but other, more direct allusions recur: a reference to the title of Balzac's novel appears later in Rhys's work, in the 1976 story 'Night Out 1925', featuring Suzy and her companion Gilbert in a bar with (what else?) prostitutes in Paris: 'Same old miseries. No splendours. Not any more' (Rhys 1979a: 106). It is not clear if Rhys read Balzac's novel in French or in an English translation, or both, but given her familiarity with the language, proven translation skills and reference to the original title ('splendours/ miseries'), one could safely speculate that Balzac's buffoonish rendition of the fake Englishman's spoken French would have both entertained and resonated with her own personal and political views on the English:

'He maddens me with his respect. If I'm at all nervy and ill-disposed, he doesn't get annoyed, he says: "I aonly wish my lady too doo as she chooooses, for I'm sure nothing is more detestable, no gentleman would thinka vitfra moment, than to say to a nice filly she was just a bale of cotton to be paid for! . . . Haw, haw, the buyer is a member of the Society for Temperance and No Slavery!" And the scoundrel remains pale, dry, cold, giving me to understand that he respects me as he would a negro, and that this doesn't come from the heart, but because of his abolitionist opinions.' (Balzac 1970: 251)

The pseudo-liberal reflexes of Balzac's clichéd 'English Baron' (or wily villain Peyrade, master of transformation) expose a hypocrisy not lost to Rhys: in her own merciless *comédie anglaise*, she associates the English not only with coldness, straightness, prejudice, snobbery, but also with a predatory, inhuman cruelty. The likening of the courtesan to 'a nice philly' in the Balzac passage may have found a subtle echo in another of Rhys's tell-tale citations in *Good Morning, Midnight* (1939), where her protagonist takes a sideswipe at the English love of animals: '"At first I was afraid they would let gates bang on my hindquarters, and I used to be nervous of unknown people and places". Quotation from *The Autobiography of a Mare* – one of my favourite books. . . . We English are so animal-conscious. We know so instinctively what the creatures feel and why they feel it . . .' (Rhys 1969: 37). This oblique reference to Anna Sewell's 1877 classic *Black Beauty: The Autobiography of a Horse* (*Translated from the Equine*) points to a prescient critique of deep ideological formation, as the evocation of a comforting, seemingly innocent example of children's Victoriana is led through Rhys's protagonist's sardonic rumination into a field fraught with gendered tension. Rhys changes the sex and age of the original 'Black Beauty' (now 'a mare', given her character's advanced years),[14] and punchily and poignantly anticipates more recent analyses of the Sewell text, such as Gina M. Dorré's reading, which places it 'in the discursive arena that sought simultaneously to promote, regulate, and fix standards for a feminine aesthetic'. In this sense, Dorré argues, 'the body in question – "Beauty" – is not simply the body of a bridled, harnessed, and eventually broken horse, but is also the corseted and bustled woman in late-Victorian England' (Dorré 2006: 95).

In this later Paris-set work, the retrospective *Good Morning, Midnight*, 'less a pilgrimage than a constant re-walking of the past', as Parsons aptly puts it (Parsons 2000: 144), Rhys revisits all the old haunts, and the linguistic and literary poses take on a spectral quality as they are refracted through memory, delusion and a different kind of longing. The very opening of the novel strikes a Rhysian pose, as great care is taken to set a meaningful spatial scene:

> 'Quite like old times,' the room says. 'Yes? No?'
> There are two beds, a big one for madame and a smaller one on the opposite side for monsieur. The wash-basin is shut off by a curtain. It is a large room, the smell of cheap hotels, faint, almost imperceptible. The street outside is narrow, cobble-stoned, going sharply uphill and ending in a flight of steps. What they call an impasse.
> I have been here five days. I have decided on a place to eat in at midday, a place to eat in at night, a place to have my drink in after dinner. I have arranged my little life. (Rhys 1969: 9)

The ubiquity of French in Rhys's writing, amounting to a two-way, mutually infecting idiom, licenses us to read the phrase 'little life' doubly, as both describing the reduced, solitary, poor state in which her character (once again) finds herself – or indeed makes for herself because there is agency in that arrangement – but also as evoking that other state perversely associated with her solitude and reduction, this time via the silent pun on *'la petite mort'*, 'the little death', sexual pleasure. In a doubly Joycean gesture, the novel's ending completes the opening scene by evoking the *petite mort*: 'Then I put my arms round him and pull him down on to the bed, saying: "Yes – yes – yes."' (Rhys 1969: 159). That exclamation has a pathetic, fantastic and (momentarily) timeless quality to it. It winks at Joyce (whom Rhys admired), both in its mimicry of Molly Bloom's great final pose, and the *Wake*'s self-contained circularity, as that 'yes' is also the answer to the room's original question at the start of the novel.

Here, then, in Paris again, Rhys strikes a literary pose and puts on yet another familiar mask. As Georg Lukács puts it in 'Longing and Form', his 1910 essay on Charles-Louis Philippe, the early twentieth-century writer of 'tales of poor love':

> Great longing is always taciturn and it always disguises itself behind many different masks. Perhaps it would not be a paradox to say that the mask is its form. But the mask also represents the great, twofold struggle of life: the struggle to be recognized and the struggle to remain disguised. (Lukács 1974: 92)

For all its reputed (and perhaps desired) 'realness', its concern with modes of display, and its criss-crossing of linguistic and literary channels, Rhys's writing seems fuelled by a 'great longing' (a phrase used by both her and Lukács), an 'eternal going back' (Lukács 1974: 99). While this is accountable partly by her known yearning for the lost (or left) paradise of her colonial childhood (another loss for which she never forgave the English), this longing, with its 'inclination towards elegy' also shades her modernism in strokes reminiscent of the idyll, as Lukács describes it:

> We should not call it a minor form. Only its format, its outward contours, are small. Its events appear arbitrary: 'merely the accidental passion of subject for subject' as Hegel puts it. Yet it is a form of the strictest necessity; and every necessity is a circle, and, as such, complete and world-embracing.... To dissolve everything in moods is banal, it can be done at any time; but when the innermost centre of the soul, pure longing, wanders through corporeal and harsh indifferent reality – even if it wanders there as a stranger, an unknown pilgrim – then this is a sublime truth and a miracle. (Lukács 1974: 104–5)

Paradoxical and perverse, Rhys's Paris idyll is the writing of that pure longing in an impure form, fashioned out of others' words and desires, but speaking its own truth to the real.

Notes

1. For critical discussions of *Smile Please*, and the autobiographical in Rhys's writings, see Delany (1983), Gilson (2004), Johnson (2006) and Savory (2004).
2. Rhys wrote to Francis Wyndham on 19 June 1964 with an account of that episode in her life: 'I went to see Maryvonne [her daughter] who was then at a convent in Weerden. . . . I found him – the writer of the book – very unhappy. He'd finished this very long and, yes, autobiographical mostly, novel in French, but made no attempt to publish it. So I took the MSS back to London and worked at it with rage, fury and devotion. Desmond Harmsworth published it' (Rhys 1984: 283).
3. See Le Gallez (1990).
4. Parsons's is one of the definitive readings in that vein: 'It is not so much that Rhys's protagonists are not placed within her texts as that they have no claim on these places for identity. Indeed, the places themselves are paradoxically places of non-place, places of the dispossessed' (Parsons 2000: 136). On associations with *flânerie* and surrealist modes, see Parsons again (2000: 135) and Britzolakis (2007: 472). On the 'liminality' of Rhys's inner and outer spaces, see Mullholland (2012). On Rhys's subversive construction of 'her own Paris', see Zeikowitz's (2005) de Certeau-influenced reading of *Quartet*.
5. On the matter of Ford's patronage of literary women, see Wiesenfarth (2005).
6. For definitions and contextualisations of these terms along the spectrum of deviant or errant female sexuality in the early twentieth century, see Marshik (2006, esp. pp. 168–200) and Thomas (1999). Betsy Draine's intertextual reading of *Quartet* is also useful in situating Rhys's *demimondaine* literary pose: 'Rhys's Marya is a half-conscious participant in the discourse of romantic concubinage that justifies the final death scene – somewhat more sordid than the death of *La Dame aux Camélias*, but an instance of the same myth' (Draine 1991: 334).
7. Erica L. Johnson reads this motif as crystallised in Rhys's autobiography and extrapolates from that 'a strategy of autoghostwriting', to argue that 'Rhys's dislocated life is best seen in its ghostly iterations and deferrals as well as in provisional references to her life as such. In a melding of modernist and postcolonial sensibilities, Rhys uses her fragments and her silences to enact a ghostly subject' (Johnson 2006: 579).
8. Peter Brooker's observation about London's bohemian scene is of relevance here: 'Cliché, therefore, somewhere along the road to the academy, hospital or morgue, was the more immediate fate awaiting the bohemian and the oppositional modern artist the figure represents. If the bohemian was too much of an outsider he was of little account, but if, on the other hand, being an artist meant little more than wearing the standard uniform then he was a tame, even comical type' (Brooker 2004: 4).

9. Ford's *bals musette* were frequented by his Paris-based acquaintances, some of whom treated them with mild contempt. Ernest Hemingway satirised them in *The Sun Also Rises* (1926), and Nina Hamnett recalled them in her memoir as a rather doomed attempt to force together incompatible desires: 'At one time Ford hired a Bal Musette once a week and invited his friends, but it ended in a disturbance between the intellectuals who wanted to talk and the dancers who wanted to dance and to drink' (Hamnett 1932: 297).
10. This point is also made by Sean Latham, in his account of Rhys's portrayal of 'an often terrifying struggle to survive on the fringes of a male bohemia' (Latham 2009: 157), and by Jennifer E. Milligan in her reading of *Quartet*: 'In a novel where the principal male characters are art dealers and collectors, vulnerable women ultimately become like the physical painting with which the novel opened: mere commodities to be bought, possessed and sold. . . . Rhys, then, refuses to endorse the popular myth of a sexually liberated Paris in which communities of women contentedly explore their own eroticism' (Milligan 1999: 282). By contrast, David Armstrong argues that while feminine objectification is supported by historical evidence, 'the *idea* of Paris as *powerfully* feminine also provides a way of understanding Rhys's female characters on new terms' (Armstrong 2013: 183).
11. This is a pastime that Rhys strategically replicates in *Voyage in the Dark*: 'I was lying on the sofa, reading *Nana*. It was a paper-coloured book with a coloured picture of a stout, dark woman brandishing a wine-glass. She was sitting on the knee of a bald-headed man in evening dress. The print was very small, and the endless procession of words gave me a curious feeling – sad, excited and frightened' (Rhys 2000: 9). Thorunn Lonsdale argues that 'Anna', the protagonist's name, is an anagram of 'Nana', making them twin characters in all respects (Lonsdale 1999: 56).
12. See Soula (2014).
13. *Pace* Paula Le Gallez who argues that Rhys uses French as a process of narrative distancing to the point of 'pure unreality', Taylor-Batty follows Elaine Savory in seeing Rhys's textual bilingualism as 'a direct reflection of the kind of plural voicing that, for a Caribbean writer such as Rhys, would be entirely natural' (Taylor-Batty 2013: 88).
14. On the 'gendered economies of ageing' in Rhys's writing, see Port (2001).

Bibliography

Armstrong, David (2013), 'Reclaiming the Left Bank: Jean Rhys's 'Topography' in *The Left Bank* and *Quartet*', in *Rhys Matters*, ed. Mary Wilson and Kerry L. Johnson, Basingstoke: Palgrave Macmillan, pp. 169–86.

Balzac, Honoré de (1970), *A Harlot High and Low*, trans. Rayner Heppenstall, Harmondsworth: Penguin.
Bowlby, Rachel (1992), *Still Crazy After All These Years: Women, Writing and Psychoanalysis*, London and New York: Routledge.
Britzolakis, Christina (2007), '"This way to the exhibition": Genealogies of urban spectacle in Jean Rhys's interwar fiction', *Textual Practice*, 21.3: 457–82.
Brooker, Peter (2004), *Bohemianism in London: The Social Scene of Early Modernism*, London: Palgrave Macmillan.
Carco, Francis (2005), *Perversity* [1928] [trans. Jean Rhys]. Rpt. Blackmask. com.
Carr, Helen (1996), *Jean Rhys*, Plymouth: Northcote House.
Delany, Paul (1983), 'Jean Rhys and Ford Madox Ford: what 'really' happened?', *Mosaic*, 16.4 (Fall): 15–24.
Dorré, Gina M. (2006), *Victorian Fiction and the Cult of the Horse*, Aldershot: Ashgate.
Draine, Betsy (1991), 'Chronotope and intertext: the case of Jean Rhys's *Quartet*', in *Influence and Intertextuality in Literary History*, ed. Jay Clayton and Eric Rothstein, Madison: The University of Wisconsin Press, pp. 318–39.
Ford, Ford Madox (1927), 'Rive Gauche', in Jean Rhys, *The Left Bank and Other Stories*, New York: Harper & Brothers, pp. 7–27.
Frickey, Pierrette M., ed. (1990), *Critical Perspectives on Jean Rhys*, Washington, DC: Three Continents Press.
Gambrell, Alice (1997), *Women Intellectuals, Modernism and Difference: Transatlantic Culture, 1919–1945*, Cambridge: Cambridge University Press.
Gilson, Annette (2004), 'Internalizing mastery: Jean Rhys, Ford Madox Ford, and the fiction of autobiography', *Modern Fiction Studies*, 50.3 (Fall): 632–56.
Hamnett, Nina (1932), *Laughing Torso: Reminiscences of Nina Hamnett*, London: Constable.
Johnson, Erica L. (2006), 'Auto-ghostwriting *Smile, Please*: an unfinished autobiography', *Biography*, 29.4 (Fall): 564–80.
Kappers-den Hollander, Martien (1984), 'Jean Rhys and the Dutch connection', *Journal of Modern Literature*, 11.1 (March): 159–73.
Kappers-den Hollander, Martien (1990), 'A gloomy child and its devoted godmother: Jean Rhys, *Barred*, *Sous les Verrous* and *In de Strik*', in *Critical Perspectives on Jean Rhys*, ed. Pierrette M. Frickey, Washington, DC: Three Continents Press, pp. 43–53.
Latham, Sean (2009), *The Art of Scandal: Modernism, Libel Law, and the Roman à Clef*, Oxford: Oxford University Press.
Le Gallez, Paula (1990), *The Rhys Woman*, Basingstoke: Palgrave Macmillan.
Lonsdale, Thorunn (1999), 'Literary allusions in the fiction of Jean Rhys', in *Caribbean Women Writers: Fiction in English*, ed. Mary Condé and Thorunn Lonsdale, London: Palgrave Macmillan, pp. 43–74.

Lukács, Georg (1974), *Soul and Form*, trans. Anna Bostock, London: Merlin Press.
Marshik, Celia (2006), *British Modernism and Censorship*. Cambridge: Cambridge University Press.
Martínez Reventós, Dolores (1997), 'Sentimental and counter-sentimental discourses in Jean Rhys' version of the popular romance', *Cuadernos de Filología Inglesa*, 611: 95–112.
Milligan, Jennifer E. (1999), 'Jean Rhys: the French connection?', *Miscelànea: A Journal of English and American Studies*, 20: 277–94.
Mullholland, Terri (2012), 'Between illusion and reality, 'who's to know': threshold spaces in the interwar novels of Jean Rhys', *Women: A Cultural Review*, 23.4: 445–62.
Parsons, Deborah L. (2000), *Streetwalking the Metropolis: Women, the City and Modernity*, Oxford: Oxford University Press.
Pizzichini, Lilian (2010), *The Blue Hour: A Portrait of Jean Rhys*, London: Bloomsbury.
Port, Cynthia (2001), '"Money, for the night is coming": Jean Rhys and gendered economies of ageing', *Women: A Cultural Review*, 12.2: 204–17.
Rhys, Jean (1927), *The Left Bank: Sketches and Studies of Present-Day Paris Bohemia* (with a preface by Ford Madox Ford), London: Jonathan Cape.
Rhys, Jean (1968), *Tigers Are Better-Looking, with a Selection from The Left Bank*, Harmondsworth: Penguin.
Rhys, Jean (1969), *Good Morning, Midnight* [1939], Harmondsworth: Penguin.
Rhys, Jean (1979a), *Sleep It Off Lady* [1976], Harmondsworth: Penguin.
Rhys, Jean (1979b), *Smile Please: An Unfinished Autobiography*, London: André Deutsch.
Rhys, Jean (1982), *Quartet* [1928], Harmondsworth: Penguin.
Rhys, Jean (1984), *Letters, 1931–1966*, ed. Francis Wyndham and Diana Melly, London: André Deutsch.
Rhys, Jean (2000), *Voyage in the Dark* [1934], London: Penguin Classics.
Sage, Lorna (1992), *Women in the House of Fiction: Post-War Women Novelists*, London: Palgrave Macmillan.
Savory, Elaine (2004), *Jean Rhys*, Cambridge: Cambridge University Press.
Soula, Virginie (2014), *Histoire Littéraire de la Nouvelle-Calédonie (1853–2005)*, Paris: Éditions Karthala.
Stewart, Susan (1993), *On Longing: Narratives of the Miniature, the Gigantic, the Souvenir, the Collection*, Durham, NC and London: Duke University Press.
Taylor-Batty, Juliette (2013), *Multilingualism in Modernist Fiction*, Basingstoke: Palgrave Macmillan.
Thomas, Sue (1999), *The Worlding of Jean Rhys*, Westport, CT: Greenwood Press.

Thomas, Sue (2001), 'Adulterous liaisons: Jean Rhys, Stella Bowen and feminist reading', *Australian Humanities Review*, 22 (June). http://australianhumanitiesreview.org/2001/06/01/adulterous-liaisons-jean-rhys-stella-bowen-and-feminist-reading/ (accessed 8 October 2019).

Wiesenfarth, Joseph (2005), *Ford Madox Ford and the Regiment of Women: Violet Hunt, Jean Rhys, Stella Bowen, Janice Biala*, Madison: The University of Wisconsin Press.

Zeikowitz, Richard E. (2005), 'Writing a feminine Paris in Jean Rhys's *Quartet*', *Journal of Modern Literature*, 28.2 (Winter): 1–17.

Chapter 6

Betray to Become: Departure in James Joyce's *A Portrait of the Artist as a Young Man*

Naomi Toth

Like many Irish writers, like many modernist writers, James Joyce left his country of origin to live in Europe: first in Paris, later in Trieste, then back in Paris again.[1] Yet few Irish writers have more insistently characterised departure from Ireland as betrayal; few modernist writers have made of such departures the very condition for a modernist poetics of the self and of the nation. Joyce does both in his second published work of fiction, *A Portrait of the Artist as a Young Man* (1914/1916). The theme of departure as betrayal is already present in his previous work, *Dubliners*, where leaving Ireland constitutes both a breach of faith and the only hope for escaping the stifling stagnation and corrosive bitterness engendered by loyalties to family, country and religion. In *A Portrait*, the link established between treacherous departure and literary creation invites us to move beyond thematic treatments of betrayal, which are dominant in critical analyses of this question in Joyce's work.[2] It encourages us to enquire instead into its role in the *textual economy* of this novel which relates how the protagonist becomes a writer. This shows betrayal to be a productive force, central to the generation of the work of art itself. *However, this work of art does not transcend the logics of betrayal that produce it, rather it perpetuates its movement.* And as betrayal implies a continuing relationship with the betrayed, the romantic vision of subjective and national identities the Joycean betrayer seeks to reject actually prove to be more persistent in their modernist reworking than might first appear. Likewise, leaving Ireland and her communities turns out to be a means of cleaving to them. For though the figure of the writer in this text does indeed quit Ireland, he never fully arrives on foreign shores. Rather he hovers, suspended, over the Channel's waves.

Etymologically, *to betray* takes us back to the Latin *tradere*: to deliver, hand over. The first definition listed in the Oxford English Dictionary is to 'disloyally . . . give up to, or place in the power of, the enemy', and this definition pervades those that follow, which can be divided into two main groups. The first involves disappointing or proving false to expectations, trust or faith. This definition sheds light on the discourse of the protagonist, Stephen Dedalus, the figure of the writer-to-be, on subjective identity formation, and helps us identify the text's critique of his discourse. The second concerns the intentional or unintentional exposure of something secret or previously invisible. This allows us to better grasp what is at stake in the novel's representation of Irish identity. Though apparently working in parallel, these two understandings of betrayal consolidate and reinforce each other.[3]

Betrayal as revenge

In the closing pages of *A Portrait*, Stephen Dedalus explains the reasons for his imminent departure for the continent to his friend Cranly:

> You have asked me what I would do and what I would not do. I will tell you what I will do and what I will not do. I will not serve that in which I no longer believe whether it call itself my home, my fatherland or my church: and I will try to express myself in some mode of life or art as freely as I can and as wholly as I can, using for my defence the only arms I allow myself to use: silence, exile and cunning. (Joyce 1992: 268–9)

This passage characterises departure as betrayal and as central to the creation of a new self. Indeed, the communal bonds Stephen seeks to sever correspond to the trinity of allegiances broken by traitors in one of the novel's more insistent intertexts, Dante Alighieri's *Divine Comedy*,[4] where those who have betrayed family, church and empire are sent to the innermost circle of hell to be eternally devoured by Lucifer, the greatest traitor of all (Dante 2008: canto 34). Stephen's reprisal of Lucifer's rebellious declaration 'I will not serve' and his announced recourse to the arms of subterfuge leave the reader in no doubt as to the sacrilegious nature of his departure. The movement from negation to affirmation in his declaration emphasises the productivity of such betrayal, and places Stephen squarely in the position of the self-generating demiurge. The proliferation of the pronoun 'I', which occurs eleven times in two sentences, underscores his ambition to achieve independent subjective agency, and the repetition of the uncontracted auxiliary verb 'will' not only suggests future possibility, but also has the noun 'will' resound in the reader's ears, conjuring up Stephen's own 'will', that, earlier in the same conversation, he has said he has not always been able to unite with God's (Joyce 1992: 261).

By declaring he *no longer* believes, Stephen inserts his gesture of departure within a temporality whose other moment is belief. The realisation that his faith in family, church and nation had been misplaced is the tipping point in this dynamic, such that the betrayed becomes betrayer in turn. Stephen's identification with Lucifer the betrayer here follows on from and is compatible with his earlier identification with the betrayed Charles Stuart Parnell[5] – that idealised figure of Irish independence abandoned by his closest allies and countrymen in his time of need – as well as with the betrayed Edmond Dantes of Dumas's *Count of Monte Cristo*, who, after being exiled, returns as a foreigner, complete with a new name adopted in exile, to exact his revenge by betraying in turn. If Stephen feels betrayed by family, nation and religion, it is because these entities have profoundly disappointed his belief in them, proving unfaithful to the ideals they profess. Home is not a haven. His father Simon Dedalus is not the gentleman the young Stephen believed he was, as he plunges his family into poverty and squalor, forcing them to move first to Dublin, then from house to house across the city to escape debtors. Catholicism, particularly its Jesuit incarnation, is shown to be incompetent in matters of truth, justice or the good. Colonised Ireland is depicted as not only unable to live up to the ideal of sovereignty that defines the very concept of the nation-state, but also, and more gravely, unwilling to do so (Joyce 1992: 220). These communities thereby seem to betray any hope the young Stephen's belief in the 'great part' that he was destined to play might have had of being realised (Joyce 1992: 64).

Each disillusionment generates bitterness, anger and shame in the young hero; each also gives rise to the desire to create a new self. Stephen's reaction to Dublin, where his family has just arrived following his father's financial downfall, is, in this respect, exemplary:

> [H]is mood of embittered silence did not leave him. The causes of his embitterment were many, remote and near. He was angry with himself for being young and the prey of restless foolish impulses, angry also with the change of fortune which was reshaping the world about him into a vision of squalor and insincerity. Yet his anger lent nothing to the vision. He chronicled with patience what he saw, detaching himself from it and tasting its mortifying flavour in secret (Joyce 1992: 69–70)

This scene may be compared with the young man's later gesture of departure in that no longer believing in his family and his country is imagined as engendering a new self. The child here 'detaches himself' from the 'vision of squalor' offered by the 'world around him', a detachment that will eventually give rise to a conception of himself as a lonely, solitary and proudly (arrogantly) independent soul, incompatible with an environment whose 'insincerities' no longer take him in. Loss of faith in family and country thereby allows for the construction of a new self by separation from and in contrast with them. The child takes provisional refuge from the rejected society in solitude, and the bitterness of this betrayal gives birth to the young man, who will later radicalise this 'detachment' in the form of active departure from Ireland's shores – such departure being, according to the young man, necessary if he is to 'express' – that is, give form to – 'himself': a new self that can only take form elsewhere, such that the project of departure and of self-invention are one and the same.

Writing as betrayal

For the child as for the young man, writing is at stake. The disillusioned child in the passage above takes up his pen for the first time in the narrative, in order to 'chronicle' what he sees in Dublin. Immediately afterwards, we see him silently recording conversation in a manner reminiscent of the 'epiphanies' Joyce himself recorded,[6] according to a literary principle Joyce theorised in *A Portrait*'s predecessor, *Stephen Hero* (Joyce 1963: 210–13) and which determines the subject matter and structure of *Dubliners*. Finding the conditions in which he could write 'freely' is the explicit motivation for the young man at the end of the novel who leaves Ireland in the name of his poetic art. Thus, implicitly for the child and explicitly for the youth, becoming a new self is synonymous with becoming a writer.

However, writing here is not only the *product* of betrayal: it is its instrument.[7] The child's writing takes for its object the very things that have disappointed belief and given the lie to his aspirations. Those to be betrayed in this manner include the old, trusting self that was once woven into this communal fabric. For 'chronicling what he sees' in Dublin allows the young Stephen to direct his anger not only towards his environment, but also towards his 'young' self. Writing is a means of delivering up this self, along with its treacherous surroundings, to an internal enemy, who is none other than the new self inaugurated by the act of writing. This explains the 'mortifying' function of Stephen's first chronicles, which both exorcise *and* reproduce the betrayal inflicted: on the one hand, recording the 'squalor and insincerity' of 'the world about him' allows Stephen to *assuage* his feelings of bitterness, anger and shame through the assertion of his own difference and independence from the object of his writing; on the other, such a gesture reproduces the 'insincerity' of the surroundings, replaying and reviving their betrayal of his gullible self. It thereby *aggravates* these same feelings while implicitly recognising his own, culpable belonging to the rejected community. In other words, writing is simultaneously a *purge*, an attempt at eliminating something that is unwanted, necessary to assure independence, and a *punishment* inflicted on a past self for having believed. Stephen's chronicles of Dublin life represent both an attempt at distancing self-creation and an abject[8] gesture of self-condemnation. Consequently, the creative process only partially disentangles the betrayer from the betrayed community, as the writing remains dependent on the object of betrayal for its content.

The function of writing for the young man about to leave Ireland at the end of the novel is no different. The text that will issue from this betrayal does not abandon the betrayed object any more than the young child's Dublin chronicles did. Indeed, to the extent to which we can identify the third-person narrator of *A Portrait* with a later version of the artist Stephen Dedalus the character,[9] the text itself testifies to the fact that the young man's writing, once he has left Ireland, will recount, from the supposed detachment expatriation provides, the very disappointing, disillusioning experience of Ireland the protagonist declares himself so eager to break free from, creating a portrait of a not entirely likeable young man, to the same 'mortifying' effects.

But the cycle of betrayal does not stop here. *A Portrait* also, and perhaps most fundamentally, debunks the very ideal of self-realisation and free subjective expression for which Stephen declares he is leaving Ireland. Indeed, Stephen's vision of himself as a proud, independent entity, free from communal bonds and endowed with poetic genius, is betrayed by the very structure of the work that sets it up, in a range of much-commented-upon ways. First, the lyrical moments of self-realisation and subjective elevation that close each chapter of the text are systematically deflated through ironic juxtaposition with passages of base, material realism.[10] This structure suggests that after the brave declarations, after the book's end, a fall is just around the corner – all the more so given the irony that discreetly but surely is directed at the meagre amount of writing the young artist produces within the novel, and upon which he nonetheless founds his pretensions of poetic glory.[11] *The character Stephen is still very much a romantic, but the narrator has gone modern*, mocking the young man's flights of somewhat naïve lyricism. The novel's final lines 'Old father, old artificer, stand me now and ever in good stead', can be read either as Stephen's identification with Dedalus, the model for classical art, or with his son Icarus, the romantic icon, destroyed by his pursuit of the sun of the ideal.[12] This ambiguity translates the tension between the modernist narrator and the romantic character, two instances that never merge entirely.[13] The ideal of self-expression is further subverted by the text's opening passage, in which the protagonist emerges not so much as the creation of an original, solitary genius but as arising from a collage of citations.[14] To rub salt into that wound, the narrator ensures that the voices which inaugurate the young man's 'self' are none other than those of the communities Stephen's departure seeks to betray: his parents (family), his aunt (church) and a nationalist Irish song (nation). Though the epigraph refers to Stephen's mythological father Dedalus, the first words of the novel are pronounced by his biological father: 'once upon a time'. Thus the Irish father who will be so forcefully rejected in favour of the mythological one is nonetheless the voice that introduces Stephen to the reader as the hero of a fable.

Betrayal of faith in familial, religious and national communities in this novel therefore leads to the birth of a romantic faith in the self, in whose name communal loyalties are to be sacrificed; this new faith is in turn betrayed by the writings of the older self-in-exile. *A Portrait* therefore both portrays the cycle of belief and betrayal and participates in it.

It might also, however, suggest a way out. For in exposing the structure of the ideal that underpins both the belief–betrayal dynamic and the romantic conception of the self, the novel simultaneously critiques it. In other words, this *künstleroman* may be the text within Joyce's work that simultaneously exhibits and exhausts betrayal as the necessary birthplace of the subject. For the idea of the self that emerges from the novel is at a far remove from the ideal of self-conscious mastery cherished by the hot-headed young Stephen. Thanks to the different narrative techniques mentioned above, another, less idealised relationship to father, nation and homeland may also be imagined. In Joyce's later work, play and humour seem to better balance the searing bitterness that characterises *A Portrait*. The fact that a larger scale of irony is played upon to a broader range of effects in *Ulysses* and *Finnegans Wake* suggests that this is the case.[15] But within the economy of this text, the relationship to the communities which constitute him remains fraught: the process of betrayal is still operative.

Forging the Irish soul from afar

For Stephen, leaving Ireland is not only the condition for his own unfettered subjective expression, but also the full expression of his nation of origin's identity: 'This race and this country and this life produced me', he declares to the Irish nationalist Davin, continuing 'I shall express myself as I am' (Joyce 1992: 220). Having established this link between personal and collective identity, he imagines himself in the role of the demiurge inventing not only his personal identity but also that of his nation, as he does in his penultimate diary entry, just before leaving Ireland: 'Welcome, O life! I go to encounter for the millionth time the reality of experience and to forge in the smithy of my soul the uncreated conscience of my race' (Joyce 1992: 257–8). This plan to create the Irish conscience within his own soul has often been read in the context of Joyce's Parnellism, in which the artist takes on the task of creating a proud, individual and independent Ireland, free from British domination, where the politician Parnell had failed to do so, because he had been betrayed by the Irish people, their conventions, their mediocrity and misplaced religiosity.[16] It has also been seen as participating in Joyce's broader critique of Celtic revivalism that attracted many of his nationalist contemporaries who fought for Irish independence, based as it was on the ideology of authenticity and a mythologising, unitary imaginary of origins that had affinities with romanticism.[17] Accounting for the references to betrayal in this declaration, however, brings a necessary counterpoint to the post-colonial readings that have been made of this primarily affirmative gesture, which see in it a form of resistance against British colonialism. At the same time, attentiveness to the tropes of betrayal allow us to nuance the modernist cosmopolitanism often ascribed to Joyce's work, for they work to keep Ireland at the centre of his preoccupations.[18]

To do so, we must first interrogate what 'encounter[ing] the reality of experience' connotes in this context and take into account Stephen's conception of the birth of souls. Throughout *A Portrait,* 'souls' are described as coming into being through 'encounters' considered sinful and which bear the name 'experience'. Two examples suffice: at the beginning of chapter 3, Stephen describes 'his own soul going forth to experience, unfolding itself *sin* by *sin*, spreading abroad the balefire of its burning stares and folding back in on itself' (Joyce 1992: 110).[19] These 'sins' refer to the young man's 'night-wanderings' in the red-light district of Dublin. The transgressive nature of the events which, according to Stephen, inaugurate the soul's existence and allow its expansion is further emphasised in his conversation with Davin earlier in the final chapter:

— The soul is born, [Stephen] said vaguely, first in those moments I told you of. It has a slow and dark birth, more mysterious than the birth of the body. (Joyce 1992: 220)

The 'moments I told you of' refers back to a conversation in which Stephen revealed to the young nationalist that he frequented prostitutes. In the Ireland of *A Portrait,* such experiences are to be kept private. Taking up the ancient metaphor of the soul as a bird, Stephen says to Davin at the end of this conversation: 'When the soul of a man is born in this country there are nets flung at it to hold it back from flight. You talk to me of nationality, language, religion. I shall try to fly by those nets' (Joyce 1992: 220). Stephen believes, then, that the souls of the Irish, born through transgression, are forced to live netted on that island's shores, and cannot find expression in the light of day. This may help explain his repeated use of the bat to characterise the Irish soul: the term 'batlike' occurs three times in the final chapter to qualify Irish souls (Joyce 1992: 198, 239, 259);[20] twice he states that this 'bat-like soul' 'wak[es] to the consciousness of itself in darkness and secrecy and loneliness' (Joyce 1992: 198, 239).

Creating the Irish soul by giving expression to those elements suppressed by religious convention in Ireland might at first appear to be a liberating gesture, one in which desire is freed from the bonds that hold it back within Ireland. However, the fact that he ascribes himself the role of the blacksmith forging 'conscience' in a 'smithy' should give the reader pause. Though this most certainly references the cunning artificer Dedalus, Stephen's patronym and mythological father, it evokes no less Lucifer and the hell fires he tends in wait for the souls of sinners, amply developed in the sermon which occupies a good part of the novel's third chapter. This potential identification of Stephen the blacksmith with Satan and punishment invites us once again to be attentive to the treachery the gesture of expressing the 'conscience' of the Irish might involve. Exhibiting for all to see that which, in Ireland, remains *shamefully* secret constitutes a compromising revelation of that which is hidden. This takes us back to the second definition of betrayal: the unauthorised exposure of secrets.

Publishing confession as a breach of faith

The comparison of Stephen with the Satanic blacksmith that both creates and damns souls though his writing is consonant with the much-quoted blasphemous image of the artist as priest Stephen also advances. This image is introduced in the following manner. Jealous of his love-interest E-C-'s intimacy with the priest Father Moran, Stephen rails against the fact that she, the 'figure of the womanhood of her country, a batlike soul', after 'tarrying awhile, loveless and sinless, with her lover' would then:

> leav[e] him [the lover] to whisper of innocent transgressions in the latticed ear of a priest. . . . To him [the priest] she would unveil her soul's shy nakedness, to one who was but schooled in the discharging of a formal rite rather than to him [Stephen], a priest of eternal imagination, transmuting the daily bread of experience into the radiant body of everlasting life. (Joyce 1992: 239–40)

Much has been made of the subversion of the ritual of communion here, in which the writer is placed in a priestly role, transforming the ordinary material experience into the permanent, eternal material of art, all the more so as it is a variant on the theme of the ordinary as a worthy subject of art, one that has traversed modernist writing since

Baudelaire's essay 'The Painter of Modern Life'.[21] Less often analysed is the fact that, in Stephen's case, the 'daily bread of experience' to be transformed into literature is not just any kind of quotidian experience, but is, very specifically, the narrative of transgression that the priest gathers in the confessional, where a young Irishwomen's 'soul's shy nakedness' is exposed to him. The artist-priest here is figured receiving the private confessions of individuals and transforming them into holy literary matter to be absorbed by the community at large at the moment of another form of communion, that involved in reading literature.

On the one hand, receiving, compiling and publishing the intimate secrets of the transgressive Irish soul may be a way for an artist-priest to grant the Irish absolution, to release the Irish soul to fly free in the light of day, proud of their desires rather than shameful of them. This subversion of religious absolution turns the publicising of confession into an anti-religious act of emancipation of the Irish people from the fetters of Catholic codes and social mores. It is consonant with Stephen's ambition to give birth to the soul through the transgression of religious rites, and the gesture is doubly transgressive in that the absolution imagined in such blasphemous terms adds sin to sin.

On the other hand, however, such an exhibition may serve as a betrayal of the penitents' good faith, one that mortifies those who have not left their communities' folds, or have not left them entirely. For Catholics *confide* in a confessor, and this confidence is betrayed when the secret is displayed for all to see. Publishing the confession of the Irish is thereby a means of compounding their shame. Stephen's departure from Ireland to write the 'uncreated conscience of [his] race' into being might therefore be imagined as a sin of disloyalty to his nation. This also helps account for the harshness of the treatment of the Irish as mediocre and of Ireland as a nation wallowing in its own misery. 'Ireland is the old sow that eats its farrow', he says to the nationalist Davin (Joyce 1992: 220).

It seems that *A Portrait* doesn't choose between the emancipatory and damning implications of the artist as the bad priest, but suggests them both at once. That is, while apparently breaking with the religious and cultural conventions, it does not entirely transcend the cycle of betrayal, but inevitably extends its logic. Indeed, if betrayal is transferring secrets to the enemy, rendering confession public is a way of sending the Irish, his Irish self, and the self narrating from foreign shores along with them, into the innermost circles of hell. For his writing as expression of the self or of his country can only be a continual confession of compromising belonging, which generates the bad confessor who is then to be condemned in turn, heaping ever more coal onto the hell fires.

Hell, of course, is a place Stephen Dedalus transports with him, for he neither belongs in the Ireland that has betrayed him, nor is his imagination ever able to fully leave his island for the continent where he has condemned his self to exile.[22] As it has often been observed, that the artist's *voluntary* departure be characterised as exile, a state normally imposed and not chosen, is telling. Unlike the immigrant, the exile is never at home elsewhere, remaining forever defined by the place he has left, by the fact of having left it, and by the impossibility, real or imagined, of return. Stephen's cutting of communal ties through his flight to Europe, structured as it is by betrayal, is a never-ending process of departure, with neither haven nor heaven as a destination.

Betraying the reader

The damnation Stephen's aesthetic project implies does not escape him. At the end of his conversation with his fellow university student friend and interlocutor Cranly, having just declared his intention to leave Ireland because he 'will not serve' its communities' ideals, he suddenly says:

> — And you have made me confess to you, Stephen said, thrilled by his touch, as I have confessed to you so many other things, have I not?
> — Yes, my child, Cranly said, still gaily. (Joyce 1992: 269)

This constitutes an avowal that the desire to depart to create his own and his country's soul is in and of itself a sin that requires confession and penitence.[23] This operation is recognised by Cranly, who playfully adopts the role of the confessor in responding with the priest's traditional 'Yes, my child'. In leaving Ireland, Stephen does not escape the reach of any nets, contrary to his own declaration: he has only transformed their cords of rope into ties of elastic that bind no less. His perversion of motifs of communion and confession lead less to liberation from the religion he thus blasphemes than to what Jacques Lacan would call, in his seminar on Joyce, *père-version*: another version of the same law, in which any apparent redemption is comprehensible only within the bounds of the relationship to the flouted authority, and not beyond it (Lacan 2005: 103).[24]

But if this avowal on Stephen's part has consequences for the role he ascribes to the reader, then the narrative of *A Portrait* itself might be taken as a confession, in which case it also implicates us as readers. Indeed, by delivering over to us the story of his younger self, he places readers in a position analogous to Cranly in this exchange: that of the priest receiving the artist's confession of his literary sins. If *A Portrait* is the exposition of an individual and nation's secret, hitherto unspoken soul in the form of a confession of sin, we are therefore forced to ask ourselves if we too feel it in us to respond, seriously or in jest, 'Yes, my child'. In other words, Stephen simultaneously dons the robes of the bad priest, the untrustworthy confessor and sacrilegious dispenser of the artistic sacrament, *and* defies his reader, situated on the other side of the textual lattice, to do the same.

For if Stephen's confession betrays and thereby creates both himself and his country, it carries the potential to betray the reader in the same movement. It does so if it catches us in the act of judging his self and his version of the Irish, taking us red-handed as we are busy absolving or condemning both him and them – for what does the critic do, if not exercise judgement? Stephen makes us uncomfortably aware of that which, in the critical gesture, still smacks of religion and the Ideal. By placing the reader in the confessional, the narrator of *A Portrait* foregrounds the religious undertones of European autobiographical writings since Rousseau's *Confessions*, which explicitly address the reader and ask him to vindicate the writer. It invites us to evaluate the extent to which we still act in accordance with the romantic conception of the critic, expounded most famously by the Schlegel brothers, who elevate the critical gesture into the site at which the truth of a work is revealed, and judged, such that, as Walter Benjamin summed it up, 'the Idea of poetry is prose'.[25]

If we comfortably take up this priestly pose, treating the literary text as linguistic bread to be transfigured into the eternal life of a critical essay, if we pass judgement on those depicted – if, in short, we stay where the young Stephen places us in his desire to create an 'authentic' self and an 'authentic' Ireland in contrast to the discourses of the coloniser, the colonised *and* the nationalist's discourses of authenticity – we are shown to be perhaps not quite as modern as we would like to think, and certainly less so than the narrator of the text, who consistently undermines all discourses of authenticity.[26] But if, on the other hand, this exposure of our position makes us blush, Stephen's betrayal of us might just become productive of a modern reader. By making us conscious of the temptations of critical priesthoods, Stephen allows us to glimpse a way out of the confessional, as well as a way out of the infernal economy of betrayal and belief in subjective and national identities it entails. It might allow us to berth our boats on one or other side of the Channel, and then to criss-cross back and forth with greater ease and delight. For it opens a door onto another, less idealised and therefore less fraught relationship to tale telling itself.[27]

Conclusion

The structure of betrayal and creation within which Stephen's departure from Ireland is embedded means that this gesture is, in this novel at least, not able to be fully realised. Turning betrayal into revenge and using writing as its instrument allows for both the creation and condemnation of new individual and national identities, but not necessarily for the critique of the very structures of belief such identities presuppose. Nonetheless, the novel does initiate this critique: first, through the modernist vision of identity the narrator articulates, and, second, though the challenge thrown down to the reader to don the robes of the priest, while making such a critical posture optional. Both gestures indicate that *A Portrait of the Artist as a Young Man* might indeed be the birthplace of a new soul, one less determined by the structures of belief and betrayal; a modernist soul, perhaps, who, after elasticising the ties that bind, cuts them altogether. It is on this condition that the artist can really leave Ireland – and that he can then really return.

Notes

1. I would like to thank Françoise Asso, whose sensitive and incisive comments were decisive in the shaping of this article, and Quentin Ravelli, whose remarks gave it greater clarity.
2. Amongst the many critical studies of Joyce that discuss the theme of betrayal, perhaps the most comprehensive is James Alexander Fraser's 2016 book, *Joyce and Betrayal*. Though Fraser seeks to understand

how betrayal can work as a 'tool' in this text and in Joyce's work more generally, he restricts his analysis of its role in *A Portrait* to the way in which it conditions the various versions of Stephen's self. This is also the case in another important study that broaches the question of betrayal in Joyce, Tony Thwaites's 2001 *Joycean Temporalities, Debts, Promises and Countersignatures*. Thwaites focuses primarily on promises made and broken in the constructions and destructions of multiple selves. Neither Thwaites nor Fraser discusses the role of betrayal in the *mises en abyme* of the creative act, which is the object of the present essay.

3. This analysis of both aspects of betrayal as mutually reinforcing each other further differentiates the argument developed here from James Fraser's discussion of betrayal in Joyce's work. Fraser focuses on conscious betrayal only, claiming, somewhat surprisingly, that Joyce was not so interested in betrayal as 'unwilled exposure' (2016: 11).
4. See notably Reynolds (1981: 181–99) where she discusses Dante's place in *A Portrait*. However, Reynolds does not discuss the *Inferno* in relation to this work, and insists upon the poetic rather than religious reading of Dante that Joyce offers. Reynold's analysis of Dante's *Inferno* in relation to the depiction of fraud in *Stephen Hero*, *A Portrait*'s abandoned first version, is complementary to the reading advanced here (see 44–51).
5. This identification is clear in the first chapter of *A Portrait*, notably the scene in which Parnell's death is reported to the young Stephen as he is imagining himself on the verge of death (Joyce 1992: 25). On Joyce's Parnellism, see Seamus Deane's Introduction to *A Portrait* (1992). James Fraser also focuses on the relationship of the young Stephen to Parnell in his chapter on betrayal in *A Portrait*.
6. On Joyce's use of 'epiphany', see Rabaté (1993: 11–23).
7. For an extended discussion of Joyce's writing *style* as an act of hatred directed towards the syntax and structures of the English language, the language of the coloniser while also being the 'native' language of the protagonist, see Verger (2013).
8. In *Pouvoirs de l'horreur* (1980), Julia Kristeva defines abjection as the state in which the process of expulsion of that which is rejected remains incomplete. The self therefore rejects something that it is not, however, capable of clearly differentiating from the self (82).
9. This is a debatable point, as many have highlighted; however, it is both a plausible and suggestive possible interpretation of the text.
10. See, amongst a vast bibliography, Rilqueme (1990: 117).
11. Be it the text for E— C— in chapter 2 (Joyce 1992: 73–4) or the villanelle of chapter 5 (Joyce 1992: 240–5).
12. On the sun as a metaphor for the ideal in Western philosophy, see Jacques Derrida's *Marges – de la philosophie* (1972).
13. Contrary to certain interpretations, cf. Cohn (1981: 49).

14. See, amongst others, Parrinder (2003) and Thwaites (2001). This clear staging of the citational nature of any individual voice develops narrative techniques already at work in *Dubliners* (see Hugh Kenner's 1978 analysis of 'The Uncle Charles Principle' in *Joyce's Voices*) and serves as a precursor to the heteroglossia Joyce's later work would foreground.
15. Exemplary of this shift in register is the passage in *Ulysses* that describes with irony the younger Stephen Dedalus, recognisable as the hero of *A Portrait*. Though explicitly directed against the priestly or saintly pose Stephen adopts in *A Portrait*, the irony here is softer and more playful (see Joyce 1990: 4). Fraser even suggests that *Finnegans Wake* is the work in which the question of betrayal itself is the least present (2016: 129).
16. On Joyce's Parnellism, see Deane (1992).
17. On this point, see Platt (1992).
18. See, for example, Cheng (1995, 2006).
19. Italics mine. Note also that at the end of the second chapter, Stephen's visit to the prostitute is the realisation of the long-dreamed-of 'encounter' in which 'inexperience' would fall from him (Joyce 1992: 67; 106).
20. Stephen refers to the 'thoughts and desires of the race to which he belonged flitting like bats, across the dark country lanes, under trees by the edges of streams and near the poolmottled bogs' (Joyce 1992: 259).
21. See Baudelaire (1992).
22. Amongst the vast bibliography dedicated to the theme of exile in Joyce's work, see the seminal work *L'Exil de James Joyce ou l'art du remplacement* by Hélène Cixous (1969).
23. He thereby confirms Cranly's previous affirmation earlier in their conversation that his refusal to take communion if only to please his mother is proof that his belief in the rite persists, in spite of his purported rejection of the faith. This is because, for a Catholic, taking communion if you are not a believer is a sin.
24. This seminar was given on 10 February 1976.
25. See Fragment 116 of Friedrich Schlegel (1971: 174) and 'L'idée de la poésie, c'est la prose' by Walter Benjamin (1986: 150).
26. Cf. Cheng (1995, 2006).
27. The reading method adopted by a critic such as Mathias Verger when faced with Joyce's work might serve as an example. Explicitly rejecting the scientific ideals of much contemporary criticism, Verger asserts that consciously taking on the subjective position of the non-authoritative reader allows for critical texts to be bound to the source text they comment upon without being bound by it. This gives rise to more creative and generative criticism precisely because the idea of critical truth and its associated risks of betrayal have been abandoned. See Verger (2016: 72–100).

Bibliography

Baudelaire, Charles (1992), *Critiques d'art*, Paris: Gallimard.
Benjamin, Walter (1986), *Le Concept de critique esthétique dans le romantisme allemand*, trans. Philippe Lacoue-Labarthe and Anne-Marie Lang, Paris: Flammarion.
Cheng, Vincent (1995), *Joyce, Race and Empire*, Cambridge: Cambridge University Press.
Cheng, Vincent (2006), 'Nation without borders: Joyce, cosmopolitanism, and the inauthentic Irishman', in *Joyce, Ireland, Britain*, ed. Andrew Gibson and Len Platt, Gainesville: University Press of Florida.
Cixous, Hélène (1969), *L'Exil de James Joyce ou l'art du remplacement*, Paris: Grasset.
Cohn, Dorrit (1981), *La Transparence intérieure*, trans. Alain Bony, Paris: Seuil.
Dante Alighieri (2008), *The Divine Comedy*, trans. C. H. Sisson, ed. David Higgins, Oxford: Oxford University Press.
Deane, Seamus (1992), 'Introduction', in James Joyce, *A Portrait of the Artist as a Young Man*, London: Penguin.
Derrida, Jacques (1972), *Marges – de la philosophie*, Paris: Minuit.
Fraser, James Alexander (2016), *Joyce & Betrayal*, Basingstoke: Palgrave Macmillan.
Joyce, James (1963), *Stephen Hero* [1944], ed. Theodore Spencer, New York: New Directions.
Joyce, James (1990), *Ulysses*, New York: Vintage.
Joyce, James (1992), *A Portrait of the Artist as a Young Man* [1916], London: Penguin.
Kenner, Hugh (1978), *Joyce's Voices*, Berkeley: University of California Press.
Kristeva, Julia (1980), *Pouvoirs de l'horreur*, Paris: Seuil.
Lacan, Jacques (2005), *Séminaire XXIIIe, Le sinthome*, ed. Jacques-Alain Miller, Paris: Seuil.
Parrinder, Patrick (2003), 'A portrait of the artist', in *James Joyce's* A Portrait of the Artist as a Young Man*: A Casebook*, ed. Mark A. Wollaeger, Oxford: Oxford University Press, pp. 85–128.
Platt, L. H. (1992), 'Joyce and the Anglo-Irish revival', *James Joyce Quarterly*, 29.2 (Winter): 259–66.
Rabaté, Jean-Michel (1993), *James Joyce: L'Œuvre de Joyce ou la trame d'une vie*, Paris: Hachette.
Reynolds, Mary T. (1981), *Joyce and Dante: The Shaping Imagination*, Princeton, NJ: Princeton University Press.
Rilqueme, John Paul (1990), '*Stephen Hero, Dubliners*, and *A Portrait of the Artist as a Young Man*: styles of realism and fantasy', in *The Cambridge Companion to James Joyce*, ed. Derek Attridge, Cambridge: Cambridge University Press, pp. 103–30.

Schlegel, Friedrich (1971), *Freidrich Schlegel's* Lucinde *and The Fragments*, trans. Peter Firchow, Minneapolis, University of Minnesota Press.

Thwaites, Tony (2001), *Joycean Temporalities, Debts, Promises and Countersignatures*, Tampa: University Press of Florida.

Verger, Mathias (2013), 'La Haine de la langue maternel: Une lecture de James Joyce, Jean Genet, Thomas Bernard', doctoral dissertation in Comparative Literature, Université Paris VIII Saint-Denis.

Verger, Mathias (2016), 'La Haine et la traduction. Une lecture à l'affect de Joyce', *L'Atelier*, 8.1: 72–100.

Interlude: Mediating

Jane Goldman

When we hit the English Channel that night, choppy and wind-blown as it was, I began to be seasick for the first and only time in my life. But I thought I was going to die. I rocked! And the sea rocked! And the boat rocked! And the world went round and round! When we got out of the Channel, we ran into one of those North Atlantic gales that lasted half-way to New York. And for over a week, every time the boat would sway, my stomach would sway, too. That cured me of ever again drinking too much gin. (Hughes 1993: 140)

Modernist Channel crossings may sometimes become narrow straits, a sort of critical shorthand for experimental exchanges between London and Paris. And traffic may in some received opinion likewise be considered preponderantly one way, particularly in view of Paris's postwar status in 1919 as the locus for the Peace Conference, and therefore for a while capital city of the political world, as well as the capital city of the international, transnational, cultural avant-gardes. But, recalling a nauseating and hungover Channel crossing, *rough* in many senses (see Virginia Woolf's hilarious cross-Channel mistranslation of this word cited in our Introduction [Woolf 1975–80, vol. 4: 197]) and made while he was working on 'a big, clean-looking freighter' on a regular run between Rotterdam and New York (1993: 139), Langston Hughes reminds us, in an aqueous autobiography, *The Big Sea* (1940), that it is possible to cross through the English Channel in many other directions too, and not only to other European destinations besides France and Belgium, the amorphous 'Flanders', metonym for all the Great War battlefields. For the English Channel/French 'la Manche' in fact mediates in the east with the North Sea (also the site of huge naval conflict), which incidentally was known until the Great War as the German Ocean on British and German maps alike (see Scully 2009), and hence east to Scandinavia and Russia, and in the west with the Celtic and Irish seas and the Atlantic Ocean.

Even in the most reductively binary inscriptions of the Channel as an historically unquestioned bifurcating trench between England and France, or between an isolationist Britain and the rest of the world, such as Algernon Swinburne's poem 'A Channel Passage' (1855), this 'channel that sunders England from shores where never was man born free' (Swinburne 1905: 280, line 21) is also flashing and coursing and flowing with multi-directional energies and confluences, 'clothed with the likeness and thrilled with the strength and the wrath of a tropic sea' (line 22):

> Sudden, sublime, the strong storm spake: we heard the thunders as hounds that bark.
> Lovelier if aught may be lovelier than stars, we saw the lightnings exalt the sky,
> Living and lustrous and rapturous as love that is born but to quicken and lighten and die.
> Heaven's own heart at its highest of delight found utterance in music and semblance in fire:
> Thunder on thunder exulted, rejoicing to live and to satiate the night's desire. (279–80, lines 8–12)

Swinburne's 'sudden' storm perhaps anticipates here the queer erotic charge of Woolf's reported howler, 'la mer brusque' (Woolf 1975–80, vol. 4: 197). Perhaps we might understand cross-Channel modernisms to be rewriting and subverting Matthew Arnold's great (proto-Brexiteer perhaps) paean to the English Channel, 'Dover Beach' (Arnold 1885: 63–4), and its opening Anglocentric observation enunciated by a lonely, isolationist lover to his love: 'The sea is calm tonight' (line 1) – *au contraire*, queer modernism counters: the sea is *sudden* tonight/la mer est *brusque* cette nuit! And the world that 'Hath really neither joy, nor love, nor light, / Nor certitude, nor peace, nor help for pain', that other world, 'Swept with confused alarms of struggle and flight, / Where ignorant armies clash by night' (lines 33–7), is *not*, as the tidal movement of Arnold's lines itself intimates, only to be found somewhere else remote from us on the other shore of the poem, threatening the Home Counties like his ebbing 'Sea of Faith' (line 21).

Anthony Hecht's 'The Dover Bitch: A Criticism of Life' (1967), offers an urbane, somewhat jaundiced cosmopolitan riposte to Arnold. Its archly ironical speaker, affecting acquaintance with Arnold's addressee, channels a world-weary ironic modern(ist) feminism of sorts, in pointing up the gender politics of Arnold's co-opting of nature and elision of the woman addressee, who 'told me later on' how 'she got to looking out

> At the lights across the channel, and really felt sad
> Thinking of all the wine and enormous beds
> And blandishments in French and the perfumes.
> And then she got angry. To have been brought
> All the way down from London, and then be addressed
> As a sort of mournful cosmic last resort
> Is really tough on a girl, and she was pretty. (Hecht 1967: lines 11–20)

But in this dramatic monologue, channelling too Robert Browning's 'My Last Duchess' (1842), the speaker's chilling ennui infects the poem with, and enacts, a world-weary critique of experimental modernist aesthetics, eliding with those clichéd French 'blandishments', wine and sex, the modernist Channel crossings that intervene between Arnold's era and poetic mode and Hecht's. And 'The Dover Bitch' also enacts a critique too of the sort of bland and pat feminist critiques that insist on reductively reading all poetry, including experimental modernist and avant-garde poetry, through the lens of a bourgeois identity politics; and Arnold's poem now seems to get off lightly.

What is this 1960s New Yorker *doing* on Dover Beach anyway? He surely needs to catch up with 'those who had gone down to pace the beach' in 'Time Passes', the middle part of *To the Lighthouse* (1927), dreaming of 'finding in solitude on the beach an answer', discover that 'to pace the beach was impossible; contemplation was unendurable; the mirror was broken' (Woolf 1927: 208) – war has already broken the sea-mirror, and the richly palimpsestic textual sea of 'Time Passes', in so far as it corresponds to geography at all, is simultaneously referencing both the English Channel off Cornwall and the inner Hebridean sea north of the Irish Channel and east of the Atlantic. Readers of *To the Lighthouse* would do well to consult Lauren Elkin's stimulating chapter on Elizabeth Bowen, which recontextualises the work of this Anglo-Irish modernist writer by opening up her Irish Channel, so to speak, to a newly imagined Anglo-Hibernian European space.

'Time Passes', in its drafts between English and French and English, may be understood as conducting a proxy cross-Channel war with the French symbolism of Woolf's translator, Charles Mauron (see Goldman 2017). But *To the Lighthouse*, like all of Woolf's

Hogarth publications, also has eyes for New York, its first edition bifurcating into two simultaneously published first editions with significant 'willed' variants on each side of the Atlantic (Gabler 2015: 154). New modernist studies has been tracing such complex channels of publication and dissemination for some time now, mapping the mediating activities of publishing houses and journals. Laura Marcus's chapter on the little magazine *Close Up* is exemplary in its exploration of the modernist magazine as a cross-Channel genre itself, mediating, theorising and disseminating the achievements of the newly arrived modernist genre, or 'tenth muse' – cinema (Marcus 2007). *Close Up* seriously explores cinema's potential in the era of silent films to fulfil a dream of a common (visual) language, free of the nationalism adhering to verbal language. Indeed *Close Up*, whose editors were in Switzerland, had tremendous international reach with correspondents all over Europe and the Soviet Union as well as in America. Through its far-reaching channels, Marcus considers both familiar and less well-known modernists.

If there was once a dominant set of binaries operating in twentieth-century modernist criticism where all eyes were on Americans in Paris, such as Ernest Hemingway, F. Scott Fitzgerald and Gertrude Stein, more recently Afromodernists (Sweeney and Marsh 2013) have productively switched focus to explore the paradoxes and complexities of an elided Paris–America binary experienced by artists such as Langston Hughes and Josephine Baker (who both crossed the English Channel as well as the Atlantic). Baker's massively popular signature song 'J'ai Deux Amours' (1930), for example, starkly delineates the racist gulf between her 'two loves' in the refrain: 'J'ai deux amours / Mon pays et Paris' ('I have two loves / My country and Paris'). As well as the Peace Conference, Paris was also host in 1919 to the Pan-African Congress convened by W. E. B. Du Bois. Hughes, meanwhile, when returning from New York to Rotterdam in 1924, suffers an incident 'to cap the climax of misfortunes, [when] in mid-ocean, this trip, our wireless operator went crazy', rendering the crew without 'use of wireless in mid-Atlantic in one of the worst storms in years'. When finally 'we reached the Channel' and then Rotterdam, Hughes fled the jinxed ship and 'packed my bags, and caught the night train for Paris. Good-bye, old freight boat!' (Hughes 1993: 143). Hughes writes of the unforgettable 'thrill of *La Frontière*':

> In the middle of the night the French customs inspectors came through, throwing open all the many doors of our third-class coach, and letting in the snow and the cold night wind that swirled about the little station. I was in France.

La Frontière!
La France!
The train to Paris. A dream come true. (Hughes 1993: 143)

Perhaps all modernist Channels eventually do cross to Paris after all. Yet consider how distinctly Hughes's third-class Channel crossing differs from the eased passage back to Paris of Gertrude Stein and Alice B. Toklas at the outbreak of the Great War, when they were in London as the guests of the philosopher Alfred North Whitehead, as related in Stein's queerly self-reflexive *Autobiography of Alice B. Toklas* (1933), written in the voice of her lover and amanuensis who finds herself the wife of a 'genius' in the company of the wife of another 'genius':

> I remember the leaving London very little, I cannot even remember whether it was day-light or not but it must have been because when we were on the channel boat it was daylight. The boat was crowded. There were quantities of belgian soldiers and officers escaped from Antwerp, all with tired eyes. It was our first experience of the tired but watchful eyes of soldiers. We finally were able to arrange a seat for Mrs. Whitehead who had been ill and soon we were in France. Mrs. Whitehead's papers were so overpowering that there were no delays and soon we were in the train and about ten o'clock at night we were in Paris. We took a taxi and drove through Paris, beautiful and unviolated, to the rue de Fleurus. We were once more at home. (Stein 1933: 168–9)

In the Great War, modernist Channel crossings were dominated by the military presence glimpsed here by Toklas and Stein in their retreat to Paris, and such crossings increasingly, then for ever, are haunted by the thronging ghosts of the non-returning war dead, who constituted for the belligerent governments a new category of population in need of management (see Sherman 2014: 93).

Meanwhile, the avant-garde music of Claude Debussy's pacifist composition for children, *La Boîte à Joujoux*, as Charlotte de Mille's chapter compellingly explores, was soon crossing the Channel in the other direction from Stein and Toklas for its premiere in London's Omega Workshops, itself newly transfigured as a site of pacifist resistance and haven for war refugees. De Mille's research has enabled a number of centenary performances of *La Boîte à Joujoux* at various modernist studies events (recent British Association for Modernist Studies and Woolf conferences, for example), and beyond into schools. For, alas, there still remains a pressing cultural need to mediate the horrific realities of warfare to children.

The revenant figure of the war dead was made officially manifest in the synecdochic corpse of the Unknown Warrior shipped back across the Channel to be ceremonially interred on Armistice Day 1920 in Westminster Abbey, London. Its French counterpart, the Unknown Soldier, was simultaneously interred on the same day at the Arc de Triomphe, Paris. These national sites of allied mourning, mediating channels of state-sanctioned grief for those bereaved by the war yet without access to the remains of their loved ones, are the focus of the closing chapter in this collection. Patrizia Muscogiuri here ferries us back to further instances of Woolf in transmanche mode, inscribed this time in three much neglected brief essays on crossing the Channel, literally so in one case. She offers a new reading of *Jacob's Room* (1922), alongside the war poetry of Wilfred Owen and Thomas Hardy, in the context of war writings and artworks by E. M. Forster, Ford Maddox Ford, Mulk Raj Anand, C. R. W. Nevinson and many others.

What will these cross-Channel modernist revenants make, we might wonder, of Isabel Waidner's experimental novel, *We Are Made of Diamond Stuff* (2019), set in the English Channel and exploring queer, working-class and migrant experiences, for whom the sea is neither calm nor brusque:

> Incidentally, the sea is YELLOW (yellow for volatile). I'm not going in this I say. The polar bears survey the coastline for a while, the reebocks get halfway to the fort before they abort. Let's regroup tomorrow, Shae says.
>
> The polar bears are novelists (infantry soldiers), the reeboks are poets (intelligence operatives). Given how busy Shae and I are, toiling, that's a beautiful thing. (Waidner 2019: 15–16)

Bibliography

Arnold, Matthew (1885), *Poems*, London: Macmillan.
Gabler, Hans Walter (2015), 'From memory to fiction: an essay in genetic criticism', in *The Cambridge Companion to* To the Lighthouse, ed. Alison Pease, Cambridge: Cambridge University Press.
Goldman, Jane (2017), '"Time passes" between "le temps passe" and "time passes": translation, secondary rendering, and textual genesis', in *Trans-Woolf: Thinking Across Borders*, ed. Claire Davison and Anne-Marie Smith-Di Biasio, Perugia: Morlacchi Editore.
Hecht, Anthony (1967), *The Hard Hours*, New York: Alfred A. Knopf.
Hughes, Langston (1993), *The Big Sea: An Autobiography* [1940], New York: Farrar, Straus and Giroux.

Marcus, Laura (2007), *The Tenth Muse: Writing about Cinema in the Modernist Period*, Oxford: Oxford University Press.
Scully, Richard J. (2009), '"North Sea or German Ocean"? The Anglo-German cartographic freemasonry, 1842–1914', *Imago Mundi*, 62.1: 46–62. DOI: 10.1080/03085690903319291.
Sherman, David (2014), *In a Strange Room: Modernism's Corpses and Mortal Obligation*, Oxford: Oxford University Press.
Stein, Gertrude (1933), *The Autobiography of Alice B. Toklas*, London: John Lane.
Sweeney, Fionnghuala and Kate Marsh, eds (2013), *Afromodernisms: Paris, Harlem, Haiti and the Avant-Garde*, Edinburgh: Edinburgh University Press.
Swinburne, Algernon (1905), *The Poems*, London: Routledge.
Waidner, Isabel (2019), *We Are Made of Diamond Stuff*, Dostoyevsky Wannabe Originals.
Woolf, Virginia (1975–80), *The Letters of Virginia Woolf*, ed. Nigel Nicolson assisted by Joanne Trautmann, 6 vols, London: The Hogarth Press.
Woolf, Virginia (1927), *To the Lighthouse*, London: The Hogarth Press.

Chapter 7

Close Up and Cross-Channel Cinema Culture

Laura Marcus

The film journal *Close Up* was published between 1927 and 1933 and edited by Bryher [Annie Winifred Ellerman] and Kenneth Macpherson (the young Scottish artist with whom Bryher entered into a 'marriage of convenience' in 1927, after he and her life-long companion, the poet Hilda Doolittle (H.D.), who also contributed substantially to the journal, began a relationship). The journal played a significant role in the development of film culture at a time of rapid expansion and transformation in cinema history, traversing as it did the uncertain years of the transition from silent to sound film. The perceived backwardness of films, film theory and film culture in Britain compared to France, Germany and the Soviet Union was one of *Close Up*'s main concerns; the location of its editors in Territet, Switzerland provided rapid access to international cinema, with Switzerland and Germany relatively unaffected by the censorship which prevailed elsewhere.

Close Up's internationalism is revealed in its spread of correspondents across Europe and the USA, its wider pool of contributors, many of whom were participants in film industries in a range of national contexts, and its extensive coverage of European and, to a lesser extent, British and American cinema. It also published articles by some of the most important film-makers and theorists of the period, making available the first English-language versions of articles by Sergei Eisenstein. Soviet cinema became of particular importance to the journal, which published numerous stills from films that were banned in Britain. Bryher's *Film Problems of Soviet Russia*, one of the first studies of Soviet film, was published under the POOL imprint which included *Close Up*.

Close Up's cultural and national identifications have been a matter of some debate, in part because of its highly critical attitude towards British cinema, film culture and criticism and its missionary zeal in relation to their improvement, both of which stances have tended to be poorly received by historians of British film who have, with good reason, pointed to significant films and dimensions of British film culture overlooked by the journal's often hyperbolic criticisms.[1] Recent American critics writing on the journal, in particular Genevieve Abravanel and Michael North, have approached the issue rather differently, though they also point to *Close Up*'s alleged 'elitism' and 'anti-populism'. Abravanel, who looks at *Close Up* in a chapter of her book *Americanizing Britain*, focuses on a British–US axis for the journal, framing the debates in its pages over the coming of sound film as determined by British hostility towards the Americanisation (and proletarianisation) of the English language, with its threat to 'British linguistic hegemony' (Abravanel 2012: 93). Michael North's earlier discussion of *Close Up* in his *Camera Works* also addressed the journal's contributors' critiques of Hollywood cinema and their responses to the coming of sound, but offered a more complex account of the ways in which the 'international modernism' represented by the journal came into conflict with both the 'cultural specificity' overtly introduced by sound technologies and 'the new media and the popular audience' (North 2005: 89).

The years of *Close Up* were indeed those in which questions of translation, multilingualism and linguistic difference were inflected by the coming of sound to the film medium; this raised vexed questions about the loss of the idealised (and, in North's account, 'oxymoronic') 'universal language' of silent film (North 2005: 91). Reflecting some decades later on 'the collapse of the silent film', which she calls in retrospect 'the art that died', Bryher writes: 'We felt we could state our convictions honourably in the twentieth-century form of art and it appealed to the popular internationalism of those so few years because "the silents" offered a single language across Europe' (Bryher 1963: 265, 248). Bryher's 'popular internationalism' puts into question the 'forcefully British' identifications which Abravanel finds in *Close Up*'s negative responses to Hollywood (Abravanel 2012: 97). It might, furthermore, be noted that the journal was significantly less hostile to Hollywood cinema than the US journal *Experimental Cinema* (1930–4). In *Close Up*'s first issue Macpherson referred to a 'mediocrity' of Hollywood film 'flashed across, now and then, with greatness', while *Experimental Cinema* was, in an editorial statement in 1931, declaring its commitment to the production of films 'which will also serve to counteract amongst these masses [of movie-goers] the stupefying opiate of the Hollywood product'.[2]

Many *Close Up* contributors were, over the years of the journal, converted to the possibilities opened up by sound technologies. Others – including H.D. and the novelist Dorothy Richardson, who wrote a regular column – were not willing to follow the film into this next stage of its history.[3] Macpherson became a partial convert, recognising the potential of 'sound-sight aesthetics' (Macpherson 1929: 262), but he nonetheless lamented the alteration of 'the world situation with regard to films' brought about 'with the establishment of the talking film':

> Whereas, during the period of silent films, world distribution was fluid, now films are becoming more and more tied up within national limits. Circulation has to an enormous extent come to an end . . . Newcomers to the talking screen will be known only in those countries where their own language is spoken. Blockage. (Macpherson 1930: 367–8)

The changes brought about by the coming of sound were massive for the film industry in all its dimensions. *Close Up* was by no means alone amongst the communities of *cinéastes* in lamenting the 'fall' into linguistic fragmentation brought into being by 'the talkies', but it was one of the most vocal in exploring its implications for the forms of internationalism and cosmopolitanism espoused by the journal, at a juncture in history in which nationalism was threatening Europe itself.

Macpherson's arguments clearly relate to questions of the production and distribution of films which go beyond purely aesthetic concerns. The contrast is one between the free (or relatively free) circulation of an image-based medium and the constraints of a language-dominated (or mutually dependent visual–verbal) medium. This also bears, in subtle but significant ways, on the linguistic and discursive dimensions of *Close Up* itself which was as strongly committed to producing a critical language fitted to the 'art of film' as it was to affording its readers awareness of cinema from Europe and beyond.

To look exclusively at a Britain–America axis for the journal and to overlook its European exchanges and interchanges is to omit a great deal of its significance, in its own time and beyond. My particular focus in this chapter is that of the channels between London and Paris in the life of the journal, with an awareness of the ways in which these were mediated through the editors' location in Switzerland and their frequent visits to Berlin: the cinema of Soviet Russia, though the country was never visited by Bryher or Macpherson, also came to play a crucial role in the journal's constructions of a future for film. The United States enters the frame, but in ways which are often routed through Europe and are not limited to Hollywood culture. The journal's contributors – and perhaps particularly Macpherson – further reveal an aspiration towards what would now be termed 'world cinema' (including explorations of Turkish, Argentinian and Japanese film).

Close Up: London and Paris

Close Up's editors stayed somewhat aloof from the contemporary developments in Britain closely related to its project, such as the London-based Film Society, founded in 1925 by Ivor Montagu, along with the film critic Iris Barry and the cinema proprietor Sidney Bernstein, which was also committed to making European films better known in the United Kingdom. Nonetheless, London was an important base from which to report on films, and *Close Up*'s three most consistent and active contributors, in addition to Bryher, Macpherson and the American-born H.D., were British and primarily located in the city. The film critic Robert Herring, who became *Close Up*'s London correspondent in 1927, had joined the *London Mercury* as its assistant editor in 1925 and became the *Manchester Guardian*'s film critic in 1928. Oswell Blakeston, who became *Close Up*'s 'assistant editor' in 1931, was a writer and critic with training in the British film industry, as assistant cameraman at Gaumont Studios; he was also involved in the making of a number of avant-garde and abstract films. The novelist Dorothy Richardson, a close friend of Bryher, wrote a regular column, *Continuous Performance*, in which she explored the conditions of film spectatorship, in the country and in London, producing a highly original account of the ways in which cinema was acting as a 'training for modernity' and of its particular appeal for women viewers. She stood apart from the commitment to experimentalism espoused elsewhere in the journal (in particular in Macpherson's editorials, 'As Is'), commenting on her film going in local cinemas in England and celebrating popular film and spectatorship. Nonetheless, her constructions of film viewing as a new mode of travelling and transport – 'The film, by setting the landscape in motion and keeping us still, allows it to walk through us' (Richardson 1931: 185) – and her representations of embodied or 'haptic' spectatorship were fully continuous with *Close Up*'s project.

For the American Marxist film critic Harry Alan Potamkin, who became a regular contributor, *Close Up* was an 'English project . . . continually stern with England, the one constantly critical voice' (Donald et al. 1998: 13). Examples of such strictures in the journal are legion, as in Bryher's polemical piece 'What Can I Do!', in which she refers to the slew of letters she has received 'from all over England. Telling me of difficulties, desires, enthusiasms'. Nearly all of them, she writes, ask why there is an absence of a cinema in London 'that will give us daily an intelligent programme':

> And to think that there are four or five cinemas in Paris that fulfil that wish! Only a few weeks ago when I was there I had the choice of going to *La Rue*, *Bett und Sofa*, or a revival of *Dr. Caligari*.
>
> In Berlin the general level of films shown is so much higher that without going to a special cinema there are at least two films shown weekly worth consideration.
>
> Even in this little Swiss town we can choose most weeks a film from three different nationalities, French, German or America and we can always count upon seeing several excellent films each month.

With 'co-operation and enthusiasm' in the development of a film culture in England, Bryher argues, 'I see no reason why we should not reach the standard of Paris cinemas, such as the Ursulines, in a couple of years if we do the thing ourselves' (Bryher 1928: 32–3).

Bryher's practical suggestions in this article were followed by H.D.'s intense and lyrical account of watching the Russian film *Expiation* (*Sühne*) in 'the Palace of Lausanne' cinema – 'The Russian', she writes, 'takes the human mind and spirit, *further* than it can go' (H.D. 1928: 49) – and then by Robert Herring's 'A Letter from London', which begins in Paris:

> A man at the Vingt-Huit waving a chair about because he disapproved of the Gance triptych [in *Napoléon*], a film taken off from the Studio des Ursulines because protests were made, a cinema that exists to give reprises of historical value and, above all, *La Tragédie de la Rue* . . . Let us leave Paris, enough of this gallivanting in foreign parts. After all, I am your London correspondent. (Herring 1928: 49)

Herring's conclusions are very similar to Bryher's: 'There is no place in London where good pictures can be regularly seen' (Herring 1928: 57).

From the outset, the journal thus looked to European models for British film and film culture to follow, with France often perceived to be leading the way in film criticism. As Robert Herring wrote in the same (May 1928) issue: 'Where is our *Photociné?* And what English paper has written such a sane account of a film as did *Cahiers d'Art* of *The Way of All Flesh?*' *Close Up*'s precedents were predominantly French, and they included both early cinema journals and film culture and the Anglo-French and transatlantic magazines of the early twentieth century. Announcing itself as the first magazine to be devoted to 'film as an art', it showed some resemblance to French film journals,[4] which had burgeoned from the 1910s onwards. *Le Film*, founded in 1914, but interrupted by the outbreak of war, was relaunched in 1916, with input from Abel Gance and film criticism written by Colette. In 1917, Louis Delluc took over the editorship for a year before creating, in 1920, his own *Journal du Ciné-club*. Although this closed in 1921, a number of other specialised journals were launched arounds this time, including *Cinéa* (1921) and *Ciné pour tous* (1919) (which merged in 1923, running under the hyphenated title until 1932). *La Revue du cinéma*, which started publication in 1928, took a distance from much early writing about film when its editor, Jean George Auriol, declared: 'Le Cinéma n'est pas un art, ou s'il en est un, c'est, au même titre que tous les autres, comme subterfuge plus ou moins fragile qu'il s'agit de briser au premier moment qu'il devient un refrain, un refrain qui n'aurait plus rien à dire, une habitude qui n'aurait plus rien à soutenir.'[5]

L'art cinématographique, published between 1926 and 1931, was an important series of article collections, with substantial contributions from, amongst others, Marc Allégret (a central figure for the *Close Up* editors), Abel Gance, André Maurois, Léon Moussinac and André Levin. There were also literary magazines with sections on cinema, such as the very influential *Nouvelle Revue française*. While *Close Up* became closer in form to some of these journals, they were not, however, identified as models that they followed. One possible reason for this was that Bryher, though substantially based in Paris during the mid-1920s, was not engaged with cinema at this time and was participating very fully in the literary scene.

The 1920s saw the emergence of literary journals whose lines of connection were drawn between the United States and Europe, including but not limited to France, taking over from the British–French axis of a number of earlier journals, such as John Middleton Murry's *Rhythm* (1911–13), which sprang from his encounters with the literature and art being produced in Paris, and Ford Madox

Ford's influential *English Review*. This was substantially modelled on the *Mercure de France*, which was founded in 1889 by a group of writers including Alfred Vallette and Rémy de Gourmont and was notable for its successful combination of mainstream and experimental writing. Mark Morrisson has pointed to letters written immediately before the first issue of the *English Review*, in which Ford expressed his wish to exchange advertisements with the *Mercure* and to have French 'diplomatic contributions' included in the journal. Ford's broader ambition, Morrisson suggests, was to emulate 'a cohesive French culture', conceived in Enlightenment terms, and understood as defined by intellectual and cultural community (Morrisson 2001: 33). France becomes 'the imaginary culture that Ford desired for England, a myth of the whole through which Ford could promote the literature he admired' (Morrisson 2001: 340).

The modernist 'little magazines' of the 1920s which developed out of the experiences of expatriate, predominantly American, writers living in Europe between the world wars included Ford Madox Ford's short-lived *the transatlantic review* (1924), *The Little Review*, printed in Paris between 1923 and 1929, though edited by Jane Heap in New York, *transition*, *Broom* and *Secession*. Other transatlantic journals of the period included *This Quarter* (which published French, German, Italian and Russian works in translation), *Pagany* (which included a 'London Letter' and a 'Paris Letter', the latter written in French by Gertrude Stein's friend Georges Hugnet), *Tambour* and *Gargoyle*, which set out 'to publish the best work obtainable from the Latin Quarters of London and New York as well as Paris'.[6] The proliferation of such journals coincided with a new (or renewed) nativism in the United States: a confidence about the strengths, national and regional, of a specifically American literature and culture, which resulted in a variety of cultural attitudes. The artistic production of Europe (and particularly France) was at times seen as the highest model for emulation, not least as a result of its resistance to a materialism which had come to define US culture, while in other contexts it was perceived to be rivalled by its American counterparts. 'France was the birthplace of our creed,' Malcolm Cowley wrote in *Exile's Return* (1934), but he also noted the fact that, on coming to France, 'the American writers who admired French literature were confronted by young French writers who admired American civilization' (Cowley 1956: 102–3).

Broom, edited (from 1922 in Berlin) by Harold Loeb and Matthew Josephson (who was also a contributing editor to *transition*), drew its energies from the Parisian Dadaist and Surrealist passion for all things American. Film played a central role here, acting as a reflecting and refracting mirror-screen for each country's perceptions both of itself and of the other national culture; this construction of the film as a cultural and national mirror was also at work in *transition*, which was founded in 1927, the year in which *Close Up* began publication, and which ran most regularly until 1933, the year in which *Close Up* ceased.

transition, edited by the Franco-German-American Eugene Jolas, with Elliot Paul and Robert Sage, had a particular commitment to new developments in word–image relations and to the ways in which photography and film were shaping new writing. The journal also published a number of film scenarios written by French Surrealist writers, including Antonin Artaud, Philippe Soupault and Georges Ribemont-Dessaignes. Jolas's ambition was, as Michael North points out, for a new language which would bridge the gap between the verbal and the visual; a revolutionised word which would act as 'an inter-racial language . . . to express the collective inner vision of mankind' (North 2005: 71). The word–image relationship became intertwined with the question of translation between different languages.

The *Close Up* editors undoubtedly saw a connection between their new project and that of *transition*, and between their potential readerships, when they took out a page advertisement in *transition*'s July 1927 issue, announcing POOL, its 'new hope' concerning books, its 'new beginning' concerning cinematography, and the first part of *Close Up*, 'a monthly magazine to begin battle for film art'. The avant-garde rhetoric – of newness and of action – was an aspect of the 'dynamic discourse' which defined *Close Up*'s model of good film writing, most apparent in the extensive editorials and other articles written by Kenneth Macpherson, in an echo of *transition*'s focus on 'writing in motion'. Over the next six years, there would be further significant connections between *transition* and *Close Up*, including both journals' publication of articles by Sergei Eisenstein and by Harry Alan Potamkin, as well as writings on and images from Surrealist, experimental and abstract film, including stills from Man Ray's 'anthropological' film *Emak Bakia*. The later issues of both journals presented uncaptioned, 'ethnographic', photographs and film stills, taking the (now talking) cinema away from words and back to a silence which had become identified with the 'native' subject.

There were also, however, marked differences between the projects of the two journals. While for its first issues *Close Up* sought, and published, contributions from a number of literary figures, including 'film poems' by H.D. as well as prose-poems written by

Gertrude Stein, it developed as a cinema rather than an inter-arts journal, focused on film production and exhibition as well as criticism, commenting on developments in film culture in world contexts, and communicating with film societies across Europe as well as the United States. Moreover, while it included discussions of Surrealist and abstract films, *Close Up*'s editorial commitments were much more fully to the psychological realism, and social commentary, represented by the cinema of G. W. Pabst and the Soviet film-makers.

Bryher in Paris

Bryher was in part based in Paris in the 1920s, during her brief marriage (undertaken in order to gain freedom from her parents) to the American writer Robert McAlmon. The financial support given to McAlmon by Bryher's father, the industrialist and financier Sir John Ellerman, funded the production of the Contact Publishing Company. This extended the little magazine *Contact* (co-founded by McAlmon in 1920 with William Carlos Williams) and included the imprint Contact Editions, which published work by writers including Joyce, H.D., Mary Butts, Mina Loy, William Carlos Williams and Gertrude Stein. Contact Editions used Darantière, the Dijon-based printer which had produced Sylvia Beach's 1922 edition of Joyce's *Ulysses*. This was also the printer chosen for the publication of the first issues of *Close Up* (before the move to England's Mercury Press in 1928), for the privately circulated numbers of H.D.'s autobiographical novellas and short stories, written during the years of the journal's publication and in part experiments in creating cinematic vision in prose form, and for a number of books, including works on cinema, produced under the POOL imprint.

In her autobiography, *The Heart to Artemis*, Bryher describes her connections with France, and Paris in particular, both as a child and as a young woman. With her father's encouragement, she learned French at an early age: 'I thought and dreamed in French for a large portion of my childhood, but it was, alas, before the days of phonetics and as the rules of pronunciation were never explained to me, my accent remains Churchillian, my inflections incurably British, to this day' (Bryher 1963: 32). France's writers, Bryher suggests, were central influences on her, from Flaubert and Stendhal through to Mallarmé ('my master'), Gide and Colette. Of the last of these, Bryher writes: 'the two writers of the generation that preceded me who most truthfully expressed the atmosphere of my childhood were

Colette and Dorothy Richardson, one from each side of the Channel. I caught, I think, the last influences of their age' (Bryher 1963: 33). Richardson's novel-sequence *Pilgrimage* was, Bryher wrote, 'the Baedeker of all our early experiences':

> it was the first time that I realised that modern prose could be as exciting as poetry and as for continuous association, it was stereoscopic, a precursor of the cinema, moving from the window to a face, from a thought back to the room, all in one moment just as it happened in life. (Bryher 1963: 173–4)

At a point where the constrictions of her life, and the narrow expectations for her sex, had become unbearable, Bryher had encountered Mallarmé in the pages of Harold Monro's *Poetry and Drama* and 'his ideas exploded in my head': 'There was a sense of infinite adventure in the words . . . He had felt intuitively some of the steps taken later by Freud to liberate the mind from purely conscious thought' (Bryher 1963: 158). Mallarmé's poetry, and Imagist 'free verse' after it, represented to Bryher the possibilities of sexual and experiential as well as poetic freedoms. Her passion for Imagism, and in particular for H.D.'s volume *Sea Garden*, would lead her to H.D. herself (who was living in Cornwall after some years spent in London avant-garde artistic circles) and 'the moment that I had longed for during seven interminable years' (Bryher 1963: 188).

While Bryher and H.D. were partly based in Switzerland during the five years – 1922 to 1927 – of Bryher's marriage to McAlmon, she spent time in both London and Paris, and met the circle of modernist writers and artists living in the Paris of the 1920s. McAlmon, she writes in her autobiography, 'introduced me to my lifelong friend, Sylvia Beach, to Joyce, Hemingway, Gertrude Stein, Berenice Abbott, Man Ray, and many others . . . He received, in his turn, the freedom of the Paris of the twenties' (Bryher 1963: 206). Bryher describes herself as 'a Puritan in Montparnasse', distanced from the bohemian group to which McAlmon belonged, but there were strong and lasting attachments to Beach and Adrienne Monnier, who ran the Shakespeare and Company bookshop; 'there was only one street in Paris for me, the rue de l'Odéon' (Bryher 1963: 211). Beach, an American by birth, had lived in France during her childhood; she was, Noel Fitch writes, 'committed to introducing the Americans, the English and the French to each other' (Fitch 1983: 101). For André Chamson, Beach 'carried pollen like a bee', doing more 'to link England, the United States, Ireland and

France than four great ambassadors combined' (quoted in Ford 1975: 27).

André Gide was a close friend of Beach, though Bryher's meeting with him, during which, she records, she was too shy to speak, came about through Marc Allégret, who was employed in 1923 and again in 1924 as tutor-companion for John Ellerman junior, Bryher's brother (Billard 2006: 249).[7] A letter from Bryher to H.D. of 18 June 1923 reads:

> Dear Horse,
> Such a joke. Dada [Sir John Ellerman] trotted all over Paris to get a nice conventional tutor for John. He was at lunch yesterday and I thought I'd get in a little practice in French! Found he was the nephew of André Gide and an intimate friend of Cocteau, Rodriguez, Man Ray, Miss Beach 'et tout le mouvement dada'. He knew about Robert's [Robert McAlmon's] book, knew Waldo Frank and is mad to visit America. Into what a nest have the family fallen!
> He has given me a list of dada literature because as we both agreed one had to be 'dans le mouvement' even if one did not care about it.[8]

Allégret's father had been Gide's tutor and Gide was known to the Allégret children as Uncle André, a label under which he and Marc Allégret sometimes presented their sexual relationship to strangers. They made a cross-Channel trip together in 1918, spending the summer in Cambridge, visiting London and meeting Conrad, Arnold Bennett, Diaghilev and members of the Ballets Russes and the Bloomsbury Group.[9] Gide was taught English by Dorothy Bussy, daughter of Lady Strachey, married to the French artist Simon Bussy, and Allégret's studies were arranged by a teacher at the Perse School in Cambridge, at whose house he lodged.

In *Heart to Artemis*, it is Allégret who is represented as forming a link between the Paris years of the early to mid-1920s and the Swiss and German years of *Close Up*'s production. Bryher describes the formation of *Close Up* in the following terms, making a connection between the Paris 'fashion' of film-making by avant-garde cinema groups and the production of 'little magazines' by writers:

> We lived at Territet and one day as we were walking beside the lake and Kenneth compared the ripples drifting across the water with an effect that should be tried on the screen, I remembered my Paris training of the early twenties and said, 'If you are so interested, why don't you start a magazine?'
> So *Close Up* was born on a capital of sixty pounds. (Bryher 1963: 264–5)

Travelling to Berlin, 'the first person we met on arrival was Marc Allégret, come like ourselves to see the new German films'. Visiting the studio at Neu-Babelsberg, they watched the making of a documentary. Bryher commented that it was 'perhaps the true expression of that time. Such films caught the everyday and revealed it as unfamiliar' (Bryher 1963: 250). It was also during this stay in Berlin that Bryher and Macpherson met the Austrian film director G. W. Pabst, whose film *Joyless Street*, with Greta Garbo, was a touchstone for Bryher and H.D., and the psychoanalyst Hanns Sachs, who became Bryher's analyst and who wrote a number of articles on film and psychoanalysis for *Close Up*.

Allégret, who was listed as *Close Up*'s Paris correspondent from the second issue of the journal (joined by Herring as London correspondent from issue 5, November 1927 onwards), was active in attempting to place its first issues in the Paris bookshops, as a letter written to Macpherson on 25 July 1927 reveals:

> J'ai demandé à la librairie Gallimard comment avait marché la vente: il parait que ça n'a pas mal marché du tout. Ils ont reçu quelques abonnements ... Je vais passer chez Sylvia pour lui demander si elle ne peut pas faire un arrangement avec les librairies anglaises de Paris. Vous pourriez toucher une clientèle de touristes qui pourraient peut-être faire des abonnés. De mon côté je n'ai pas fait grand chose pour le premier numéro parcequ'il n'y avait pas de textes français et que je crois qu'il vaudra mieux donner deux numéros spécimen en même temps.[10]

The first number of *Close Up* included an article, written by the French writer and critic Jean Prévost and translated by Macpherson, on the film *Voyage to the Congo*. In this documentary film, the camera was operated by Allégret, with André Gide contributing to the scenario. Film material was gathered on the year-long trip Gide and Allégret made to sub-Saharan Africa, in part inspired by Conrad's *Heart of Darkness* – Gide dedicated his journal of the time to Conrad – which resulted in Gide's account of the journey, titled *Voyage au Congo*, and a second book, *Retour du Tchad*. Léon Poirier, who commented that *Voyage au Congo* displayed the qualities of a talented cinematographer but had all the faults of a first film (Billard 2006: 250), had himself completed a film, *La Croisière noire*, of a journey across the Sahara lavishly funded by Citroën to display their brand, accompanied by a large film crew. Allégret would go on to become a highly successful film director, amongst whose many films was *Zouzou* (1934), Josephine Baker's first sound film.

The making of *Voyage au Congo* almost certainly acted as an encouragement for the POOL group's own film production, which culminated in their only extant film, *Borderline* (1930). Their first film, *Wing Beat* (with H.D. and Macpherson acting parts in this 'film of telepathy') was in preparation in 1927 and stills from both films appeared on facing pages in *Close Up*'s first issue. In his article on *Voyage au Congo*, Prévost (a friend of Allégret's) commended the ways in which the film set out not to astonish, like so many 'documentaires', but to put 'things back in their natural place':

> He wants, all the time, to help us understand. For instance, up to the present, negro dances have always been shown to us as diabolic and possessed. Allégret for the first time, makes us feel in them natural motive and expression. Through pictures carefully unhurried, one sees the contagion of joy in movement. (Prévost 1927: 38–41)

Beach and Monnier had first encountered Prévost as a young critic and reviewer in 1924. Monnier subsequently invited him to become the literary editor of her journal *Le Navire d'argent* (named after the ship in Paris's coat of arms) which ran for twelve issues between June 1925 and May 1926. The significance of the journal, which was not financially successful, lay in large part in its publication (and, on occasion, translation into French) of new works by Anglo-American writers.[11] The poet, novelist and critic Valery Larbaud, introducing Walt Whitman in the first issue of the journal, referred to 'les Parisiens nés hors de France, c'est-à-dire les étrangers qui ont pu ou qui peuvent contribuer à l'activité matérielle de Paris et à sa puissance spirituelle . . .' (Larbaud 1926: 20).[12]

Larbaud also acted as a literary adviser to the journal, providing Prévost with references to British and American literatures in French translations which were then listed in extensive bibliographies in the journal, which saw one of its primary roles as that of giving its French readers information about foreign, and particularly English, literature. Prévost's interests included not only literature and literary criticism but the 'spectacles' and performance-cultures of theatre, cinema and sport: his long-standing interest in body-culture was expressed in two books, *Plaisir des Sports: Essai sur le corps humain* (Gallimard, 1925) and *Maîtrise de son corps* (Flammarion, 1938) His articles on the cinema and film reviews appeared in journals in the 1920s including *Les Nouvelles littéraires*, *La Nouvelle Revue française*, which opened up its pages to cinema reviewing with Prevost's contributions, and *Le Crapouillot*. Along with a great many of his French literary contemporaries, Prévost was fascinated by Charlie Chaplin, whom the French called 'Charlot'. The 1920s saw writings on Chaplin/'Charlot' from French writers and cinéastes including Philippe Soupault, Henry Poulaille, Louis Delluc, Henri Michaux, Jean-Paul Sartre, Robert Desnos, Max Jacob and Francis Ponge. Prévost explored Chaplin's art in an essay titled 'Comme l'homme primitif au milieu de la nature', published in *Le Navire d'argent* in 1926 and reprinted in his study of pantomime, *Polymnie ou les Arts mimiques* (1929).

It was through Prévost's contributions to *Close Up* that discussion of Chaplin most fully entered the journal. *Close Up* did not, for the most part, embrace Chaplin, celebrating him neither as exemplary of the modern energies of US popular culture, unlike a number of the French writers associated with Surrealism, such as Philippe Soupault, nor as an embodiment of cinematic art itself, as he became for Delluc, Poulaille, the art historian Elie Faure, and many others. Chaplin's reception is indeed a central example of cross-Channel complexity, with the French claiming, and renaming, this British-born, US-based, cultural phenomenon as their own, even as some celebrated his 'American' modernity.[13]

Prévost's articles appeared in the first year of *Close Up*, published (with the exception of his piece on *Voyage to the Congo*) in the original French. His article for the journal's second issue was entitled 'Lettre au Metteur en Scène', in which he warned film directors against certain pitfalls in the use of visual effects such as those involving falling bodies. The article was followed by a short summary in English (in which the term used is 'film-producers'). The predicament of the director, bringing together a number of specialists without film experience, is a recurrent theme in the journal. Prévost followed this with a series of four articles on 'La Face Humaine à l'Écran', subsequently also published in *Polymnie*, with Allégret making the introduction to the *Close Up* editors.

Recognising that 'the screen is a magnifying glass' in which the smallest movements become expressive, Prévost discussed and explored the play of musculature and facial movement, including Chaplin's; his concern was 'technical' rather than conceptual. Nonetheless, these articles share a commitment to the 'aesthetic of proximity' at the heart of the film theory of French critic and film-maker Jean Epstein, with its focus on the 'penetration' of life and on the close-up of the face. For Epstein, as for many other early writers on the film medium, it was the 'close-up' that defined the nature of this new art: 'The almost godlike importance assumed in close ups by part of the human body,' Epstein writes, 'or by the most lifeless elements in nature, has often been noted' (Epstein 2012: 295).[14] In 1921 Epstein had written: 'A face is seen under a magnifying glass, exhibiting itself; it flaunts its fervent geography' (Epstein 2012: 272).[15] The focus on the face, and the representation of film as a physiognomic medium, was present in much early film theory: it was, to take one prominent example, at the heart of the film writings of the Hungarian-born Béla Balázs, whose 1924 work *Der sichtbare Mensch* (*Visible Man*) argued for the close-up as 'film's true terrain' (Balázs 2010: 38). 'No art is as well qualified to represent this "face of things" as film. For film presents not just a once-and-for-all rigid physiognomy, but a mysterious play of expressions' (Balázs 2010: 46). On the one hand, this 'physiognomic' focus relates to an 'expressionist', and vitalist, perception of the life of the object-world. On the other, the focus on 'the face' and faces in this period can be understood as a response to the conditions of urban modernity and the modern metropolis, in which individuals orient themselves not by the *recognition* but by the *observation* of faces.

In adopting the title *Close Up* for their journal, Bryher, Macpherson and H.D. (who wrote extensively for the journal in its first years) were entering into a nexus of cultural, aesthetic and cosmopolitan values and concerns, including a 'modernist' interplay between proximity and distance and the concept of the 'penetration' of reality by the camera-eye, as by the forms of analysis at work in the 'new' science of psychoanalysis (see Balázs 2010: 38).

Cross-Channel languages

The publication of Prévost's articles in the original French indicates the editors' confidence in their address to a French-speaking readership on either side of the Channel. The French cinema journal *Cinéa-Ciné pour tous* had carried an advertisement for *Close Up* in its 15 June 1927 issue and greeted its foundation in terms which suggest its perception as a bilingual journal:

> Un petit groupe de cinéastes et d'artistes vient de fonder une nouvelle revue, qui paraîtra mensuellement à partir du 1er juillet, et qui publiera des textes en français et en anglais . . .
>
> 'Close Up' est la première revue de cinéma qui, dirigée par des non-professionnels représente le point de vue des intellectuels et des artistes en temps [*sic*] que public de cinéma. Nos metteurs en scène

pourront sans doute y trouver de grands enseignements. 'Close Up' entend que le cinéma ne soit plus considéré comme un art inférieur. C'est pourquoi nous sommes contents de tendre la main à notre nouveau confrère et de lui souhaiter bonne chance.[16]

Close Up included regular accounts, also in French, of films shown in Paris and Geneva, by its correspondents the director Jean Lenauer (who had moved from Vienna to Paris at the age of nineteen and was based in Paris until 1936, when he moved to New York) and by Allégret, who, as the Paris correspondent, wrote two short articles on films shown in Paris and on the reconstruction of the 'Vieux Colombier' cinema,[17] which had brought Renoir's films to public attention and thereby counteracted the prejudice that the cinema was 'la plus grande entreprise d'abrutissement publique' (Allégret 1927: 65). He also reported on current initiatives in France, such as the cinema founded by Jean Tedesco and René Clair, and on recent films. An appreciation of the films of Clair by Lenauer was published in English: Lenauer defines Clair's 'spirit' as 'entirely French', while also drawing a comparison between his work and that of Chaplin in its 'pure cinematography':

> So cinematographic that everything is lost when it is presented in stills for his quality is to be found only in his rhythm, his astonishing sense of movement; so cinematographic that any attempt to reproduce in words what exists only in gesture must be abandoned as hopeless. (Lenauer 1928b: 35–6)

Whether in French or in English, then, writing about film can only approximate the art of motion, rhythm and gesture that is cinema.

Lenauer also wrote a review (which appears in English) of Clair's first sound film, *Sous les toits de Paris*, in which he commented that Clair, 'one of the few French directors that deserve to be studied closely, has known how to adapt his genius to the talking film' (Lenauer 1930: 496). The article appeared in an issue in which there was a substantial discussion by H. A. Mayor of the differences between English and French film criticism (with the latter represented as sophisticated, literary and emphatic, by contrast with the sobriety of the former) and of sound film in general, with lengthy articles by Kenneth Macpherson, Ernest Betts (a regular British contributor to the journal) and Robert Herring on 'talking films', all of whom suggested that they might have a future but that they had little or no present. Freddy Chevalley returned to Clair's film in an issue of the journal six months later, writing of the director's success in producing 'cinéma intégral 1930', with 'images, rythme et sons': 'Nous n'avons pas si souvent que cela l'occasion de prôner les talkies, en général, et les parlants français en particulier.'[18]

Chevalley, who managed *Close Up*'s Geneva office, and reported on the film scene in Geneva and in the rest of Switzerland, reviewed a significant number of films. He also wrote more general articles, on 'Vie du Film et Vie Réelle', 'Littérature et Film' and a 'Comment and Review' on the same theme, 'Apôtres et Multitude' and some rather sardonic responses to sound cinema. In his account, the silent film, basing its art on images, has barely established itself before it is overtaken by sound, leading cinema to imitate theatre at the risk of losing its way (see Chevalley 1929, 1930a). Chevalley translated Clifford Howard's report on Hollywood and probably the immediately following reports, also in French, by W. M. Ray on Japanese and by H. P. Tew on Argentine cinema.[19]

Apart from Robert Aron, who reviewed three of Alberto Cavalcanti's films and was one of the organisers of a conference of independent film producers in 1929, and the surrealist writer and poet René Crevel, who had moved in expatriate circles in Paris during the 1920s, the other French-language contributors were practitioners. Crevel commented on the pretentious décor of cinemas. He also pointed out that, unlike the theatre, which along with the classical French rule of the three unities (time, place and action) also imposed on the actors the 'unity of the face' and made it difficult for them to change their appearance radically in the course of a performance, cinema, 'par les étranges franchises des gestes, du rythme, des expressions, nous force à voir la vraie richesse des êtres, leur imprévisible multiplicité' (Crevel 1927: 56–7).[20]

The other contributions in French were for the most part written by Lenauer. His first two articles concerned a blistering critique of the absence of a film culture in Vienna and the contrast between the similarly poor situation in Belgium and the much better scene in the Netherlands, noting the international orientation of the Amsterdam-based *Filmliga*, which had an office in Paris, and writing appreciatively of the Dutch documentary film-maker Joris Ivens's *Regen* (see Lenauer 1928a).[21]

It is worth noting that, despite *Close Up*'s close attention to the German film scene,[22] material in German was confined to occasional notes and brief descriptions of films, such as those discussed by Ivor Montagu. The Berlin correspondent, Andor Kraszna-Krausz, editor of *Film für Alle* and *Filmtechnik*, contributed from late 1928 to early 1933. His rather upbeat last piece, 'Beginning of the Year in Germany', however, ends on a warning note about Ufa's monopoly position and 'the darkness of the situation in Europe' (Kraszna-Krausz 1933: 76); it is dated January 1933, presumably before Hitler became Chancellor. Kraszna-Krausz left Germany in 1936 and established Focal Press in London.

The issues raised by incorporating untranslated material (primarily in French) into a predominantly English-language journal have received little or no attention, either in the pages of *Close Up* and the correspondence relating to its production or in subsequent discussions of the magazine. It was by no means unprecedented amongst early twentieth-century journals, but the volume of French-language material in the pages of *Close Up* is substantial. I suggested earlier that the journal's editors seemed happy to assume a readership with knowledge of French (an assumption that would confirm, for the journal's detractors, its essential elitism). Marc Allégret's letter (quoted previously) indicates that the inclusion of material in French was necessary to attract a French readership. Furthermore, given the pressures of producing a monthly, and then quarterly magazine (much of the labour falling on Bryher), it was perhaps seen as more important to translate from Russian and German where necessary.

While *Close Up* was by no means a fully bilingual journal, its partial Franco-British linguistic and cultural axis, its early adoption of Paris and London correspondents, its very full engagement with French film and film culture, and its inclusion of advertisements for Parisian bookshops, film journals and distributors all contribute to its placing in a cross-Channel framework. At the same time, this cross-channelling was rendered more culturally and geographically fluid by the fact of the journal's location in neither Britain nor France but Switzerland, a country which, though French-speaking in the region inhabited by the group, possessed porous linguistic borders. Moreover, its situation in provincial Switzerland – albeit close to Lausanne and Geneva – placed it outside the metropolitan centres of film culture. POOL's films, directed by Macpherson, were all made in this immediate location; the most ambitious of the films, *Borderline*, explores questions of belonging and exclusion, transit and stasis. Its title encompasses, just as the film transgresses, the 'borderlines' of culture, identity and nationalism.

Close Up ceased publication in December 1933. Bryher's final named article in the June 1933 issue, 'What Shall You Do in the

War', uttered a warning about the dangers in Europe to come and the need to fight for peace, not least with cinema:

> The film societies and small experiments raised the general level of films considerably in five years. It is for you and me to decide whether we will help to raise respect for intellectual liberty in the same way, or whether we will plunge, in every kind and colour of uniform, towards a not to be imagined barbarism. (Bryher 1933: 192)

Close Up's dream of a common language, as represented both in international cinema and in multilingual film commentary, may have shared the unfulfillable utopianism of contemporary movements of linguistic unification – H.D. referred on more than one occasion to cinematic 'Esperanto' – while the terms of some of its resistance to sound film, in the first years, may well be open to political critique. Nonetheless, *Close Up* was undoubtedly a pioneer in its transnationalism, entering not only into a cross-Channel dialogue but also into an international conversation whose reverberations did not cease with its demise.

Notes

1. Andrew Higson and Sarah Street offer nuanced discussions of this issue in their histories of British cinema. See Higson (1995) and Street (1997).
2. *Experimental Cinema*, 1.3 (1931): 3. *Close Up* was distributed in North America from 1928 and found common cause with US journals celebrating avant-garde and political cinema. Véronique Elefteriou-Perrin writes that *Close Up* responded to the financial imperatives and moral prescriptions of the 'studio system' by defending 'une culture filmique composite, cosmopolite et responsable'. See Elefteriou-Perrin (2011).
3. This was in part a gendered response – something which neither Abravanel nor North brings into their considerations.
4. For a very full account of French film culture at this time, see Gauthier (1999).
5. *Revue du cinema*, 1 (1928): 1. 'Cinema is not an art, or if it is, it is just like the others, as a more or less fragile subterfuge to be broken as soon as it becomes a refrain, a refrain which would have nothing more to say, a habit with nothing left to uphold.'
6. Editorial, *Gargoyle* (July 1921): 4–5. See Brooker and Thacker (2012: 632).

7. H.D.'s correspondence with Bryher includes references to meetings with Allégret, who corresponded with Macpherson in July 1927.
8. Beinecke Rare Book and Manuscript Library, Yale University. H.D. Papers – BL YCAL MSS 24 I Box 3, Folder 81.
9. See Billard (2006).
10. 'I asked at the Gallimard bookshop how sales had been: it seems that they've gone pretty well. They have had some subscriptions . . . I'll call in on Sylvia to ask her if she couldn't set up an arrangement with the English bookshops in Paris. You could reach a clientele of tourists who might perhaps become subscribers. I haven't done much myself for the first issue because there were no French articles and I think it would be better to provide two specimen copies at the same time.' Beinecke, GEN MSS 97 VIII Box no 169, Folder 5658.
11. These included the first French-language translations of T. S. Eliot's 'The Love Song of J. Alfred Prufrock' and of work by Hemingway, as well as sections of Joyce's 'Work in Progress' (the early version of *Finnegans Wake*). Special issues were dedicated to William Blake, with material by late nineteenth-century English writers Swinburne and Arthur Symons, and to the work of American writers, including Walt Whitman, William Carlos Williams, e. e. cummings and Ernest Hemingway.
12. 'the Parisians who were born outside France, that is, the foreigners who have contributed or may contribute to the active life of Paris and its spiritual power'.
13. When America rejected Chaplin, on political grounds, it was to Switzerland that he turned, living on Lake Geneva (not far from Bryher's home 'Kenwin') until his death in 1977.
14. Original in Epstein (1928).
15. Original in Epstein (1921).
16. 'A small group of cinéastes and artistes has set up a new journal which will appear monthly from July 1st and will publish texts in French and in English . . .

    'Close Up' is the first cinema journal which, directed by non-professionals, represents the viewpoint of intellectuals and artistes as a cinema public. Our directors will certainly learn a lot from it. 'Close Up' contends that cinema should no longer be seen as an inferior art. For this reason we are happy to reach out to our new companion and to wish it good luck' (*Cinéa-Ciné pour tous*, 15 June 1927, p. 27).
17. The Vieux Colombier was Gide's friend Jacques Copeau's theatre, which he made available to the film director Jean Tedesco and where *Voyage au Congo* was first shown.
18. 'We do not often have occasion to support talkies in general and French dialogue films in particular' (Chevalley 1930b: 276).
19. See 'Revue du Premier Semestre', *Close Up*, 6.6 (June): 498–504. See Munro (2006: 50).

20. [Cinema affords a] 'strange freedom for gestures, rhythm, and expression, [which] obliges us to see the true richness of human beings, their unpredictable multiplicity.'
21. *Filmliga* also occasionally published articles in French, English and German.
22. See also Arnold Bennett's belief that 'The future of the films seems to me to be in Germany' (Bennett 1927).

Bibliography

Abravanel, Genevieve (2012), *Americanizing Britain: The Rise of Modernism in the Entertainment Empire*, New York: Oxford University Press.
Allégret, Marc (1927), 'Lettre de Paris', *Close Up*, 1.4 (October): 65–8.
Balázs, Béla (2010), 'The visible man', in Béla Balázs, *Early Film Theory*, ed. Erica Carter and trans. Rodney Livingstone, New York: Berghahn.
Bennett, Arnold (1927), 'The film "Story"', *Close Up*, 1.6 (December): 27–32.
Billard, Pierre (2006), *Le roman secret: André Gide et Marc Allégret*, Paris: Plon.
Brooker, Peter and Andrew Thacker (eds) (2012), *The Oxford Critical and Cultural History of Modernist Magazines*, Vol. 2: *North America 1894–1960*, Oxford: Oxford University Press.
Bryher (1928), 'What can I do!' *Close Up*, 2.5 (May): 32–7.
Bryher (1933), 'What shall you do in the war?', *Close Up*, 10.2 (June): 188–192.
Bryher (1963), *The Heart to Artemis: A Writer's Memoir*, London: Collins.
Chevalley, Freddie (1929), 'Le Cinéma et la trompette de Jericho', *Close Up*, 4.6 (June): 60–4.
Chevalley, Freddie (1930a), 'Il Parle, la Belle Affaire', *Close Up*, 7.1 (July): 63–5.
Chevalley, Freddie (1930b), 'Sous les toits de Paris', *Close Up*, 7.1 (July): 276–8.
Cowley, Malcolm (1956), *Exile's Return: A Literary Odyssey of the 1920s*, New York: Viking.
Crevel, René (1927), 'Les Hommes aux mille visages', *Close Up*, 1.2: 56–7.
Donald, James, Anne Friedberg and Laura Marcus (eds) (1998), *Close Up 1927–1933: Cinema and Modernism*, London: Cassell.
Elefteriou-Perrin, Véronique (2011), 'Contre "Hollywood": Close Up et ses combats', in *Revues modernistes, revues engagées*, ed. Benoît Tadié, Céline Mansanti and Hélène Aji, Rennes: Presses Universitaires de Rennes.
Epstein, Jean (1921), 'Le cinéma et les lettres modernes', in Jean Epstein, *La Poésie aujourd'hui, un nouvel état de l'intelligence*, Paris: Éditions de la Sirène, pp. 169–80.

Epstein, Jean (1928), 'Les approches de la vérité', *Photo-Ciné* (15 November to 15 December), reprinted in Jean Epstein, *Écrits sur le cinéma*, Paris: Seghers, pp. 191–3.
Epstein, Jean (2012), *Critical Essays and New Translations*, ed. Sarah Keller and Jason N. Paul, Amsterdam: Amsterdam University Press.
Fitch, Noel (1983), *Sylvia Beach and the Lost Generation: A History of Literary Paris in the Twenties and Thirties*, New York: Norton.
Ford, Hugh (1975), *Published in Paris: American and British Writers, Printers, and Publishers in Paris, 1920–1939*, New York: Macmillan.
Gauthier, Christophe (1999), *La passion du cinéma: Cinéphiles, ciné-clubs et salles spécialisées à Paris de 1920 à 1929*, Paris: AFRHC.
H.D. (1928), 'Expiation', *Close Up*, 2.5 (May): 38–49.
Herring, Robert (1928), 'A letter from London', *Close Up*, 2.5 (May): 49–58.
Higson, Andrew (1995), *Waving the Flag: Constructing a National Cinema in Britain*, Oxford: Clarendon Press.
Kraszna-Krausz, Andor (1933), 'Beginning of the year in Germany', *Close Up*, 10.1 (January): 74–6.
Larbaud, Valerie (1926), 'Paris de France', *Le Navire d'Argent*, 1.1: 20.
Lenauer, Jean (1928a), 'Impressions de Belgique et Hollande', *Close Up*, 2.6 (June): 26–30.
Lenauer, Jean (1928b), 'René Clair', *Close Up*, 3.5 (November): 34–8.
Lenauer, Jean (1930), 'Sous les Toits de Paris', *Close Up*, 6.6 (June): 495–8.
Macpherson (1929), 'As Is', *Close Up*, 5.4 (October): 257–63.
Macpherson (1930), 'As Is', *Close Up*, 7.6 (December): 367–70.
Montagu, Ivor (1928), Title, *Close Up*, 2.1 (January): 83.
Morrisson, Mark S. (2001), *The Public Face of Modernism: Little Magazines, Audiences, and Reception 1905–1920*, Madison: University of Wisconsin Press.
Munro, Emily J. (2006), 'The language problem in European cinema: discourses on "foreign-language films" in criticism, theory and practice', PhD thesis, University of Glasgow.
North, Michael (2005), *Camera Works: Photography and the Twentieth-Century World*, New York: Oxford University Press.
Prévost, Jean (1927), 'André Gide and Marc Allégret's *Voyage to the Congo*', trans. Kenneth Macpherson, *Close Up*, 1.1 (July): 38–41.
Richardson, Dorothy (1931), 'Narcissus', *Close Up*, 8.3 (September): 182–5.
Street, Sarah (1997), *British National Cinema*, London: Routledge.

Chapter 8

Debussy at the Omega Workshops

Charlotte de Mille

'But who in music has tried to do what Strauss is doing, or Debussy?' (Woolf 1977: 18). Virginia Woolf's comment in her article for *The Times*, 'Impressions at Bayreuth' from August 1909, is remarkably prescient of a schism in the reception of contemporary music in the United Kingdom between those who championed Richard Strauss, and those who favoured Claude Debussy. Debussy's reputation in Britain had been growing since 1907, the product of enthusiastic programming by Sir Henry Wood and Sir Edgar Speyer, but Woolf's attention to Debussy in 1909 follows the premiere of his opera *Pelléas and Mélisande* at Covent Garden that year, and two concert visits to Britain by the composer, the first in 1908. Whilst these were not an unreserved success – Victor Segalen recalled Mme Debussy's comments after a rehearsal for *La Mer*: 'the sea in lumps', she complained, dinted by 'labourious [sic] chewing' (quoted in Nichols 1992: 219)[1] – the scene was at least prepared for Debussy's reception by a cultured artistic elite, for whom the performance of allied international composers became an increasingly important part of a stance of European solidarity during the First World War.

Woolf's interest in and detailed knowledge of music has been the subject of an authoritative analysis by Emma Sutton in *Virginia Woolf and Classical Music* (2013), a study which explores Woolf's record of music through her diaries and letters, the role of music for key themes in her novels, and the transposition of musical forms to her own writing. Bloomsbury's engagement with music more generally, however, has had less attention. An appeal for work on this subject in the *Charleston Newsletter* of 1984 stimulated reminiscences from Barbara Strachey Halpern of music in Oliver Strachey's household, and the activities of passionate Wagnerian Saxon Sydney-Turner.[2] A few months later, a short article considered Duncan Grant's activities as a stage designer, including his commission by the French director

Jacques Copeau for designs for a production of Debussy's *Pelléas et Mélisande* in New York in 1917 (performed 1918), and later commissions in London for the Camargo Ballet. However, the musical – or indeed theatrical – activities of the Omega Workshops are seldom more than mentioned, not least since archival material is scant where one-off live performance events are concerned. Partly, no doubt, this has been a casualty of wartime, but it is also the case that aside from the formal events of the Omega Club founded in 1917, many more informal soirées occurred from the earliest days of the Workshop, and by their very nature these are harder to trace. My subject here is one such informal performance. Overlooked by Debussy scholarship and sparse in Bloomsbury and Omega literature, the example of a staged production of Debussy's *La Boîte à Joujoux* at the Omega Workshops in January 1915 asks more questions than it answers. The story around Roger Fry's foundation of the Omega has been well rehearsed in art-historical literature, particularly by Judith Collins and Isabelle Anscombe.[3] With the outbreak of war, Fry's zeal for his workshops as a site of affordable modern design that provided a stipend for emerging avant-garde artists was transformed to become a home for pacifist resistance and political debate, as Grace Brockington has shown.[4] Central to Fry's vision for an open, European forum was the Workshop's provision for artist refugees, who contributed to a performing arts programme established to counteract the lack of cultural events in wartime London.[5]

The immediately pre-war context for the Omega's staging of *La Boîte à Joujoux* was a Ballets Russes commission and production of *Jeux*, which used a score by Debussy and premiered at the Théâtre des Champs Elysées on 15 May 1913. In 1912 Ottoline Morrell had invited the ballet's chief dancer, Vazlov Nijinsky, and designer, Léon Bakst, to a dinner party at her house in Bedford Square. Morrell later claimed that it was watching Duncan Grant play tennis in the square that gave Nijinsky the idea for *Jeux*, a ballet that explored the trivial character of love in the modern age through the metaphor of a game of tennis.[6] The score by Debussy is significant for its use of remote harmonies producing dissonant sound, in accord with the sudden movements of Nijinsky's choreography. While plans for the ballet were already under way in the summer of 1912, this does not negate the impact Grant made. The theme had a further output in two murals executed by Grant at 38 Brunswick Square, figure sketches for which reside at the Courtauld Gallery, and others for John Maynard Keynes, who was later to marry Ballets Russes dancer Lydia Lopokova. From its first London season in 1911, the Russian ballet became a compelling fixture, its often bold Post-Impressionist sets asserting the fashionable status of bright jarring colours and flat planes.[7] As if to cement the connections between the arts, Rupert Brooke claimed that *Jeux* was 'a Post-Impressionist picture put in motion' (quoted in Reed 2004: 101).

By 1914, Bloomsbury had forged solid relations with a large number of colleagues living across the Channel, Matisse and Picasso amongst them. At home, the group had embraced Nina Hamnett and her Norwegian husband Roald Kristian (born Edgar de Bergen, he adopted his middle names on the outbreak of war, fearing to be mistaken as German).[8] It is Kristian who was largely responsible for *La Boîte à Joujoux*, one of the more peculiar feats of the Omega Workshops, performed as part of the series of Friday concerts arranged by the Omega Art Circle at the Workshops at 33 Fitzroy Square to raise funds for Belgian refugees, and to introduce 'Belgian and French artists who were across in the War, to London Society and hostesses'.[9] Winifred Gill recalled five evenings, including

> one great evening when we produced one of those Goldsworthy Lowes Dickenson's plays with puppets. It wasn't a puppet play, but we did it with puppets. I think it was something allegorical and something to do with Peace and Nina Hamnett's husband, de Bergen, designed and made the puppets which were in felt with over-lapping limbs so that they moved.[10]

This was Dickinson's pre-war allegory *War and Peace: A Dramatic Fantasia*, a transcript of which (in King's College Cambridge library) gives a cast list of James and Lytton Strachey and Saxon Sydney-Turner in addition to 'Winnie', but makes no reference to the use of puppets.[11] Either Winifred conflated the Dickinson and Debussy events, both of which concerned the theme of war and peace, or the use of puppetry was commonplace at Omega.[12] Either way, as Brockington has emphasised, these informal performances were intended as a means to draw together a 'beleagered' artist community, promoting pacifist ideas and reminding attendees of the long-shared European history in the face of jingoistic sentiment (Brockington 2007: 52). On a memorable occasion, in spite of '2 or 3 pumps and a large cloud in the space', the cellist Madame Suggia entertained the audience unabated whilst firemen put out flames in the roof (Diamond 1966: 4–5).[13] However, it is Kristian's staging of Debussy's *La Boîte à Joujoux* in early 1915 that is truly remarkable, for according to the Debussy scholarship the piece was still incomplete, and available only in a piano score.¹⁴ This intriguing anomaly between the Debussy and Omega research suggests that Kristian, or one of his fellow refugees, had access to Debussy or his work in progress, although details of this remain elusive. Moreover, it gives the Omega performance the weight of a previously unrecognised premiere.

In February 1913 Debussy had been approached by the artist and children's book illustrator André Hellé to write a children's ballet after his play. The piano score was complete by the end of 1913, but the orchestration was only partially finished on Debussy's death in 1918, and the acknowledged premiere in the Debussy literature is 1919, at the Théâtre Lyrique du Vauderville in Paris, with adult dancers. In spite of this, Kristian gathered a small orchestra of Belgians for a performance complete with dancing puppets made and worked by Omega artists.¹⁵ As Hamnett recalled in her autobiography:

> Edgar suggested to Mr Fry that they should have a musical performance of Debussy's 'Boîte a joujoux' [sic], and that he should make and work the marionettes for it. This he did. We all worked the marionettes. We lay on our stomachs and pulled the wires. He cut them out of cardboard with a knife. We had a fine orchestra of Belgians and a good audience and made some money. (Hamnett 1932: 81)

Judging by different recollections of marionette shows at the Omega, this audience may well have included H. G. Wells, Arnold Bennett and George Bernard Shaw, all of whom were frequent visitors.¹⁶ Collins also references reminiscences by David Garnett and a letter from Walter Sickert to Ethel Sands that mention performances with puppets, suggesting they too may well have been at this performance. In Garnett's autobiography, *The Flowers of the Forest*, he wrote of going 'to the Omega Workshops to see a performance or marionettes made by a mysterious figure called de Bergen, the husband of Nina Hamnett, the painter' (Garnett 1955: 25). Sickert's letter is less precise, only mentioning 'marionette shows' (quoted in Collins 1984: 102).

Given that Debussy's work was not yet published, it can only be assumed that Kristian was working with close inside knowledge. This possibility can be evidenced further by an uncanny statement from Debussy in a letter from the end of October 1913, where the composer wrote that 'only marionettes could interpret the meaning of the text and the expression of the music' (Vallas 1973: 240).¹⁷

Surely Kristian's staging is too close to Debussy's vision to be entirely independent, although tracing a finite connection between the two figures has so far proved elusive.

A mysterious figure, Kristian met Hamnett in Paris, where both artists lived until the war forced Hamnett to return to England with Kristian in tow. Their French sojourn goes only some way to explaining Kristian's coup in arranging the performance. Other 'Bloomsburies', of course, had many literary connections in France. Duncan Grant had produced designs for a production of *Twelfth Night* for Jacques Copeau at the Théatre du Vieux Columbier in autumn 1913, a modernist design for which resides in the Courtauld Gallery.[18] Another possible source could have been the Omega artist (and friend of Fry) Henri Doucet, who contributed some pottery designs to the Omega Workshops before the war. There is a wonderful anecdote from artist and later manager of the Workshops, Winifred Gill, of Doucet hurriedly stencilling red artichokes on the walls on the day the Workshops opened (Collins 1984: 49). It was also Doucet's death at the front in April 1915 that led Fry to join his sister Margery in France to work as a Red Cross ambulance driver, leaving Omega in the hands of Virginia Woolf's sister Vanessa Bell and Winifred Gill, who described herself as a 'maid-of-all-work'.[19] Gill herself produced detailed designs for jointed children's toys, now in the Courtauld collection, which are significant points of comparison for Hellé's original scenario, particularly in the absence of extant designs by Kristian.

In brief, the story related in *La Boîte à Joujoux* tells of the lives of the inhabitants of a box of toys when people are absent. It falls into four tableaux: 'The Toy Shop', the 'Field of Battle', the 'Smallholding for Sale', and 'Twenty-eight Years Later, After Making a Fortune'. The chief characters are a little English soldier, a young girl and a Pierrot, with a side cast of Policeman, Mayor, Negro, Harlequin, and general Pierrots and soldiers. The Soldier is in love with the girl, but she has given her heart to the 'frivolous Pierrot'. The soldiers and the Pierrots have a large battle, and the soldier is injured. The girl nurses the soldier back to health, marries him and has many children, while the Pierrot's life continues in the box. With brilliant wit, Debussy gives each character their own musical leitmotif so it is easy for listeners to follow the drama of the story in the music, including a classic cake-walk for the English Soldier, and a 'Hindu' song for the elephant. It is charming and whimsical and entirely in keeping with Omega's interest in developing bright-coloured fun nursery toys, and valuing the spontaneous freedom of children's art, of which they organised exhibitions.[20]

Debussy at the Omega Workshops 189

The 1913 Omega collaboration between Vanessa and Winifred Gill for a nursery showroom at the workshops included bold stencilling on walls and ceiling, and was accompanied by a short story by Gill bringing the animals on the walls and jointed toys to life.[21] The story tells of a happy afternoon had by a group of rhinos, camels and elephants (the animals stencilled on the nursery wall and made into jointed toys), picnicking, and playing in a pool with fish. Gill anthropomorphises the animals to describe their pleasure in their very Post-Impressionist jungle habitat. It opens with the eldest brother rhino discovering a 'beautiful' jungle of 'yellow trees with red trunks, and blue pools with yellow mud. On hot days I can slosh yellow mud all over myself and look handsomer than ever.' His experience is paralleled by eldest brother camel who finds 'red, white, and yellow flowers, and blue trees with purple dates on them' (Kato 2009: 72). Also in this vein, the Omega entered the 'Allies Doll Show' at the Grafton Galleries with a set of caricatures of the Kaiser, the Crown Prince, Lord Kitchener, General Joffre and the King of the Belgians.[22] Whilst none of these are extant, we can look to Gill's designs for Jellicoe and the 'Fat Military figure' at the Courtauld for an idea of how these may have been realised (see Figures 8.1, 8.2 and 8.3).

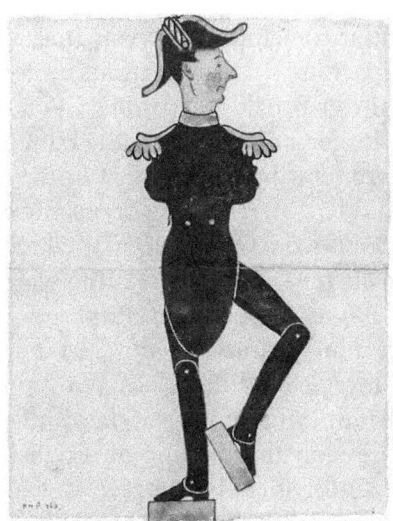

Figure 8.1 Toy design (Jellicoe) (verso), attrib. Winifred Gill, 1914–16 © The Samuel Courtauld Trust, The Courtauld Gallery, London © Bodleian Libraries, University of Oxford.

Figure 8.2 Toy design (Jellicoe) (recto), attrib. Winifred Gill, 1914–16 © The Samuel Courtauld Trust, The Courtauld Gallery, London © Bodleian Libraries, University of Oxford.

Figure 8.3 Toy design (fat military man), attrib. Winifred Gill, 1914–16
© The Samuel Courtauld Trust, The Courtauld Gallery, London © Bodleian Libraries, University of Oxford.

La Boîte à Joujoux tells a reassuring story of peace, happiness and fulfilment after war. No doubt essential for children in wartime, it nonetheless had its grown-up counterpart in Fry's publications under the auspices of the Omega: Arthur Clutton-Brock's *Simpson's Choice* (on evil and death); a translation by Roger Fry of a carefully edited selection of anti-war poems from Pierre Jean Jouve's *Men of Europe* (1915), both illustrated by Kristian; and R. C. Trevelyan's translation of parts of *De Rerum Natura* as *Lucretius on Death* (1917), which counselled a long-term perspective on current events by relating wars long since fought and forgotten. It is with appropriate resonance that Kristian was unable to produce illustrations for this last due to his arrest and deportation as an unregistered alien. As Winifred Gill recalled in a letter to Grant in 1966, Nina made the 'fatal mistake of marrying him under the impression that having an English wife might be an advantage to him. Unfortunately the reverse was the result and Nina not only lost her nationality but became an enemy alien, subject to many tiresome restrictions.'[23] The situation must have felt a pointless interruption to the internationalist artistic endeavour of the Workshops.

The conservatism of *La Boîte à Joujoux*, where the soldier representing the state triumphs over the Pierrots, who true to their function in traditional *commedia dell'arte* represent subversiveness, is at odds with both Debussy's and Bloomsbury's creative, intellectual and political positions.[24] The key is perhaps Hellé's initial idea that 'toy-boxes are really towns in which the toys live like real people. Or perhaps towns are nothing else but boxes in which people live like toys' (Vallas 1973: 239). In a town mechanised for warfare with strict and apparently arbitrary laws which restricted both civil and intellectual liberty – as, for example, those concerning unregistered aliens or conscientious objectors – the latter half of this statement must have appeared very prescient, particularly to the Belgian refugee performers, and to Kristian as designer. It would be all too easy for many refugees to perceive the automaton soldiers at the front as often manoeuvred from afar by superiors who could see the larger picture but not conditions on the ground. Moreover, conscripts were in some cases performing a war ostensibly for democratic freedom, but one it was not necessarily their choice to fight.[25] To this extent the production of *La Boîte à Joujoux* can be regarded as part of a wider resistance across Bloomsbury, of which the staging of Goldsworthy Lowes Dickinson's play *War and Peace: A Dramatic Fantasia* at the Workshops in 1917 is the most obvious. As Brockington has said, these events arguably function as 'pacifist dissent through performance' (Brockington 2009: 66).[26]

The use of marionettes was critical to the distancing of individual agency from action, reminding us why Debussy said 'only marionettes could interpret the meaning of the text'.[27] We only have one (poor) image of a marionette by Kristian, which is why Gill's toy designs are an important part of reconstructing how this event might have appeared. Her simple forms, bright primary colours, and implication of rhythm and dynamism in her carefully jointed sections compare favourably with Hellé's original illustrations. But Gill's designs are only a part. It is difficult to get an accurate impression of the scale of Kristian's marionettes. Collins has suggested they were 'a couple of feet' tall, but also notes that Grant made eight-foot marionettes for a show of Racine's *Bérénice* at Clive and Vanessa Bell's New Year Ball for the start of 1915 (Collins 1984: 102). These giants would undoubtedly have ridiculed individual action purely by their scale and the practical demands made on those who operated them. A substantial if not gigantic scale is suggested by Hamnett's recollection that those manipulating the marionettes lay on their stomachs, so it was clearly not performed at a scale where they could crouch behind a false stage or box.

Reliance on simplified profiles and rhythmic gestures was a hallmark of Omega visual work, but these attributes were also central to Debussy's musical innovations. In *La Boîte à Joujoux* he deploys musical cameos for his characters, and clearly 'paints' changes in mood or action. Writing on *Pelléas et Mélisande*, Debussy contended that 'there should be expressive variety, though in places it is necessary to paint in cameo . . . Nothing should impede the progress of the drama: all musical development not called for in the words is a mistake' (quoted in Orledge 1982: 50). Whilst *La Boîte à Joujoux* is of an entirely different character, Debussy's principle holds. The music is directed by Hellé's text and through composed: the melodic line is at the service of events, clearly indicated by the second tableau, the battle. Even though written for children, Debussy does not shy away from harmonic complexity, using remote, unfamiliar and extreme harmonies to indicate the emotional intensity of the events with clarity. The second scene, the 'Field of Battle', is marked 'slow and mysterious'. Debussy opens with a deceptively simple modal A minor line played in octaves, but evidence of the coming skirmish in the form of a triple mordent flourish in bar 4 gives an eerie sense of foreboding, as if a camera shot cuts from an overview to a close-up and back again. This is further manifested by a comparatively fast sequence of modulating staccato demi-semi-quavers, a 'grandmother's footsteps' kind of effect. Throughout the movement the perpetually unsteady key and extensive chromaticism renders the unsettled atmosphere of battle. The soldiers arrive with regular staccato quavers in 4/4 time, marked 'noise in the wings of a troupe marching', then soon disrupted by the arrival of the Polchinelle, in 'rapid' 3/4 accidentals. As the Polchinelle returns with others, artillery and canons, the music is marked 'animated and ferocious'; the dissonant sequences culminate in two abrupt staccato chords using the extreme registers of the bass. Debussy's tactics in composing *La Boîte à Joujoux*, fearlessly expanding what was regarded as possible for musical structure, could remind us here of Grant's description of his scene design for Copeau's *Twelfth Night*, which was 'meant to look flat but at the same time to give one a feeling of space'.[28] In other words, Grant intended to highlight the contradictions implicit in theatre: the equivalence of events on stage, and yet the intellectual expansion of an immersive artistic experience. Debussy similarly educates the ears of a young audience away from the strictures of what was acceptable to the academy, asking instead for validation through the emotional response to the listening experience.

So where does this leave Debussy and music more generally in relation to Omega? The step to set design which engaged Grant and Bell in the 1920s would have been a natural one following their experiments in interior decoration, both formally through Omega, and informally in their homes and those of their friends. Returning to this interior decoration, it is worth remembering that despite his death in 1918 Debussy remained a prominent composer for Bloomsbury in this context. Debussy featured conspicuously in the opening of the 1932 exhibition at the Lefevre Gallery of designs by Bell and Grant: the *Music Room*. Financially the exhibition was a mixed success, heavily underwritten by Virginia Woolf. The designs included a gramophone painted by Bell, an embroidered piano stool designed by Grant, a decorated baby grand piano, and a screen with nude instrumentalists. On the walls, six large murals of vases of flowers were intended to suggest composers – Bach, Mozart, Chopin, Debussy and Stravinsky. At the private view, Cyril Connolly recalled that the 'room vibrated to a Debussy solo on the harp' which produced a 'rare union of intellect and imagination, colour and sound, which produced in the listener a momentary apprehension of the life of the spirit' (quoted in Reed 2004: 272). On this estimation, Bloomsbury's combination of decoration with music was significant: obviously more than a homely domesticity, music and art could be the expression of personality, purveyor of hope – above all, the articulation of the 'aesthetic emotion' of Fry's 1909 'Essay in Aesthetics'.[29]

In a number of significant articles in 1912–13, Roger Fry specifically compared the visual and musical arts, finding in music an inspiration for the move towards abstraction in painting. In an aesthetic statement-cum-explanation written for the Post-Impressionist Exhibition catalogue of 1912, he famously argued that the Post-Impressionists aimed at finding 'an equivalent for life' which was 'a new and definite reality', achievable if one were to 'create a purely abstract language of form – a visual music' (Fry 1988: 353). Fry had praised the 'abstract and musical quality' of designs by Picasso, which aimed for the 'construction of a fugal arrangement of forms' (Fry 1912: 395). Later, in 1913, he again returned to the theme, extolling 'pure visual music . . . I cannot any longer doubt the possibility of emotional expression by such abstract visual signs.'[30] Returning to my opening quotations on Debussy from Woolf and the context of his reception in Britain from 1907 to 1908, it is clear he was understood to be a radical composer, the *Observer* reviewer finding him 'unquestionably one of the most original of the "moderns"'. Even with this praise, the reviewer could not help criticising the structure of *La*

Mer: 'regarded as programme music – of the special Debussy kind – the three sections are all too much of the same tone'.[31] Avant-garde composers could not win here – an 'original' modern is still analysed through a conservative un-modern genre and is found lacking, writing bad programme music. Equally, it is true that the music that was heard – *La Mer, Pelléas et Mélisande, L'Après midi d'un faune* and *La Damoiselle élue* – is all descriptive of particular events or locations. Debussy conjures images in sound – a 'visual music', to adopt Fry's term. To Debussy, these pieces were anything but abstract, which serves as a timely reminder that Fry's call to abstraction did not necessarily entail non-figuration.

The exact circumstances surrounding the performance – potentially the public premiere – of Debussy's *La Boîte à Joujoux* at the Omega Workshops will probably never be discovered. Regardless of the grey areas, this curious episode in Omega history cements the significance of the Workshops as one of the most forward-thinking and well-connected avant-garde venues in London, a meeting place for progressive artists, thinkers, musicians and writers of all nationalities who on this smaller, more domestic scale fought for European solidarity through cross-Channel artistic collaboration in the face of the nationalist politics of wartime.

Notes

1. Victor Segalen to his wife, 31 January 1908. Segalen is familiar to art historians for his proximity to Paul Gauguin. See particularly Forsdick (2000, 2010). Debussy also recalled an appalling rehearsal, after which he was asked to conduct it himself, thereby making his conducting debut. Debussy letter to Victor Segelan, 15 January 1908, in Lesure and Nichols (1987: 186).
2. Mr Lee, 'Bloomsbury and music', *Charleston Newsletter*, April 1984, p. 20; response Barbara Strachey Halpern, August 1984, 19–21; Asya Chorley, 'Duncan Grant as stage designer', *Charleston Newsletter*, August 1984, pp. 6–9.
3. See Anscombe (1999) and Collins (1984). Both mention the performance in passing but without recognising its status as a premier.
4. See Grace Brockington's excellent 2010 study, particularly pages 107 and 240.
5. In addition to Brockington's more recent work, Collins and Anscombe cover the war years at Omega. Collins records Vanessa Bell's dressmaking department which employed women from the Marne and Meuse. Examples of their work can be found in the V&A from the Friends' War Victims Relief Committee. See Collins (1984: 106).

6. A comprehensive account is given by dance historian Millicent Hodson (2010) and by Frances Spalding (1997).
7. Diaghilev started working in France with an exhibition of Russian painting in 1906; 1909 was the first summer visit of what was to become the Ballets Russes. To London's Royal Opera, he brought *Carnival* (1911), *The Firebird* (1912) and *L'Après midi d'un faune* (1913). Other performances at Drury Lane and the Alhambra took place between 1912 and 1919.
8. Winifred Gill recalled Nina and Kristian changed his surname 'from von Bergen to de Bergen, as it 'sounded better'. Letter to Duncan Grant, 4 August 1966, p. 3, Tate Gallery Archives, duplicate transcript in the Courtauld Gallery.
9. Winifred Gill in conversation with Pamela Diamond and Stephen X, 13. Transcript in the Courtauld Gallery.
10. Winifred Gill in conversation with Pamela Diamond and Stephen X, 12.
11. Kings College Archive GLD/ 4/3. Annotations show parts read by Saxon Sydney-Turner, James and Lytton Strachey and Winnie (Winifred Gill).
12. Grace Brockington reproduces notes on Dickinson's play on Omega headed paper (2010: 109).
13. The fire brigade 'still wore these splendid helmets worthy of Roman Legions, and Mr Robinson (the manager) asked if they would hide them under their cots as they went past the door of the showroom so that the audience could not see them and panic.' See Diamond (1966: 4–5). Also referred to in Spalding (1999: 180). Spalding does not give a source.
14. Robert Orledge does not list the Omega performance in his otherwise detailed chronology. Orledge lists the piano score as written July to 30 October 1913, orchestration started April 1914, and completed by André Caplet October to November 1919. Orledge's handwritten annotations to his published information include a private performance with piano by Guido di Madran, 24 March 1915; a performance by Ballet Sulois 1914–15; a possible public performance at Neighbourhood Playhouse, New York early in 1917; question marks surrounding a possible performance at the Red Rooster Café; a performance by the State Moscow Chamber Theatre, 21 December 1917, with score orchestrated by Henri Forterre, dir. Aleandre; a performance with marionettes designed by Otto Morach in Zurich, 29 January 1918; and a performance at Theatre Français de San Francisco, 21 and 22 February 1918, directed by André Ferrier. I am immensely grateful to Robert Orledge for sharing these annotations with me. See also Orledge (1982: 177–85).
15. Anon., *Colour Magazine*, February 1915: 'all the figures and scenery designed and executed by him' (Kristian). In January 1915, Debussy was himself engaged in activities to support Belgium, writing *Berceuse heroique* for Hall Caine and the *Daily Telegraph*'s initiative, *King Albert's*

Book, a collection of music including contributions from Debussy, Saint-Saëns, Liza Lehmann, Elgar, Stanford and Smyth. See Debussy letter to Robert Godet ,1 January 1915, in Lesure and Nichols (1987: 295n).

16. Winifred Gill lists the first three in a vague sweep incorporating 'anyone who was anyone'. W. Gill in conversation with Pamela Diamond and Stephen X, transcript held at the Courtauld Gallery, 14. Also Collins (1984: 151); Anscombe (1999: 30).

17. 31 October 1913. Other letters refer to marionettes for the scenario. Writing to publisher Jacques Durand, Debussy warned that 'the third tableau is going slowly. The soul of a doll is more mysterious than even Maeterlinck imagines; it doesn't easily tolerate the kind of humbug so many human souls put up with' (letter 27 September 1913, in Lesure and Nichols 1987: 278); later, again to Durand: 'Can you image those poor marionettes in a setting normally reserved for the demands of Ariane or the fury of Golaud . . . as for La *Boîte*, we must slow it to retain its unaggressive aspect and present it in some fairly novel manner' (Lesure and Nichols 1987: 285). Peculiarly, a letter from April 1914 suggests children might play the parts (Lesure and Nichols 1987: 289).

18. Duncan Grant, Design for a backdrop for Jacques Copeau's production of *Twelfth Night*, Courtauld Gallery, D.1958.PD.99.

19. Winifred Gill, in conversation with Pamela Diamond and Stephen XX, 14. Transcript the Courtauld Gallery.

20. For example, the *Omega Workshops Catalogue* of 1914 includes a page of jointed toys, available in various sizes. These included designs for a camel, rhinoceros, elephant and tiger, two of which can be seen in photographs of Vanessa Bell's nursery. There is also an extraordinary poster for 'Exhibition of sketches by M. Larianov, and drawings by the girls of Dudley High School' in February 1919, reproduced in Collins (1984: 91).

21. Winifred Gill: 'Story written by me to popularise the jointed ply-wood animals we sold at the Omega.' The Bodleian Library, Gill family papers MS 6241/37 Folder 1, no page numbers. Also referenced in Kato (2009: 72, 77).

22. Gill, possibly conflating the two schemes, recalled 'plywood limbs that over-lapped with a turning point and stood up. There was a Kaiser among them and a Crown Prince – Crown Prince Willie and various animals, a rhinocerous, a giraffe and an elephant'. W. Gill in conversation with Pamela Diamond and Stephen X, transcript held at the Courtauld Gallery, N.D. 13.

23. Winifred Gill to Duncan Grant, Letter 4: 18 August 1966, Tate Gallery Microfiche TAM 24M (copy consulted at the Courtauld Gallery).

24. In a complex area, Brockington (2010) describes the nuanced reasonings for Bloomsbury members' pacifism; likewise, Arun Rao (2015) has distinguished Debussy's nationalism from his modernist, anti-institutional music.

25. Conscription in Britain was not brought in until the Military Service Act of January 1916; the 'Three Year Law' in France, passed in 1913, required all men of eligible age to undertake three years of military training. In August 1914, the French army consisted of regular soldiers, men who had completed the three years, plus reservists and later territorials. Belgians were conscripted into forced labour during the German occupation.
26. Brockington also compares Margaret Morris's Kings Road Theatre Club as another centre of resistance, one that focused more on dance. Other marionette performances did occur, produced by John Rodker and the Choric School. See Brockington (2010: 115–29, 163–91).
27. Debussy in Vallas (1973).
28. Duncan Grant, letter to Jacques Copeau, 18 August 1913, BNF, reproduced in Gerstein (2009: 153).
29. See Fry (1937).
30. Roger Fry, 'The Allied Artists', *The Nation*, 2 August 1913, in Bullen (1988: 459).
31. *The Observer*, 2 February 1908, *The Guardian* archive online: https://www.theguardian.com/music/2016/apr/19/debussy-most-original-of-moderns-review-1908 (accessed 13 March 2019).

Bibliography

Anon. (1908), 'Debussy the most original of moderns' *The Observer*, 2 February 1908.
Anscombe, Isabelle (1999), *Omega and After: Bloomsbury and the Decorative Arts*, London: Thames & Hudson.
Brockington, Grace (2007), 'Translating peace', in *Publishing in the First World War*, ed. Mary Hammond and Shafquat Towheed, Basingstoke: Palgrave Macmillan.
Brockington, Grace (2009), 'The Omega and the end of civilisation: pacificism, publishing and performance in the First World War', in *Beyond Bloomsbury: Designs of the Omega Workshops 1913–19*, ed. Alexandra Gerstein, ex. cat., London: The Courtauld Gallery.
Brockington, Grace (2010), *Above the Battlefield*, New Haven, CT and London: Yale University Press.
Bullen, J. B. (ed.) (1988), *Post-Impressionists in England*, London: Routledge.
Collins, Judith (1984), *The Omega Workshops*, London: Secker & Warburg.
Diamond, Pamela (1966), 'Some recollections and reflections on Omega', privately bound collection of letters, National Art Library, V&A.
Forsdick, Charles (2000), *Victor Segalen and the Aesthetics of Diversity: Journeys between Cultures*, Oxford: Oxford University Press.

Forsdick, Charles (2010), 'Gauguin and Segalen: exoticism, myth and the "aesthetics of diversity"', in *Gauguin: Maker of Myth*, ed. Belinda Thomson, ex. cat., London: Tate Publishing.
Fry, Roger (1912), 'Art: the Grafton: an Apologia', *The Nation*, 9 November, pp. 249–51.
Fry, Roger (1937), *Vision and Design*, London: Pelican.
Fry, Roger (1988), 'The French Group, Catalogue of The Second Post-Impressionist Exhibition', in *Post-Impressionists in England*, ed. J. B. Bullen, London: Routledge, pp. 353–5.
Garnett, David (1955), *The Flowers in the Forest*, London: Chatto & Windus.
Gerstein, Alexandra (ed.) (2009), *Beyond Bloomsbury: Designs of the Omega Workshops 1913–1919*, London: The Courtauld Gallery.
Hamnett, Nina (1932), *Laughing Torso*, New York: Ray Long and R. Smith.
Hodson, Millicent (2010), *Nijinsky's Bloomsbury Ballet: Reconstruction of the Dance and Design for Jeux*, Hillsdale, NY: Pendragon Press.
Kato, Akiko (2009), 'The Omega Workshops: Roger Fry's search for community', in *Beyond Bloomsbury: Designs of the Omega Workshops 1913–1919*, ed. Alexandra Gerstein, ex. cat., London: The Courtauld Gallery.
Lesure, François and Roger Nichols (eds) (1987), *Debussy Letters*, Cambridge, MA: Harvard University Press.
Nichols, Roger (1992), *Debussy Remembered*, London: Faber.
Orledge, Robert (1982), *Debussy and the Theatre*, Cambridge: Cambridge University Press.
Rao, Arun (2015), 'Claude de France: Debussy's Great War of 1915', in *France and Ireland, Notes and Narratives*, ed. Una Hunt and Mary Pierce, Bern and Oxford: Peter Lang.
Reed, Christopher (2004), *Bloomsbury Rooms*, New Haven, CT and London: Yale University Press.
Spalding, Frances (1997), *Duncan Grant*, London: Chatto & Windus.
Spalding, Frances (1999), *Roger Fry*, Norwich: Black Dog Books.
Sutton, Emma (2013), *Virginia Woolf and Classical Music: Politics, Aesthetics, Form*, Edinburgh: Edinburgh University Press.
Vallas, Léon (1973), *Claude Debussy: His Life and Works*, Mineola, NY: Dover Publications.
Woolf, Virginia (1977), 'Impressions at Bayreuth', in Virginia Woolf, *Books and Portraits*, London: The Hogarth Press.

Chapter 9

Across the Other Channel: Elizabeth Bowen and Modernist Mediation

Lauren Elkin

The Anglo-Irish writer Elizabeth Bowen has always presented a problem to critics who have wished to place her. Politically conservative but socially liberated, Irish but English, the author of novels and short stories that are experimental narratives of social life, an heir to both Virginia Woolf and Jane Austen, she wrote deeply strange narratives that can and have been understood as expressions of a permanent self-estrangement. She lived between her two countries, feeling English in Ireland and Irish in England, as one of her friends described her, and was, according to her one-time lover, the writer Sean O'Faolain, 'heart-cloven and split-minded' when it came to the question of national loyalty (O'Faolain 1982: 15). She is, in this sense, an intensely complex writer of mediations. How can we understand this 'clovenness', this 'split', of both body and heart, life and text, in Bowen's work? What are the material and textual ways in which it embodies this mediation?

On the question of nationality, Elizabeth Bowen was Irish by birth and English by marriage. But simply describing her as 'Irish' does not tell the whole story; she was Anglo-Irish, a product of the Protestant ascendancy, and grew up in one of the Big Houses that were so often targeted during the troubles, finding themselves at the business end of a torch. Even the label 'Anglo-Irish' did not quite suit her; Bowen stresses that her father's family, the Bowens, came from Wales, where they were the ap Owens (the name change occurred early in the reign of Elizabeth I), while her mother's people were 'pure Irish' – to the extent an Anglo-Irish family could be Irish-Irish (Bowen 2010: 235). This should be explained to the editors of the 1993 *North Cork Anthology*, who chose to include Bowen in their table of contents with a line through her name, to underscore their total rejection of her as an Irish writer. This crossing-out is just one example of a lifetime, and an afterlife, of crossings for Bowen, her work and our understanding of her as a cross-Channel writer.

Bowen's ambivalent, ambiguous relationship to Ireland may be typically Anglo-Irish, as the historian J. C. Beckett claims, though it may have been exacerbated by the times in which she lived, challenged by Irish bids for independence and two world wars.[1] She spent the Second World War in both England and Ireland, but clearly experienced an increased loyalty to England, working in London as an air raid warden, and comparing the solidarity of English city life positively against the 'cut-off' life of the Protestant ascendancy in Ireland (Bowen 1999: 126). She went to neutral Ireland to spy for the British Ministry of Information, attempting to learn, among other things, whether Ireland would allow Britain to use the Treaty Ports. And yet she vigorously supported Ireland's policy of neutrality, believing it to be in that country's best interest.[2] Clearly, we are dealing with a writer whose sense of herself as belonging to two nations was more complicated than simply feeling 'Irish in England and English in Ireland'. She liked to say that the Anglo-Irish only ever feel 'at home in mid-crossing between Holyhead and Dun Laoghaire' (Cronin 1991: 143). In an attempt to better clarify Bowen's relationship to both countries, I propose we read Bowen as a cross-Channel writer – referring not only to the English Channel, which she writes into many of her texts, but St George's Channel (sometimes called the Irish Channel, a term I will use for the sake of symmetry), the body of water that separates Ireland and the United Kingdom. I will argue that the Irish Channel has a permanent presence in her texts, on a formal if not an explicit level.

The ferry Bowen took so many times during her young life left from Pembrokeshire (Holyhead, Wales to be precise) and crossed the Irish Channel to enter Ireland at Cobh Harbour to make its way up the river Lee towards Cork. Bowen's identity and subjectivity and writing was formed out of this movement back and forth, the roughly twelve hours it took to travel by boat from Ireland to Wales, and back. In his study *The Philosophy of Walking* (2014), the philosopher Frédéric Gros argues that in the work of great walkers, like Nietzsche and Rousseau, you can feel that it has been composed on foot, out in the open air, rather than hunched over a desk in a library. By this line of reasoning, Bowen's work carries within it some sense of the back-and-forth journey, the constant movement from one place to another. In what follows I will suggest that Bowen's writing embodies this sensation of movement, this feeling of never being at home anywhere, or, on the contrary, of having too *many* homes.

Edwina Keown has read Bowen as a 'seaside modernist', a writer who 'responded to the English seaside as a place of shifting identities, and made it the site of her most probing investigations of class mobility and consumerism between the wars' (Keown 2011: 179). But Keown's cultural history-inflected discussion stops at the English coastline, whereas I want to head out into the water, across the Channel, and back again, and then up through England into Wales, across the other Channel, St George's Channel, through which Bowen had to pass to get from England to Ireland. I want to look at crossings and correspondences in Bowen's fiction, and ask how we may conceptualise this cross-Channel experience as a formal component of her work, and ask whether this takes a particular shape in the modern moment, suggesting that a modernist notion of mediation may help us understand this dimension of Bowen's work. In their study of the literary channel and the invention of the novel, Margaret Cohen and Carolyn Dever argue for a liminal 'Channel zone' between England and France, where 'the processes of literary and cultural exchange that occurred across the English Channel' enabled the novel to flourish (Cohen and Dever 2002: 2). We might borrow this notion of a Channel zone as the place where Bowen's own novels flourish – the *other* Channel zone. My readings of these crossings and correspondences counters O'Faolain's metaphor of the split with the logic of the fold, focusing on Bowen's 1935 novel *The House in Paris* and the personal recollections of her last book, *Pictures and Conversations* (1975). Looking at these movements across two channels will allow us to free Bowen from the back-and-forth motion of the Anglo-Irish binary, and to open up the many passages, connections and encounters her novels and short stories enact. More broadly, this chapter aims to widen our understanding of modernist exchanges and mediations across an Anglo-Hibernian-European space.

Origins and encounters

Bowen acknowledged that place is the pre-eminent aspect of her work, and expressed confusion and dismay when critics missed this: 'Am I not manifestly a writer for whom places loom large?' (Bowen 1975: 34). In the decades since her death, many critics have commented on the constant toing and froing in Bowen's work: the planes, trains and automobiles, the trips, the holidays, the encounters.[3] Bowen is aware that this is a habit imposed on her in her youth; in an essay from her unfinished autobiography, written in her final years, she speculates that it came about through being 'transplanted' (her word) from Ireland to England '[a]t an early though conscious age' (Bowen 1975: 23), and in a 1949 preface to a reprint of her first story collection, *Encounters* (first published in 1923), she recalls: 'Motherless since I was thirteen, I was in and out of the homes of my different relatives – and, as constantly, shuttling between two countries: Ireland and England' (Bowen 1962: 86). As an adult, travel would provide a means of getting perspective, or a valuable distraction; she wrote *A Time in Rome* (1960) when she was realising that she had to sell Bowen's Court. In his introduction to *Pictures and Conversations*, Bowen's literary agent Spencer Curtis Brown calls this 'good therapy for her. It meant not only going to a completely different place, but immersing herself in two thousand years of the past' (Bowen 1975: xxxv). When she finished writing, the decision had to be made about Bowen's Court. She went to New York to make it, where she had 'a bad breakdown of health' (Bowen 1975: xxxvi). One might go so far as to suggest that it was the combination of transplantation, of encounter, and avoidance offered by travel that drove her to write, and that is such an integral part of her writing itself.

The act of writing is as much of an encounter, Bowen writes, as a transplantation to a new country. In the 1949 preface, she looks back to her early years as a writer, composing the stories that would become *Encounters*, and recalls the 'first uncanny complicity with one's physical surroundings' that arises from the writing-table, with its specific 'objects, sounds, colours and lights-and-shades'. Every aspect of the writing room is 'hyper-significant': 'The room, the position of the window, the convulsive and anxious grating of my chair on the board floor . . . here were sensuous witnesses to my crossing the margin of a hallucinatory word' (Bowen 1962: 83). Here, Bowen speaks of writing as a kind of crossing. If the story is the encounter, the act of writing is the passage towards that encounter, and it signifies within the story itself.

One way of apprehending this involves a Channel crossing. The contrast between Ireland and England first took the form of two contrasting 'mythologies'; Bowen emphasises the strangeness of England, which far from being a return to some colonial motherland was in fact a land 'totally alien to that of my forefathers, none of whom had resided anywhere but in Ireland for some centuries, and some of whom may never have been in England at all: the Bowens were Welsh'

(Bowen 1975: 23). She would thenceforth feel a 'cleft' – the lot of any immigrant, she writes – between the old country and the new. It was this new 'mythology' which invited investigation, into 'the ways, manners, and views of its people, round me: those, because I disliked being at a disadvantage, it became necessary to probe' (Bowen 1975: 23–4). She explains that she eventually lost interest in society, and became 'affected' by 'the lie of the land . . . that cool, clear light falling upon it, which was extraordinary' (Bowen 1975: 24), pointing specifically to the 'dramatisable' Kent coastline as having a formative influence on her imagination. She muses, with a horror I am not convinced is feigned: 'Suppose, for instance, some Cousin Lilla or Cousin Isabel had siren-sung us into the Midlands, with their soporific monotony? Or, for that matter, into the West Country, with its rainy semi-resemblances to Ireland?' She leaves the threat unarticulated, but the reader seems meant to deduce – had she been 'siren-sung' into the Midlands, she never would have become a writer. Or at least she would have been a very different writer. She was amazed by the difference between the 'new' land and the old:

> Gone was the changing blue of mountains: instead, bleached blond in summer, the bald downs showed exciting great gashes of white chalk. Everything, including the geological formation, struck me as having been recently put together. Trees were smaller in size, having not yet, one could imagine, had time for growth. (Bowen 1975: 25)

Yet there is something 'precarious' about this new landscape. '*Would* it last?' she asks, imagining it subject to 'landslides, subsidences and tidal waves' (Bowen 1975: 25). Far from being some established, irrevocable border, Bowen imagines the coastline as vulnerable, changeable, subject to the vagaries and violence of the elements (and, perhaps, climate change). It is the memory of the place of origin that allows her to see the coastline this way, the comparison with the old, enduring landscape of Ireland draws the dramatic new Kentish coastline into stark relief. Through Bowen's perceiving eye, the Irish landscape is replaced with the Kentish one, not as if the Channel had been erased, but rather as if the two had been enfolded, creating not a 'cleft,' but an encounter. Then, too, we might remember that the word 'cleaving' describes not only a separation, but a bringing together. The crossing, and all its many resonances in Bowen's work, provides a rich source of perspective on the way places and nations relate to one another; it creates a borderland where one is never fully in one place, nor fully in another.

St George's Channel

A channel, the OED tells us, is 'a (comparatively) narrow piece of water, wider than a mere "strait", connecting two larger pieces, usually seas'. A channel is a conduit, encouraging flow. It does not divide, it connects; and this connection is not simply a question of joining two disparate places. Between two countries it is an elemental, intermediary space, neither one nation nor another, but creating strange collusions, mixings and overlaps.

It is also a space charged with meaning, political, historical, cultural. St George's Channel connects the Irish Sea to the north and the Celtic Sea to the south. The Welsh call it Sianel San Siôr, Channel Saint George. The Irish, on the other hand, call it Muir Bhreatan: British Sea. Which is to say: if you are living in Ireland, the Irish Channel is the English Channel. But though 'Muir Bhreatan' translates as 'British Sea', it also carries connotations of Welshness, since in Ireland, until the seventeenth century, 'British' and 'Welsh' were interchangeable. In which case, Bowen's distinction between being English or Welsh, viewed from the Irish coast, is a moot point; the two countries blend into one, 'that place across the sea', Britishness as hybrid identity encoded into the Irish world-view and nautical nomenclature.

Bowen's 1935 novel *The House in Paris* is formally and thematically a novel about crossings, which coincide in the house of the title. The first and the third parts of the novel concern two children: Henrietta is stopping over at Mme Fisher's home in between journeys from London and the South of France. Leopold has journeyed from Italy, where he lives with his foster parents, to Paris, to meet his mother for the first time. He is poised on the quay, so to speak, waiting to see if the train that arrives will carry him off with her, or back to his foster parents. For all its apparent solidity, the house is a transitory space, a channel between these different geographical locations.

But it is the crossings in the middle part of the novel that will be my focus here. The middle section is set ten years earlier than the sections that surround it, and allow us to meet Karen, Leopold's mother, and to understand the circumstances that led to his birth, of which he is unaware. The Channel crossings Karen makes – between England and Ireland and England and France – suggest that the middle section of the novel is not (or not only) about a look backward to understand the events leading up to the present day; it is about crossings themselves, and about the overlaps and encounters they generate.

A channel is a shifting kind of boundary, like time, like memory, and Bowen uses St George's Channel to move the narrative from the present to the past that created that present. The middle section begins on board a boat: 'Morning comes late at sea, when you lie in your berth under the porthole, hearing the sea sough past' (Bowen 1976: 69). Karen has left the night before on an overnight ferry from a Welsh port, and is now entering Ireland at Cobh Harbour in the morning, before sailing up the tidal river towards Cork and getting off at Rushbrook (today spelled with an 'e' at the end). Just as we the readers cross the boundary into the past, Karen has nearly completed her channel crossing, and perceives here that time is moving at a different pace as well. As she sits up in bed on the boat, she can see 'green hills beginning to slip by', followed by trees. In the following extended passage, Bowen develops this cognitive dissonance of travelling by boat past land, after being on the open sea:

> The ship, checking, balanced uncertainly up the narrowing river, trees on each side, as though navigating an avenue, leaving a salt wake. Houses asleep with their eyes open watched the vibrating ship pass: against the woody background those red and white funnels must look like a dream. Seagulls, circling, settled on mown lawns. The wake made a dark streak in the glassy river; its ripples broke against garden walls. Every hill running down, each turn of the river, seemed to trap the ship more and cut off the open sea.
> On the left shore, a steeple pricked up out of a knoll of trees, above a snuggle of gothic villas; then there was the sad stare of what looked like an orphanage. A holy bell rang and a girl at a corner mounted her bicycle and rode out of sight. The river kept washing salt off the ship's prow. . . .
> Smells of wood-smoke from cottages on the waterfront overhung the spongy smell of the tide; the smoke went melting up white against the woods.
> The river still narrowing, townish terraces of tall pink houses under a cliff drew in. In one fanlight stood a white plaster horse; clothes were spread out to dry on a briar bush. Someone watching the ship twitched back a curtain; a woman leaned out signalling with a mirror: several travellers must be expected home. A car with handkerchiefs fluttering drove alongside the ship. (Bowen 1976: 71–2)

The passage works to emphasise the strangeness of this encounter, between land and sea, the sea become land ('as though navigating an avenue'), the hills 'trap[ping]' the ship in the purview of land, 'cut[ting] it off from the open sea', as if the meeting of boat and land risked becoming a running aground rather than a travelling alongside. In this collection of things usually seen on land but perceived here from the water, the channel is prolonged; the sea does not stop at the boundary of a country; salt is washed away by freshwater, in an ongoing organic process with no origin and no absolute destination. The travellers, who might expect to be greeted upon docking at the port, can here be signalled to before they have properly arrived. For Karen, standing still on board the ship as the earth itself slides by, the passage takes on the surreal quality of an encounter, prefiguring the life-altering encounters that will come as a result of her trip to Ireland. Many years later, Bowen tells us, the place would still hold for Karen a 'troubling strangeness, a disturbing repose' (Bowen 1976: 76).

The ship's progress across the channel and up the river has instigated a process of enfolding between land and sea, town and ship, and, perhaps, Karen and the world. This overlapping could be seen in the light of Gilles Deleuze's concept of the fold, the unit of matter which divides into 'smaller and smaller folds that always retain a certain cohesion', the numerous ways in which the sea seems to delineate from land collapsing, or folding, in on each other to an infinite degree (Deleuze 2006a: 6). The fold brings together locations – say on a piece of paper – that do not usually touch, creating unexpected continuities. Writing on Deleuze's understanding of the Leibnizian concept of the fold, Elspeth Probyn has commented that subjectivity itself is constituted through this ongoing process of folding and refolding: 'The act of pleating or folding ("*la pliure*") is thus the doubling-up, the refolding, the bending-onto-itself of the line of the outside in order to constitute the inside/outside – the modes of the self' (1993:129). This raises two key issues: Karen's spatial perspective in the context of Bowen's formal writing of crossings, and Karen's own subjectivity.

The previous citation contains the following section in the fold I created through an ellipsis:

> Then, to the right, the tree-dark hill of Tivoli began to go up, steep, with pallid stucco houses appearing to balance on the tops of trees. Palladian columns, gazeboes, glass-houses, terraces showed on the background misted with spring green, at the tops of shafts or on toppling brackets of rock, all stuck to the hill, all slipping past the ship. Yes, this looked like a hill in Italy faded; it stood in that flat clear light in which you think of the past and did not look like a country subject to racking change. (Bowen 1976: 72)

Although for Karen this is a crossing from England to Ireland, it is in fact a writing in reverse of Bowen's impressions journeying from Ireland to England. The crossing forward is in this way a crossing back, collapsing the notion of either country as totally unknowable. Bowen underscores the strangeness of the juxtaposition of land, water and boat, in those houses that 'appear' to be balanced on the tops of trees, the various elements of everyday living 'stuck to the hill', the comparison between Ireland and Italy, the invocation of the unchangingness and continuity between past, present and future seemingly broken in on by Karen's perception of it, and the strange second person Bowen uses at the end of the paragraph. Who is speaking? Who is being addressed? And most importantly, when with regard to the boat ride is this happening? Are these the observations Karen makes to herself while on the boat? We have been so firmly in Karen's consciousness throughout this passage, and yet this awareness of Italy, of time, of the unchangingness of Ireland seems to belong to someone with more life experience. The question of this ambiguous second-person form of address in the second section of the novel is a problem to which I will return below. For the moment, it is sufficient to note the way Bowen writes the same scene two ways at once: there is the moment of the scene, and perhaps the suggestion of the scene being simultaneously revisited, retold, at a later point; this feeling of movement and stasis and recollection suggests this is a description not only of one journey from England to Ireland, but of many, made over a long period of time. If Bowen's characters are perpetually in transit, as she concedes in *Pictures and Conversations*, they are always in transit '*consciously*' (Bowen 1975: 41).

Bowen uses this seemingly uneventful section of *The House in Paris* in a late essay on craft, included in *Pictures and Conversations*. 'Staticness', she says, is the enemy of the novelist; it can be avoided by

> showing scene in fluidity, in (apparent) motion ... The greater the speed, the more liquefying the process. . . . [The beholder] does not merely – as he would were he at a standstill – *see* scene, he *watches* its continuous changes, which act upon him compulsively like a non-stop narrative. (Bowen 1975: 40)

This movement can be discerned on the level of the sentence as well, and constitutes another form of channel crossing in Bowen's work. Critics often note the strange syntax of Bowen's sentences: John Banville describes Bowen's prose as a kind of 'Hiberno-English', 'as if English held her Irish tongue hostage' (quoted in Hepburn 2010: 9).

Maud Ellmann spots the theme of conflict in Bowen's work 'insinuat[ing] itself into the very structure of her sentences, which often seem to be contending with an unseen obstacle', or, as Bowen herself put it, 'a never quite dislodgeable something to push against' (Ellmann 2003: 11). I suggest this relates to the movement embodied in her writing, the never-ending voyage out and back in again that is an intrinsic part of Bowen's Anglo-Irish identity. 'Something in Ireland bends one back on oneself', Karen writes in a letter to her fiancé (Bowen 1976: 89); it is this 'something in Ireland', I suggest, that makes the novel bend back upon itself, to include this middle section in such a recursive, ambiguous way. Neil Corcoran describes this as 'a reflexive turning back in upon itself rather than a committed motion forward' (Corcoran 2004: 3). But it is, in fact, both at the same time: the ship steaming forward to Ireland, irrevocably forward in time, and at the same time a journey backward to the point of origin, Deleuze's fold operating at the level of the sentence.

A boat making its way upriver: there is nothing officially strange about this image. Boats travel on rivers, if they're deep enough, as easily as on seas. It takes Bowen's eye to notice the oddness, and to transform it into a kind of 'epistemological suspension', to use Susan Osborn's term, that challenges the notion of both departure and arrival (Osborn 2009: 9).

The English Channel

The weirdnesses and dislocations continue throughout Karen's section of the novel, and culminate in Karen's affair with Leopold's father, Max, which takes place in a series of trysts on either side of the English Channel. They meet first in Boulogne where, as Karen's boat nears port, France 'met her approach coquettish, conscious, gay' (Bowen 1976: 145). Then, a week later, Max crosses the Channel to meet Karen in Hythe, on a rainy, sunless, horizonless day, and they spend the night together in a hotel. At three o'clock in the morning – an hour of crossing from night to day, a phenomenon usually unobserved for those of us who sleep through the night – Karen wakes up and asks: 'What have I done?' (Bowen 1976: 151). She has no awareness of having slept apart from the hour having advanced on her watch: 'She thought, how frightening luminous watches are, the eye of time never stops watching you . . . Her sleep of an hour had let to-morrow in' (Bowen 1976: 152). This moment recalls the feeling of stasis in movement Bowen described on the boat to Ireland, though here the movement is temporal rather than spatio-temporal; they are in the same hotel, but it is as if they have advanced miles in one evening.

As Karen attempts to weigh the consequences of her action, the narrative begins to act very strangely, presenting the reader with another, more pronouncedly eccentric problem of voice. Although previously the novel has been told mostly in an omniscient third person, here in the hotel at three in the morning, the text shifts again into the second person – another crossing. The narrative slips from a conventional Bowenian narrative voice ('The street lamp still lit up the chestnut tree, cut out its fingered leaves on the dark above and cast the same inescapable barred square on the ceiling over the bed') to directly address Leopold: 'Having done as she knew she must she did not think there would be a child: all the same, the idea of you, Leopold, began to be present with her' (Bowen 1976: 151). This time it is certainly not Karen addressing herself, but clearly some other voice referring to Karen in the third person and addressing Leopold for the first time as interlocutor. Whose is this new voice? It is someone who appears to know Leopold, who does not speak with authorial detachment. Are we meant to infer that this is Naomi telling Leopold what happened to 'make [him] be', as he longs to find out (Bowen 1976: 67)? But then we were told at the beginning of part two that this is the story Karen *would* have told Leopold, if she had come that day; in which case why is Karen referred to in the third person? Possible readings are plentiful, but if we continue to consider it through this motif of crossing, employing the logic of the fold, we might consider this narrative moment to be born of Karen's phenomenological experience of 3 a.m. as a kind of fold in time, a moment that conjugates Leopold somehow come into being through intuitive means, as Karen imagines her child for the first time.

This builds an epistemological uncertainty around narrative, tense, speaker and addressee. Bowen eschews the traditional flashback technique, legible in terms of clearly pinning the narrative down in time, and instead employs a strange, shifting kind of flashback to depict these events, presenting the flashback as the story Karen *would have* told Leopold if she had gone to meet him. In this sense, Bowen creates a potential flashback, a *récit manqué*, a past-tense narrative pitched in the past conditional tense. But with this narrative indeterminacy, Bowen also enacts an oneiric crossing that prompts the reader to wonder whether we have set out yet, or if we are still back where we started.

In his book on Foucault, Deleuze is fascinated by the way Foucault seems to be 'haunted' by the 'theme of an inside which is merely the fold of the outside, as if the ship were a folding of the sea':

> An Outside, more distant than any exterior, is 'twisted,' 'folded,' and 'doubled' by an Inside that is deeper than any interior, and alone creates the possibility of the derived relation between the interior and the exterior. It is even this twisting which defines 'Flesh,' beyond the body proper and its objects. (Deleuze 2006b: 110)

The unfolding of the narrative – in the sense that events unfold in textual time – is also a folding, expressing a relationship between inside and outside. A fold is created when what we might have taken for interiority is revealed to be exteriority – both at once, folding and unfolding.

Deleuze turns to *Madness and Civilization* to make reference to the madman who was put to sea in a boat. As Foucault writes, 'he is put in the interior of the exterior, and inversely . . . a prisoner in the midst of what is the freest, the openest of routes: bound fast at the infinite crossroads. He is the Passenger *par excellence*: that is, the prisoner of the passage' (Deleuze 2006b: 97). Karen, too, is to some extent always a prisoner of the passage, held fast even as she is in movement, unable to escape from the bounds of propriety, except in the one daring act which has Leopold for a consequence. Still interpreting Foucault, Deleuze calls the individual's 'cod[ing] or recod[ing]' within a moral knowledge, a fold which appears unfolded (though unfolding is, he argues, another kind of folding), a passage from 'subjectivation' to 'subjection' in which the subject is, as Foucault puts it, '"tied to his own identity by a conscience of self-knowledge"'.' Sexuality is similarly 'organized around certain focal points of power' which becomes 'integrated into an agency of "power-knowledge", namely Sex' (Deleuze 2006b: 103). There is no escaping the binds of the social system that hold Karen, even when she reacts against them; she is like the madman set out to sea, a 'prisoner of [her] departure' (Foucault 2005: 8). The hours she spends with Max are 'only hours', not an escape route; she had tried to swim out to sea but 'was washed back ashore again' (Bowen 1976: 152).

And yet in the making of Leopold some escape *would* be effected, Karen thinks: 'I should not have rushed on to nothing. He would be the mark our hands did not leave in the grass' (Bowen 1976: 153). Leopold is a child of his parents' crossings, which are in turn the reason Karen refuses to marry Max: 'We have been people darting across the sea to each other; there has been no time yet to be anything else' (Bowen 1976: 165). They have no common ground, but they have reached each other on the plane created when two places touch together; the power of that fold is enough to generate new life. The moment when the narrator addresses Leopold is a disruption in the text that is also the text itself; Karen's desire to keep her worlds separate, divided by the English Channel, collapses here, just as her actions remind her of something her Aunt Violet said in Ireland, wondering 'did she want this for me?' (Bowen 1976: 153). Both channels are, for a moment, filled in, or folded over, as Karen contemplates the possibility of Leopold existing. The house in Paris – setting of parts one and three, around which is enfolded part two – expands to contain both waterways.

Crossings

From the apartment where I write this in Liverpool, I have a view of the mouth of the River Mersey and the Birkenhead to Belfast ferry, the Stena Line which leaves several times a day. I watch the boats as they move sternly downriver, out to the Irish Sea, which, on a clear day, I can almost see from my window. It is impossible not to think of constant crossings; impossible not to, somehow, cross in my writing, to Ireland. There is something very strange in this stasis, when outside all is movement – the river, the boats as they come and go, the sea birds (Liver birds?) darting past the window or gliding over the water. My own stay here is temporary, as I am always coming and going between Liverpool and Paris, never in either place long enough to settle in. But the possibility of crossing a sea to go home is also never far from my mind; my own point of origin is across the Atlantic, which I can also almost see from my window.

These displacements are doubtless part of why I am fascinated by the question of crossing in Bowen's work, as well as how she understood herself to be forever in a sort of translation. Her deeply strange narrative line can be understood as an expression of a permanent self-estrangement. One reason more critics did not consider the role of place in her work, she speculates, may be because she was not a 'regional writer in the accredited sense . . . The Bowen terrain cannot be demarcated on any existing map; it is unspecific' (Bowen 1975: 35). It exists, as I hope I have shown, in the folds created by channel crossings, and unexpected connections between people. The 'unspecificity' of her writing is at the very heart of what makes it so visionary, so important in the history of modernism, both in terms of Bowen's achievement as well as in helping us reconceptualise modernism as a transnational phenomenon, further inscribing passages between Ireland, England and France.

Deleuzian theory has much to offer readings of Bowen's work, and though I have only had space to touch briefly on the fold, Deleuzian readings of crossings and hybridity in Bowen's work must include analyses of such key words as 'deterritorialisation', becoming 'minoritarian', and the notion of smooth and striated spaces. I have chosen to focus on the fold as a means of making new connections between *The House in Paris*, Bowen's hybridity and our understanding of transnational modernism. Deleuze's reading of the baroque, in his study of Leibnitz, *The Fold*, reveals it to be a highly mediated and mediating tendency, one of processing and rethinking the previous movement. This strikes me as an appropriate concept for working through Bowen's prose, which has often been called 'baroque' with regard to its style and syntax, which frequently doubles back on itself to reframe, restate or even contradict what has come before: another example of back-and-forth movement in Bowen's work.[4]

Bowen's work provides an important counterpoint to the usual stories we hear of modernism, nationalism and expatriation. *The House in Paris* is not *The Voyage Out*; it is a voyage back and forth. As opposed to a modernist impetus forward towards the future, onward to new territories, Bowen's late modernist mediation shows us the surprising folds and juxtapositions which can be created between two, or three, well-known and familiar locations.

Notes

1. J. C. Beckett, a historian specialising in Anglo-Irish civilisation, has written that the 'most pervasive Anglo-Irish quality is a kind of ambivalence, or ambiguity of outlook, arising from the need to be at once Irish and English, and leading sometimes to detachment, sometimes to a fierce aggressiveness that may, on occasion, mark an underlying sense of insecurity' (quoted in Ellmann 2003: 10).
2. Maud Ellmann notes: 'it is evident that Bowen's contradictory relationship to her two nations was never resolved. In old age, she is reported to have snapped, with a vehemence that startled her friends: "I *hate* Ireland"' (Ellmann 2003: 10).
3. See, to name only a few, Brassard (2007), Magot (2013), Parkins (2009), Ridge (2017).

4. On Bowen's 'baroque' syntax, see Bennett and Royle (1995), Bryant Jordan (1992), Ellmann (2003), Glendinning (1978), among others. Bowen herself professed to a love of the baroque (as an architectural style) in her 1948 BBC radio broadcast 'Impressions of Czechoslovakia,' in Hepburn (2010: 89).

Bibliography

Bennett, Andrew and Nicholas Royle (1995), *Elizabeth Bowen and the Dissolution of the Novel*, Basingstoke: Palgrave Macmillan.
Bowen, Elizabeth (1962), *Afterthought: Pieces About Writing*, London: Longman.
Bowen, Elizabeth (1975), *Pictures and Conversations*, New York: Alfred A. Knopf.
Bowen, Elizabeth (1976), *The House in Paris* [1935], Harmondsworth: Penguin.
Bowen, Elizabeth (1999), *Bowen's Court & Seven Winters: Memoirs of a Dublin Childhood* [1942, 1943], ed. Hermione Lee, London: Vintage Classics.
Bowen, Elizabeth (2010), 'Portrait of a woman reading' [1968], in *Listening In: Broadcasts, Speeches, and Interviews by Elizabeth Bowen*, ed. Allan Hepburn, Edinburgh: Edinburgh University Press.
Bowen, Elizabeth, Graham Greene and V. S. Pritchett (1948), *Why Do I Write?: An Exchange of Views [by letter] between Elizabeth Bowen, Graham Greene, and V.S. Pritchett*, London: Percival Marshall.
Brassard, Geneviève (2007), 'Fast and loose in interwar London: mobility and sexuality in Elizabeth Bowen's *To the North*', *Women: A Cultural Review*, 18.3: 282–302.
Bryant Jordan, Heather (1992), *How Will the Heart Endure? Elizabeth Bowen and the Landscape of War*, Ann Arbor: University of Michigan Press.
Cohen, Margaret and Carolyn Dever (eds) (2002), *The Literary Channel: The Inter-National Invention of the Novel*, Princeton, NJ: Princeton University Press.
Corcoran, Neil (2004), *Elizabeth Bowen: The Enforced Return*, Oxford: Oxford University Press.
Cronin, Gerald (1991), 'The Big House and the Irish landscape in the work of Elizabeth Bowen', in *The Big House in Ireland: Reality and Representation*, ed. Jacqueline Genet, Dingle: Brandon, pp. 143–61.
Deleuze, Gilles (2006a), *The Fold: Leibniz and the Baroque* [1988], trans. Tom Conley, London: Continuum.
Deleuze, Gilles (2006b), *Foucault* [1986], trans. Seán Hand, London: Continuum.
Ellmann, Maud (2003), *Elizabeth Bowen: The Shadow Across the Page*, Edinburgh: Edinburgh University Press.

Foucault, Michel (2005), *Madness and Civilization: A History of Insanity in the Age of Reason* [1961], trans. Richard Howard, London: Routledge.
Glendinning, Victoria (1978), *Elizabeth Bowen*, New York: Alfred A. Knopf.
Gros, Frédéric (2014), *The Philosophy of Walking*, trans. John Howe, London: Verso.
Hepburn, Allan (ed.) (2010), *Listening In: Broadcasts, Speeches, and Interviews by Elizabeth Bowen*, Edinburgh: Edinburgh University Press.
Keown, Edwina (2011), 'The seaside flâneuse in Elizabeth Bowen's *The Death of the Heart*,' in *Modernism on Sea: Art and Culture at the British Seaside*, ed. Lara Feigel and Alexandra Harris, Oxford: Peter Lang, pp. 179–90.
Magot, Céline (2013), 'Prosthetic goddesses: ambiguous identities in the age of speed', *Textual Practice*, 27.1: 127–42.
O'Faolain, Sean (1982), 'A reading and remembrance of Elizabeth Bowen', *London Review of Books*, 4.4: 15–16.
Osborn, Susan (ed.) (2009), *Elizabeth Bowen: New Critical Perspectives*, Cork: Cork University Press.
Parkins, Wendy (2009), *Mobility and Modernity in Women's Novels, 1850s–1930s: Women Moving Dangerously*, Basingstoke: Palgrave Macmillan.
Probyn, Elspeth (1993), *Sexing the Self: Gendered Positions in Cultural Studies*, London: Routledge.
Ridge, Emily (2017), *Portable Modernisms: The Art of Traveling Light*, Edinburgh: Edinburgh University Press.

Coda: 'You, who cross the Channel': Virginia Woolf, Departures and the Spectro-Aesthetics of Modernism

Patrizia A. Muscogiuri

> Let's ferry back our souls across the Channel.
> Wilfred Owen, 'A New Heaven' ([MS] 1916)

> A specter is always a revenant and thus it begins by coming back.
> Jacques Derrida, *Specters of Marx* (1993)

> The sea has another voice than this.
> Virginia Woolf, 'The Royal Academy' (1919)

> I think that the dead are with us.
> John Berger, 'Interview' (2015)

In Woolf's writings, the marginal space of the coast unexpectedly brings about 'the silent apparition' (Woolf 1927: 207) of material aspects of history, including warships and the many nameless soldiers who departed for and died in the Great War (the war departed), remarkably prefiguring the Derridean notion of the spectre as political dead. A Derridean spectro-aesthetics arises here in the context of a cross-Channel modernism troubled by the carnage and futility of war. Touching on *Jacob's Room* (1922), *Mrs Dalloway* (1925) and *To the Lighthouse* (1927), in constellation with works by Wilfred Owen, T. S. Eliot, E. M. Forster, Thomas Hardy, Mulk Raj Anand, C. R. W. Nevinson, among others, this chapter draws on three cross-Channel essays by Woolf: 'Heard on the Downs: The Genesis of Myth' (1916), 'The Royal Academy' (1919) and 'To Spain' (1923).

Woolf's often metaphoric treatment of the sea does not entail a dismissal of history, including maritime history, but is, on the contrary, historical-materialist, merging history with vision in ways departing from, and subverting, the visual rhetoric prescribed by the British War Propaganda Bureau to official war artists.

The concept of 'departing' in its polysemy ('depart for', 'the departed', 'depart from') brings into play the interrelation between three of its main senses: spatial movement, final demise, dissent, all involving a decentring and/or a crossing of boundaries. Woolf's frustration at the government's use of Britain's geographical insularity to keep civilians in the dark about the reality of war emerges repeatedly in her wartime writings: the Channel was used as a political barrier, facilitating state suppression of information about the conflict and its human costs. Woolf's strategic liminal stance is deeply informed, instead, by a cross-Channel perspective that is historical, political and aesth-ethical. Inherently entailing an oppositional poetics, Woolf's liminal outlook from the watery borders of Great Britain – specifically its southern edges – involves, and builds upon, metaphorical and literal crossings of the Channel, beginning, in the latter case, with her own.

Woolf's material early crossings of the Channel (in particular, in 1904, visiting exhibitions and artists' studios in Paris with her sister Vanessa Bell) contributed to shaping her artistic sensibility and understanding of aesthetics beyond the confines of a stifling Victorian tradition, and was cultivated and strengthened through regular discussions at the Bloomsbury Group's Friday Club – 'the first avant-garde exhibiting society of the century' (Beechey 1996: [1]), founded by Vanessa following the Paris experience. Bloomsbury's two Post-Impressionist exhibitions in London (1910 and 1912) were major embodiments of that cross-Channel perspective. Among the British artists exhibiting at the Friday Club was the rebel painter Christopher Nevinson (1889–1946) who had crossed the Channel not only to study art in Paris, but also to help with the Friends' Ambulance Unit in France and the Red Cross in Flanders, before becoming an official war artist, albeit a controversial one. Nevinson revolutionised visual arts in war, providing a disruptive cross-Channel view on what was actually happening on European battlefields. He and other artists and writers who had been in the war gave Woolf the possibility of metaphorically crossing those waters to 'see' the conflict, as well as an indication of an aesthetics capable of bearing witness to erased histories.

Woolf was recovering in the middle of the war from a severe episode of mental illness, and was facing a critical, epochal conundrum that is at once epistemic, political and aesthetic: how to inscribe the end of a world and channel change. A myth of Woolf's aloofness from contemporaneous events before the 1920s is perpetuated by critics disregarding or misreading her writings in this period, which in fact inscribe a powerful cross-Channel ethos. This coda recontextualises three key essays as well as her war trilogy in light of this evidence, tracing intellectual and artistic connections beyond Woolf to a spectrum of radical aesthetics that in some cases defied censorship to express the brutality and senselessness of war – all that the abstract idea of 'The Glorious Dead' inscribed on the Whitehall Cenotaph and other war memorials erases. As reflected in these modernist works, those British soldiers forever missing from their native land met across the Channel their final (un)resting place: in the modernist imagination, the departed can find no peace. As the centenary of the state memorialisation passes, we might ponder what we are to do with the still very present departed of the Great War, and the dead of ensuing wars now accreting to them: 'The past is very present to me and has been for a very long time', John Berger recalled in an interview in 2015, aged eighty-eight: 'I first became aware of this quite intensely when I was a teenager, because of the First World War. You see, I think that the dead are with us' (Maughan 2015).

In this context, Woolf's *Jacob's Room* is, I suggest, a polemical rewriting of the Unknown Warrior's crossing the Channel to return to Britain as corpse. For not only does the ghostly protagonist Jacob Flanders first appear on a beach of the English Channel in Cornwall, and later sail on its waters, but he also crosses and re-crosses it for adventures in Europe, before his final fatal crossing to Flanders, his corpse remaining on one side of the Channel, his empty civilian shoes on the other. Woolf's rewriting of the Unknown Warrior's crossing is divested of the celebratory nationalism informing Britain's commemorations on Armistice Day 1920; it becomes a potent metaphor of 'disillusionment' (a key word in relation to war, both for Freud and Woolf), pointing at the inanity of the nationalist discourse of war. The Unknown Warrior is co-opted as nationalist signifier, 'the synecdochic object of mourning for each and all of those with dead far from home' (Sherman 2014: 45), and the object of Woolf's and Wilfred Owen's political critique. For David Sherman in his compelling book chapter 'The State's Unending Vigil: Owen's and Woolf's Unknown Warrior', the narrative voice of *Jacob's Room* 'is everyone's and everyone. Like the Unknown Warrior, it is without identity, a mechanism for narrative individualization and totalization' (Sherman 2014: 100). The lost corpse of Judith Shakespeare, in

A Room of One's Own, on the other hand, becomes for Bette London a feminist counterpart to the Unknown Warrior:

> Woolf enjoins her audience to 'let flowers fall upon the tomb of Aphra Behn' – in Westminster Abbey, no less – and dedicate themselves to bringing Shakespeare's sister (back) to life, she is evoking . . . the well-established rituals of collective mourning which she then displaces with her own idiosyncratic rites. (London 2010: 50, citing Woolf 1929: 97; Sherman 2014: 98)

The political reach of this powerful synecdoche goes beyond the unknowable corpse itself, beyond its paradoxical expansionist territorial capacity – 'It is well for a nation that would be great to scatter its graves all over the world' (Forster 1953a: 31; Sherman 2014: 81) – to its marine journeys ferried across the Channel as pre-corpse and then corpse.

As metaphoric locus of vision, the sea dis-locates any pretence at localism or nationalism in its fluid geography. The stretch of water separating Britain from, and simultaneously connecting it to, continental Europe shapes itself in Woolf as locus of a double vision, prompting alternative readings of the Great War that reclaim histories erased by official historiography, and informing her aesthetics and her pacifist, anti-nationalist politics. Set against the culture of the granite memorial (paradoxically dematerialising the common embodied realities of war) and the tenet of 'beauty for ashes' embraced by the Royal Academy as an establishment institution promoting nationalist, class and patriarchal politics in the immediate aftermath of the war, the visions of Woolf's characters on 'the shore of the world' (Woolf 2015: 83) recreate a groundbreaking palimpsest of war, albeit one that is written on water. This aqueous imaginary is elusive but permeated by visions capable of undermining the nationalist, phallogocentric discourse of war, and it has the unsettling quality of the 'spectral', what Jacques Derrida calls the *'revenant'* (Derrida 1993: 96) – literally the one who returns, dead and yet repeatedly coming back to haunt us.

Such hauntings are not only visual but auditory, as demonstrated in 'Heard on the Downs' (1916), one of the first things Woolf wrote while recovering from mental illness in a world now at war. Published in *The Times* on 15 August 1916 – at a time when state censorship had already silenced some of her intellectual friends like Clive Bell and Bertrand Russell – and signed 'from a correspondent', the article develops a satirical hybrid form combining reportage, experiential narrative and allusions to classical mythology – the gothic and rural anecdotes to target and undermine the fatalistic rhetoric of the discourse of war and, more subtly, the restrictions on information underlying it, treating blind nationalist faith on a par with popular misbeliefs, namely as 'myth', both products of deliberate state disinformation. The 'correspondent', first acting as an 'earwitness' of war sounds and then giving ear to common discourses about the war, proceeds to survey other ordinary, popular 'myths'. The piece opens with the jingoistic clichés of 'two well-known writers [who] were describing the sound of the guns in France, as they heard it from the top of the South Downs' – the one as '"the hammer stroke of Fate"; the other heard in it "the pulse of Destiny"'. An alternative audio-visual image is proffered:

> More prosaically, it sounds like the beating of gigantic carpets by gigantic women, at a distance. You may almost see them holding the carpets in their strong arms by the four corners, tossing them into the air, and bringing them down with a thud while the dust rises in a cloud about their heads. (Woolf 1986–2011, vol. 2: 40)

The artillery heard from across the Channel will re-sound almost verbatim in *Jacob's Room*, where it is heard not on the south coast from across the Channel but on the east coast in Scarborough from the North Sea (known until the Great War as the German Ocean), where a sizeable and eerie four-line gap in the text appears, extending a blank white space – or channel, perhaps (see Bishop 2004) – as the narration shifts between Jacob holidaying in Greece and his mother hearing guns at sea:

> The sound spread itself flat, and then went tunnelling its way with fitful explosions among the channels of the islands.
>   Darkness drops like a knife over Greece.
>
>
> "The guns?" said Betty Flanders, half asleep, getting out of bed and going to the window, which was decorated with a fringe of dark leaves.
>   "Not at this distance," she thought. "It is the sea."
>   Again, far away, she heard the dull sound, as if nocturnal women were beating great carpets. There was Morty lost, and Seabrook dead; her sons fighting for their country. But were the chickens safe? Was that some one moving downstairs? Rebecca with the toothache? No. The nocturnal women were beating great carpets. Her hens shifted slightly on their perches. (Woolf 1922: 287–8)

First heard in 'Heard on the Downs', the sound-image reappears in *Jacob's Room* soon before the eponymous protagonist's death in the war, when the sound of the guns on the continent and the sound of the North Sea get confused in the drowsy mind of his mother, Betty Flanders, and perceived 'as if nocturnal women were beating great carpets' (Woolf 1922: 288), with the twice-recurring 'gigantic' of the original – and, hence, any possible mythical reference – now dropped, while Betty's thoughts about 'her sons fighting for their country' (288) mixed with the preoccupation for the safety of her chickens also in part recreates the connection addressed in the 1916 article between the concern for unproductive hens and the 'vibrations in the earth caused by the shock of the great guns in Flanders' (Woolf 1986–2011, vol. 2: 41). In other words, the sounds of war are not notional noises produced in a vacuum without consequences, as the Futurists, for example, typically present them – 'the violence encouraged and the carnage suppressed' (Khan 1999: 66) – but are inevitably followed by death and in any case associated with it, hence always 'sinister' (Woolf 1986–2011, vol. 2: 40).

The ghostly, ghost-making guns of Flanders appear among an abundance of centuries-old 'stories of ghostly riders and unhappy ladies' in the villages of the Downs related to 'such tricks of sound' in the morphology of the land. The essay turns to wartime and

> many phantoms hovering on the borderland of belief and scepticism – not yet believed in, but not properly accounted for. Human vanity, it may be, embodies them in the first place. The desire to be somehow impossibly, and therefore all the more mysteriously, concerned in secret affairs of national importance is very strong at the present moment. (Woolf 1986–2011, vol. 2: 40)

Bringing into play the etymon or, rather, the common historical acceptations of both words, the gradual passage from 'ghost(s)' to 'phantom(s)' shifts the emphasis from the gothic to a subtle critique of basic nationalist ideology. The ghostly (and any allusion to the spirit or soul of the departed that it might imply) is shelved in order to signpost the character of 'illusion', 'delusion', 'unreality' implied in the polysemic word 'phantom'. Addressed subsequently, instances of how these 'many phantoms' are 'embodie[d]' by 'human vanity', by the 'desire' to be 'impossibly' in the know about the war, are the common figure of the village 'wiseacre' and the local surmisers of the historical and strategic significance of the southern English landscape predicting a possible German landing in the area. Compare

Ford Madox Ford's short story 'The Scaremonger' (1914), which targets the effects of the sensationalism of newspapers at the start of the war and the government-generated atmosphere of suspicion. Subtly, Woolf's inclusion of these cases, both based on rumours (etymologically, 'noise'), is consistent with her approach to the sounds/ noises of war as generating 'myth' – a term discussed by Jane Harrison in *Themis* (1912), deriving from 'the Greek μῦθος, speech, mere word, saying, rumour, conversation, tale, narrative, fiction, anything delivered by word of mouth, word, speech, opp. to ἔργον' (Liddell and Scott 1889) – since they involve the spreading of 'circumstantial narratives' which in time could 'masquerade in solemn histories for the instruction of the future' (Woolf 1986–2011, vol. 2: 40, 41). This is truly a more sinister result than the innocuous ghost stories produced by the propagation of sound waves in the landscape. These misbeliefs and other 'mysteries' (42) were the result, in a country fighting a war overseas, of censorship and propaganda, as the government-controlled media's sanitised information generated the disconcerting awareness that it was 'no good buying newspapers . . . Nothing ever happens', as a character in 'The Mark on the Wall' (1917) laments, blurting out in exasperation: 'Curse this war; God damn this war!' (Woolf 1985: 83). The same vexation permeates 'Heard on the Downs'.

The earwitness 'correspondent' surveys other myths more ordinary and popular than the prevailing 'supernatural state of things' (Woolf 1986–2011, vol. 2: 41) produced by disinformation. They turn from ghosts and 'historical speculations' by locals to how the war is thought to affect things as varied as poultry farming (see Woolf 1975–80, vol. 2: 66; Coward 1915), the weather and even 'the behaviour of the church bell', at a time when many civilians could only conjecture about the war and its repercussions on their daily lives. Among these 'Portents at Home' (Woolf 1986–2011, vol. 2: 42n3), the one object intrinsically associated with sound production in peacetime, the church bell, is instead noted for its dissonant behaviour, when, 'dropping from the belfry' (a subversion perhaps of Marinetti's Futurist 'orchestra of the noises of war swelling under a held note of silence in the high sky round golden balloon that observes the firing'; Russolo 1986: 27), it is mistaken for a sign of imminent ceasefire, thus foregrounding its imposed silence in wartime.

Among its impingements on civil liberties and wide-ranging prohibitions punishable by martial law, the Defence of the Realm Act (or DORA) also banned 'the ringing and chiming of bells and the striking of clocks' at certain times, as they could guide enemy aircraft

(March 1916: Regulation 12^B, Pulling 2018: 91). Passed without debate on 8 August 1914 by Asquith's government, frequently amended and extended, DORA's emergency legislation gave unprecedented powers to the government on every aspect of people's lives with the aim of optimising the war effort while increasing national security. Besides specific prohibitions on sounds, including whistling and making noises, and among innumerable other injunctions, there were bans on free speech and free press (Pulling 2018: 92). Enforcing censorship on newspapers and any publications (Regs. 27^C, 51, 51^A), DORA also silenced the pacifists. Woolf's brother-in-law Clive Bell's pamphlet *Peace at Once* (1915) was soon seized and destroyed by order of the Lord Mayor of London Colonel Sir Charles Johnston (not Sir John Krill, *pace* Hussey 2016: 246; see Wynn 2016: 40, 77ff.), and her friend 'Bertie' Russell was dismissed from Trinity College, Cambridge, when he was prosecuted following the publication, in April 1916, of a pamphlet in support of Ernest Everett, a Lancashire teacher and conscientious objector sentenced under DORA to *Two Years Hard Labour for not Disobeying the Dictates of Conscience*, as the pamphlet title summarises. Like the dissonant church bells, Clive Bell's behaviour was being watched by the 'bastards from D.O.R.A.' (Bell 1923: 1), his voice having already been hushed. Not only did the silenced church bells become associated, in the common imagination, with various wartime restrictions and prohibitions – see for example the popular song 'When the Bells of Peace Are Ringing' (1917), composed by F. J. Wilson – they can be read more specifically in Woolf as an emblem of the counter-discourses of war that were censored and obliterated, whether rooted in religion or in ethics and secular pacifism. And silencing of bells was again a concern in the Second World War (Herbert 1943: 27–8; Fleming 2011: 97).

As the overpowering sound of the guns heard on the Downs eclipses 'the grasshoppers and the larks', obliterating (etymologically, literally, 'erasing written letters'; figuratively, 'erasing from memory') pacifist/dissenting voices, so wartime censorship suppressed and greatly limited many 'sounds' or (ideological) messages. Propaganda and jingoism dominated the discourse of war unchallenged. For the state-controlled media, 'nothing ever happens' beyond the Channel, the barrier between war zone and home front. Yet those sea-borne 'strange volumes of sound' were a constant manifestation of war, daily bringing conflict to the home front, channelling more than mere noise of artillery. 'Heard on the Downs' demonstrates how even the objective physical phenomenon of sound received by the ear may be manipulated by a dominant discourse which hears (and makes the public hear) it as 'mythical' amplification of that discourse itself, manufacturing consensus on war's inevitability and nobility. The state, the university (the college, as Woolf has it in *Three Guineas*), the media – in short, the dominant apparatus – 'has you by the ear'. And the ear can become 'double' (Derrida 1985: 33, 35), the receiver of both direct empirical impressions but also of targeted, ideologically earmarked discourses. Woolf's acute awareness of the ear's vulnerability and even proclivity towards those discourses particularly in wartime is expressed unequivocally in her 'The War from the Street' (1919), her *Times Literary Supplement* review of Bridgman Metchim's *Our Own History of the War. From a South London View* (1918). Here she outlines the psychology of 'that anonymous monster the Man in the Street' (Woolf 1986–2011, vol. 3: 3), whose 'mind', she says, 'has had certain inscriptions scored upon it so repeatedly that it believes that it has originated them', whereas in fact 'for four years and more you are nothing but *a vast receptacle* for the *rumours* of other people's opinions and deeds' (4, emphasis added). Those 'rumours' thus 'inscri[bed]' on the self-as-'receptacle' are none other than 'the otograph sign of State' (Derrida 1985: 19), which ear-marks the 'auto' of any possible self-written sign ('autograph'), turning it to 'oto', passive and 'quiescent' (Woolf 1986–2011, vol. 3: 3). This binary dynamic bodies forth, in Woolf's shrewd analysis, that 'you'/'they' system she lucidly exposes whose function is to legitimise the establishment.

The ear's doubleness renders it a site of dissonance (etymologically, 'disagreement in sound') and, hence, resistance. Woolf brings about a 'disagreement' in how certain sounds are perceived, precisely 'to strike a discord' (Woolf 1919: 327), subtly to trans-mute them. She radically reconfigures the sounds of war crossing the Channel from their otograph perception as the deterministic 'pulse of Destiny' and 'hammer stroke of Fate', a process begun in 'Heard on the Downs', significantly, spreading like rumour into her successive writings. The diverse 'myths' generated by sounds in similar circumstances signals for the correspondent the difficulty for someone on the home front of voicing views on a conflict fought on the other side of the Channel. In reporting sounds of war from beyond the Channel, 'Heard on the Downs' signals the pervasive presence of a war not seen, and re-echoes the effects of censorship on various perceptions of the war on the home front in stories, newspaper columns, rumours – that is, marginal war-related discourses but not the official discourse of war and accounts of history. 'No one who has taken stock of his own impressions since 4 August 1914,' Woolf observes in 'The War from the Street' (1919), 'can possibly believe that history as it is written closely resembles history as it is lived' (Woolf 1986–2011, vol. 3: 3). Accordingly, to an ear not enslaved by 'the otograph sign of State' (Derrida 1985: 19), those sounds crossing the Channel can only channel somebody's death. Even more so, then, 'the ear is uncanny'. Woolf attends to the physical reverberation of gunfire but also to what she terms, subtly, 'strange *volumes* of sound' (emphasis added), which in its polysemy encompasses the intensity of sound but also its mass, its aggregates of matter, consistent with her conception elsewhere of sound as matter (Woolf 1975–80, vol. 1: 264).

The 'strange volumes of sound that roll across the bare uplands, and reverberate' (Woolf 1986–2011, vol. 2: 40), in 'Heard on the Downs', promptly reappear, trans-muted, as 'spirit matter' in her story *Kew Gardens* (1917, Woolf 1985: 297), specifically 'the spirits of the dead', since 'now with his war, the spirit matter is rolling between the hills like thunder' (Woolf 1985: 92) according to the acoustic perception of a returned shell-shocked soldier. No wonder those 'strange volumes of sound'/'the spirit matter' should 'roll'/ be 'rolling', in tune with the etymology of volume – 'roll', namely 'roll of a manuscript', 'roll of parchment containing writing' – from which not only its sense of book but all its other meanings derive. Most of the voices of those fighting and dying beyond the Channel were silenced, as were the voices of the pacifists – but those voices were not lost. Just by crossing the Channel and 'rolling' in the landscape, to a fine ear the sounds recorded in these wartime writings of Woolf's speak volumes. The ear is indeed 'unheimlich' (Derrida 1985: 33): Woolf may have momentarily shelved the ghostly in 'Heard on the Downs', but what is at play (beyond her playing with the gothic, the uncanny) is the inauguration of a textual haunting channelling silenced voices and obliterated anti-war discourses. These keep emerging in her wartime and post-war writing, bodying forth a spectro-aesthetics of pacifism.

This haunting starts from the ear, as the cross-Channel sounds heard in 'Heard on the Downs' return to haunt a mother's sleep in *Jacob's Room*, having already rematerialised in *Kew Gardens* as 'the spirits of the dead, who, according to [a shell-shocked returned soldier], were even now telling him all sorts of odd things about their experiences in Heaven . . . known to the ancients as Thessaly' (Woolf 1985: 92). A similar aural haunting is experienced, in *Mrs Dalloway*, by Septimus Smith, also a returned shell-shocked soldier. To him, too, the war dead communicate, among other things: 'The dead were in Thessaly, . . . among the orchids. There they waited till the War was over' (Woolf 2015: 63). In *Kew Gardens* the aural ostensibly shapes a purely acoustic haunting, to the extent that, as the veteran suggests, if 'the widow applies her ear' to a 'little machine' made from 'a small electric battery' she can 'summon . . . the spirit by a sign as agreed' (Woolf 1985: 92). But in *Mrs Dalloway* it is the power of the aural to channel vision that emerges – a power already anticipated in 'Heard on the Downs' when, having listened to the sounds from across the Channel discerningly and associated them with 'gigantic women', the narrator suggests that 'you may almost see them', the women in the midst of their sound-producing actions (a crucial difference being that, in the latter case, this is an alternative but still mythical vision). Hearing in *Mrs Dalloway* (following *Kew Gardens*) combines with vision to bring about the spectral – with all its historical-political implications – literally in Septimus, but also po-et(h)ically in Clarissa. Vision more conspicuously brings about the spectral specifically in relation to Channel-crossing both in *Jacob's Room* and in Woolf's 1923 essay 'To Spain'.

Departures: 'those who have survived the crossing'

> It is natural that those who have survived the crossing, with its last scrutiny of passing faces so like a little rehearsal of death, should be shaken . . . and tremble for one intoxicating moment. (Woolf 1986–2011, vol. 3: 361)

'To Spain' (1923) is an article devoted to Channel-crossing that voices the 'excitement', having departed from Britain, of 'those who feel themselves liberated from one civilisation, launched upon an other', 'escap[ing] the hours, the works, the divisions, rigid and straight, of the old British week' for a 'more congenial civilisation' (361, 362). Significantly, in an article full of light and colour in its vibrant depiction of a train journey through France and Spain, the unpredictable, uncanny configuration of the crossing as something that has been 'survived' and 'with its last scrutiny of passing faces so like a little rehearsal of death' insinuates a jarring note that haunts the narrative, understanding Channel-crossing as departure in a deeply polysemic sense: to Europe, from British 'civilisation', as well as from (its way of) life – both journey, divergence and demise. A crucial implication may emerge, as I discuss below, that Channel-crossing involves a kind of positive and necessary death. But this unexpected image of the Channel-crosser as a nearly/try-out departed has a more immediate purport for the contemporaneous reader, since it alludes to the still fresh memory not only of ships sunk in the Channel during the recent war – of which Woolf kept a record in her diary (Woolf 1977–85, vol. 1: 4, 28) – but of those British soldiers departing for the battlefields of Europe never to return – hence, in this sense, who did not 'surviv[e] the crossing'. The recent war is never explicitly mentioned, but the article is nevertheless informed by and channels reflections on the war. Most significantly, Woolf's image of Channel-crossing as polysemous departure, specifically in the dual sense of journey and demise, echoes the wartime depiction of the Channel as Styx, the river of Hades (and river of hate) across which the newly dead were ferried by Charon to enter the Underworld, in Wilfred Owen's 'A New Heaven' (1916), where British soldiers who crossed the Channel to reach the front lines 'never found gay fairyland' (Owen 2013, vol. 1: 82), only death. Unable to forget the horrors of war, they have 'missed the tide of Lethe' (the river of oblivion), 'yet are soon / For that new bridge that leaves old Styx half-spanned' (Owen 2013, vol. 1: 82). That 'old Styx' is only 'half-spanned' immediately introduces a ghostly presence in Owen's text: having killed, the (dead) soldiers 'from high Paradise are cursed and banned', and thus cannot complete passage to the other world. Manuscript versions of its focal lines (lines 9–10) confirm that the poem is spoken by a dead soldier addressing his departed comrades: 'Let's die back to those hearths we died for. Thus / Shall we be gods there. Death shall be no sev'rance' (Owen 2013, vol. 2: 223). This suggests a longing for an impossible second death in order to find peace, and 'Let's ferry back our souls across the Channel' (also 'Let us be taken home by Death', Owen 2013, vol. 2: 224). Only half-departed after death, then, the soldiers may aspire to divine translation to the 'New Heaven' of the title, alluding to the Book of Revelation 21: 1, but they do so in the form of their souls' crossing 'back to our homes' (Owen 2013, vol. 2: 223), presumably punning on the material Sussex port of Newhaven. Thus the drafts of the poem specify an idea that Owen would later amplify in 'The Kind Ghosts' (1918), but that at first must have seemed perturbing, inappropriate or maybe ineffective. And lines 9–10 were revised for the final version of 'A New Heaven' as: '– Let's die home, ferry across the Channel! Thus / Shall we live gods there. Death shall be no sev'rance' (Owen 2013, vol. 1: 82). The ironic severing of 'severance' to 'sev'rance' in obedience of metrical authority painfully complicates this nevertheless powerful homing riposte to the imperialist thrust of Rupert Brooke's 'The Soldier' (1914). Brooke died of sepsis en route to Gallipoli, aged only twenty-seven, but never saw the battlefields nor, as Owen did later, 'the distortion of the dead, whose un-buriable bodies sit outside dug-outs all day, all night, the most execrable sights on earth. In poetry we call them the most glorious' (Owen 1985: 217).

In its realism and ambiguity, the revision brings a further sense to Channel-crossing: the subtle intimation of a departure from the dominant nationalist imperative of war 'pro patria mori', a departure that escalates in Owen's later poetry. But by the time Owen wrote 'The Kind Ghosts', Britannia – the true protagonist of this 1918 poem – was utterly haunted by ghosts of the war departed. Siegfried Sassoon's first collections of war poetry, for example, also inscribe that haunting: *The Old Huntsman and Other Poems* (1917) and *Counter-Attack and Other Poems* (1918), which was reviewed by Woolf. 'To Spain' carries traces of that haunting in its Channel crossing. But if the crux of 'A New Heaven' is Owen's emphasis on death across the Channel as 'sev'rance' for the soldiers whose bodies were severed from and never returned to Britain, Woolf's focus in 'To Spain' is instead on the deadly severance represented by Britain's secluded insularity – a critical point for Woolf during the Second World War, resurfacing in *Between the Acts* (1941) in Lucy Swithin's musings on primeval unity: 'Before there was a channel', 'when the entire continent, not then, she understood, divided by a channel, was all one' (Woolf 1941: 130, 13). The earlier essay addresses habitual Channel-crossers, who in 1923 are on vacation rather than making a one-way trip to a battlefield, yet the crossings of the former are haunted by the latter:

> You, who cross the Channel yearly, probably no longer see the house at Dieppe, no longer feel, as the train moves slowly down the street, one civilisation fall, another rise – from the ruin and chaos of British stucco this incredible pink and blue phoenix, four stories high, with its flower-pots, its balconies, its servant girl leaning on the window-sill, indolently looking out. Quite unmoved you sit reading – Thomas Hardy, perhaps – bridging abysses, preserving continuity. (1986–2011, vol. 3: 361)

Early in the Great War (December 1914) Dieppe was established as a British military station (Porter et al. 1952: 542). The opening invocation, 'You, who cross the Channel yearly', ironically invoking all those combatants who fell in the war never to make a return journey on an annual basis, let alone as a civilian on vacation, echoes T. S. Eliot's 'Death by Water' in *The Waste Land* (which Woolf hand-set for publication in September 1923): 'O you who turn the wheel and look to windward, / Consider Phlebas, who was once handsome and tall as you'. In 'To Spain', written in the aftermath of that war, crossing the Channel emerges as a radical break, from both a cultural, aesthetic and psychological perspective, almost an out-of-body experience. Defined as 'that precipice – our departure', Channel-crossing reveals 'abysses'. Language short-circuits with a 'visual beauty' that it cannot express, producing a 'chasm' in which 'the eye pours it all in' (Woolf 1986–2011, vol. 3: 361). It effects positive, if 'alarming', deterritorialisation for travellers who, '[t]aken from home, which like a shell has made them hard, separate, individual', suddenly find themselves with 'exposed brains', their 'disembodied spirit fluttering at the window' (362, 361), suggesting a kind of death of a situated somatics (the rootedness of bodies in a specific geographical, socio-historical and cultural context) and liberation of the spirit (travellers 'feel . . . liberated from one civilisation, launched upon another'), which, in a way, retraces the fate of the dead soldiers leaving their bodies behind whilst, simultaneously, reversing it.

What work by Thomas Hardy is being read by the essay's addressee? His famous poem 'Channel Firing' (1914) (Hardy 1976: 305–6), perhaps? Here 'gunnery practice out at sea' (line 10) is mistakenly imagined by the already dead buried in England as heralding the biblical end of the world:

> That night your great guns, unawares,
> Shook all our coffins as we lay,
> And broke the chancel window-squares,
> We thought it was the Judgment-day (lines 1–4)

God explains to the dead that this is merely life as normal: '"All nations striving strong to make / Red war yet redder. Mad as hatters / . . . That this is not the judgment-hour / For some of them's a blessed thing"' (lines 10–15). And the poem closes with reports of channel firing:

> Again the guns disturbed the hour,
> Roaring their readiness to avenge,
> As far inland as Stourton Tower,
> And Camelot, and starlit Stonehenge. (lines 33–6)

Meanwhile, on the other side of the Channel, the 'souls' of departed soldiers whose bodies remain in Europe are understood, in Owen's poem, to long for a crossing back to Britain as a second death. Conversely, for the 'disembodied spirit' of Woolf's travellers, Channel-crossing to Europe is absolutely vital for overcoming Britain's separation and cloistered individualism (producing conservatism and exacerbated nationalism). They depart the limits of 'one civilisation' while exploring another. Britain's 'dangerous' geographic insularity is set against the more appealing European connectedness between transnational places through what Woolf imagines as an 'eternal white road':

> [T]he French have roads. Yes, they have roads which strike from that lean poplar there to Vienna, to Moscow; pass Tolstoy's house, climb mountains, then march, all shop decorated, down the middle of famous cities. But in England the road runs out on to a cliff; wavers into sand at the edge of the sea. It begins to seem dangerous to live in England. (Woolf 1986–2011, vol. 3: 363, 362–3)

Crossing from an England relatively unscathed to a France ravaged by warfare, Woolf's essay in imagining 'one civilisation fall, another rise', shockingly reassigns 'ruin and chaos' to British stucco and celebrates the regenerative powers in the 'incredible pink and blue phoenix four stories high' of that house in Dieppe.

There were state ceremonies on both sides of the Channel, on 11 November 1920. The 'Unknown Soldier' was taken to the Arc de Triomphe in Paris, and the 'Unknown Warrior' to Westminster Abbey in London, having been drawn by gun carriage through crowd-lined streets, stopping at the Mall for the royal unveiling of the Cenotaph. The more inclusive term 'Warrior' was chosen by the British apparently in acknowledgement of their naval forces, albeit that their corpse was chosen from the remains of unknown British servicemen exhumed from four battle areas, the Aisne, the Somme, Arras and Ypres. If both nations went to great lengths to ensure the anonymity of the grotesquely unidentifiable corpses chosen for these ceremonies (Goldman 2004: 131), Owen defiantly attempts to lift the state coffin lid, as Sherman argues, in his radically thinking 'the recalcitrant materiality of the war corpse as its primary meaning ... the dead are dead bodies ... these bodies mean merely themselves' (Sherman 2014: 80). The elusive heterodiegetic narrator of *Jacob's Room* 'fulfills the rhetorical function of the Unknown Warrior', for

Sherman, whereas Jacob, 'in his opacity and final absence, fulfills the function of the Cenotaph, the empty tomb for the war dead at the other end of Whitehall' (Sherman 2014: 104). Yet the novel sets out to get to know the obviously fictitious Jacob Flanders whose very surname is proleptic of his ultimate fate as unknowable.

The state raises up the unknown combatant 'UNKNOWN BY NAME OR RANK / BROUGHT FROM FRANCE TO LIE AMONG / THE MOST ILLUSTRIOUS OF THE LAND'; Woolf's novel conversely traces the disappearance into unknowability of someone whose illustrious future is cut short. Jacob's induction into an elite education and career may suggest he is a version of Percival in *The Waves*, a personification of white Anglo-Saxon chivalry, implicit wielder the sixteenth-century crusader's sword from the Tower of London collection placed in the Unknown Warrior's coffin. But the novel is at pains to demonstrate Jacob's precarious and contested family origins (see Bradshaw 2003); and his possible Jewishness, hinted at throughout the novel, places him in uneasy relations with the pillars of the British establishment he encounters (see Stalla 2012). Woolf tests here the racial, ethnic and cultural inclusivity of the state's Unknown Warrior, but it is left to a younger generation of Bloomsbury novelist at the dawning of the Second World War to make clear that the fallen of the Great War also include combatants who did not approach the battlefields via the English Channel crossings but arrived on convoy ships 'steaming up towards the [south] coast of France, with their cargo of the first Divisions of Indian troops who had been brought to fight in Europe, a cargo stranger than they had carried before' (Anand 1940: 11). Mulk Raj Anand's *Across the Black Waters* (1940), recently explored in a brilliant chapter by Santanu Das (Das 2018: 343–66), seems to offer a new perspective on the Land's End vista of gulls and cottages in *Jacob's Room*: 'A few sea-gulls were coming out to meet them, and more seemed to be seated on the hills above the bay, but on closer view the latter proved to be houses' (Anand 1940: 13). Anand has the strange cargo disembark from the black waters and enter an Eliotic whirlpool that brings these ill-fated troops on to land:

> the quay seemed to be drowned in a strange and incongruous whirlpool: Pathans, Sikhs, Dogras, Gurkhas, Muhammadans in khaki, blue-jacketed French seamen and porters and English Tommies. And there was a babble of voices, shouts, curses, salaams and incomprehensible courtesies. He struggled into the single file which was disembarking and, before he knew where he was, stood on solid earth in the thick of the crowd. (Anand 1940: 16)

'The sea has another voice than this'

Before starting to inscribe the war more directly in her novels of the 1920s, Woolf was carefully pondering the pivotal question of the representation of war. In this context, her significant, though misinterpreted, scathing review of one of the first post-war art exhibitions at the Royal Academy, the Summer Exhibition of 1919, not only underpins this claim but also points to her perceptive understanding of representation and her acute oppositional awareness of the patriotic/patriarchal visual rhetoric inherent in official war images. Published in *The Athenaeum* (August 1919) and simply entitled 'The Royal Academy', the review is both subtle and trenchant in assessing the artworks and the event itself from an uncompromising aesthetic-political angle. The exhibition having already been covered a number of times by *The Athenaeum*, Woolf's heady cataloguing of numerous works in passing ventriloquises snatches she confesses of an unidentified 'story from Rudyard Kipling' (Woolf 1986–2011, vol. 3: 90), who, as her readers would know, was tasked by the Imperial War Graves Commission as literary adviser to recommend inscriptions. She focuses in detail on three paintings (by John Singer Sargent, John Reid and Alfred Priest) and on the Royal Academy as an establishment institution patently amplifying, through the exhibition, Britain's class, nationalist and imperialist politics. Yet, this may not be so self-evident. Maggie Humm, for instance, deems Woolf's review an 'inappropriate elitist response', marred by the 'unexpected lacuna [of] Woolf's lack of attention to women artists' and whose 'exaggerated satire is misplaced and inaccurate', in particular with regard to John Singer Sargent's famous painting *Gassed* (Humm 2009: 156). Yet Woolf shrewdly considers the politics of certain aesthetic representations of war in a world entirely changed by it, I would suggest, and at last 'disillusioned', a key word reiterated in her review, she seems perfectly aware that the artworks exhibited would not in the least have bothered the British War Propaganda Bureau during the conflict – quite the opposite, as most were paintings by uncontroversial official war artists, propaganda pieces commissioned by the Ministry of Information, including Sargent's painting, commissioned in May 1918.

Woolf, a strong supporter of women in the professions, Humm argues, should not have ignored Flora Lion's painting *Women's Canteen at a Munitions Factory*, also in the exhibition, because it is a 'critical representation of women's new, major, modern experience that is, the factory' (Humm 2009: 157). Paradoxically, Humm cites exactly the reason why Woolf, a committed pacifist, could *never* have supported a representation of women aiding the war effort: her *praising*, in *Three Guineas*, of 'the Mayoress of Woolwich for refusing "to darn a sock to help a war"' – in 1937, so not in fact a 'war time action' as Humm mistakenly dubs 'this brave act given that Woolwich at that time contained over 12,000 electors employed in armament factories (Humm 2009: 157; see Woolf 1938: 210–11). This is precisely the point. Lion was commissioned (early in 1918) by the Ministry of Information to 'paint the home-front effort' – in this case, munition workers – 'producing propaganda images which would boost [female] employment' (Speck 2014: 12) with a view to winning the conflict. By ignoring Lion's painting, Woolf too was refusing 'to darn a sock to help in a war' ideology (Woolf 1938: 210) which survived post-war in heroic representations of the home-front war effort, and in monumental memorials.

For Woolf, patriarchal constructions of class and gender are connected, underpinning discourses of nationalism, empire and war, but her main focus in this review is on class. With its display of so many portraits of high-ranking officers and members of the upper classes mixed with official war pictures, and taking into account the way in which the lower classes were portrayed in those paintings, it was the exhibition that was elitist, not Woolf's response to it. She gleefully savages no. 248, Alfred Priest's *Cocaine*, in which 'a young man in evening dress lies, drugged, with his head upon the pink satin of a woman's knee' as 'a dreary vigil' (ironic reference to the home front). When the lower classes are represented, 'it seemed certain that the artist intended a compliment in a general way to the island race' (Woolf 1986–2011, vol. 3: 91, 90). She takes no. 306, John Reid's *The Wonders of the Deep*, as typical of the latter case, depicting a fisherman's family on the shore, 'the sea itself tricked out for a fair', yet: 'The sea has another voice than this' (90, 91). More generally, Woolf complains:

> Every picture . . . seemed to radiate the strange power to make the beholder more heroic and more romantic; . . . *illusions* of all kinds poured down upon us from the walls. . . . It is indeed a very powerful atmosphere; so charged with manliness and womanliness, . . .sunsets and Union Jacks, that the shabbiest and most suburban catch a reflection of *the rosy glow*. (92, emphasis added)

'[T]he rosy glow' emanating from the upper-class portraits in particular is 'the rosy glow' of the British Empire, but it also shrewdly refers to the unusual (in war art, with the exception of some of Orpen's works) rosy tints of Sargent's painting, mentioned explicitly soon after the following quote and criticised for its 'discrepancy' (92) from reality where the English, Woolf continues,

> are, perhaps, not quite up to the level of the pictures. Some are meagre; others obese; many have put on what is too obviously the only complete outfit that they possess. But the legend on the catalogue explains any such discrepancy in a convincing manner. 'To give unto them beauty for ashes. Isaiah LXI.' – that is the office of this exhibition. Our ashes will be transformed if only we expose them openly enough to the benignant influence of the canvas. (92)

The biblical sense of what may seem a rather infelicitous, questionable caption used to identify the exhibition less than one year after the end of the conflict refers to putting aside the ashes of mourning and grief and replacing them with glory, praise, joy, which constitute a kind of 'beauty' that is not acquired but given, because it is of the nature of grace. The caption subtly intimates that mourning and grief for the war dead be put aside for what the exhibition is offering through the artworks displayed, namely a celebration of the glory of Great Britain. But Woolf goes a step further and identifies the 'ashes' with the (grieving) viewing public who is the object of that operation, in particular the lower classes, and takes issue with that: 'One is not altogether such a bundle of ashes as they suppose, or sometimes the magic fails to work' (92), she comments. And here that 'magic' – the transformative 'rosy glow' she has mentioned – is immediately identified with the one painting that 'at last pricked some nerve of protest, or perhaps of humanity' (92) by its 'over-emphasis', rosy tints and inconsistent lighting (diffuse illumination typical of composite 'realist' paintings). The 'last straw' (93) that makes Woolf's speaker flee the exhibition, citing Baudelaire's famous suicide poem 'N'importe où hors de ce monde' (1867), 'Anywhere, anywhere, out of this world!' (93), is Sargent's *Gassed*.

While 'at last pricked some nerve of protest, or perhaps of humanity' has occasionally been interpreted as a positive reaction, Woolf unambiguously identifies this as one of the questionable artworks exhibited, representing nothing but '[h]onour, patriotism, chastity, wealth, success, importance, position, patronage, power' (93). Praised by Churchill at the banquet opening the exhibition, *Gassed* was unsurprisingly crowned 'Picture of the Year' by the Royal Academy. Woolf was not its only detractor. E. M. Forster's review of the 1926 Sargent memorial exhibition at the Royal Academy provides a more detailed reasoning behind his dissent from establishment acclaim, and follows exactly Woolf's line of argument, describing the change of atmosphere and milieu between the streets outside and the inside of the Academy, highlighting economic inequality by focusing on clothes, and emphasising the social chasm created by class and maintained by power. Forster too singles out Sargent's *Gassed* as a reassuring picture for the establishment in its depicting '[a] line of golden-haired Apollos', young men 'of godlike beauty – for the upper classes only allow the lower classes to appear in art on condition that they wash themselves and have classical features' (Forster 1953b: 39): 'It was all that a great war picture should be, and it was modern because it managed to tell a new sort of lie', allowing the viewing public 'to say, "How touching," instead of 'How obscene"' (Forster 1953b: 39–40).

Forster, a Red Cross volunteer in Alexandria, Egypt in the war, viewed this painting as a 'rosy' picture of war celebrating silent endurance and patriotism. Compare *Gassed* with the shocking lines of Wilfred Owen's 'gas poem' of 1917 (pub. 1920), 'Dulce Et Decorum Est', to realise how the horror lived by soldiers exposed to mustard gas is edulcorated and sanitised in Sargent's painting. Like Forster, Owen too unmasks belligerent patriotism as 'The old Lie: Dulce Et Decorum Est / Pro patria mori' – in his own translation: 'It is sweet and meet to die for one's country. Sweet! and decorous!' (Owen 1994: 29–30). Or, compare *Gassed* with Gilbert Rogers's painting of the same name, *Gassed. In Arduis Fidelis*, also painted in 1919. (Its subtitle 'Faithful in Adversity' is the motto of the Royal Army Medical Corps in which Rogers served as a medical orderly in France and Flanders.) The difference couldn't be greater, '[w]ith its close tonal range and a palette limited to ochres and umber this is an image of utter bleakness' (Gough 2013: 416).

Rogers's *Gassed*, painted after the war when the ban on painting dead bodies had been lifted, owes much to Christopher Nevinson's *Paths of Glory* (1917), censored for daring to show the reality of war, namely dead bodies (see Sherman 2014: 73–4). Nevinson too was an official war artist, but more controversial than Sargent. He had served in the Royal Army Medical Corps, then as a Red Cross volunteer ambulance driver in Flanders, becoming an official war artist in 1917. Sargent did not really see the war and was sent to France for a few weeks towards the end to paint commemorative work. Like Sargent, Nevinson was commissioned after the armistice to produce a large canvas for the planned and never realised Hall of Remembrance: *The Harvest of Battle* (1919). In striking contrast with Sargent's piece, the green-khaki hue of Nevinson's painting, so pervasive and nauseating, evocative of mustard gas, recalls the 'thick green light' of Owen's poem: 'As under a green sea, I saw him drowning' (Owen 1994: 29). There are no rosy tints here, no composed Britons of 'godlike beauty', but wounded Tommies and German soldiers alike, all victims of that horror, a devastated landscape, an horizon darkened by the black smoke of battle and dead men in the foreground. Nevinson had started out as a Futurist, but his art was radically changed by first-hand experience of war.

Woolf knew Nevinson. The two were introduced by Clive Bell at an exhibition of Walter Sickert's paintings in February 1919, as recorded in her diary (Woolf 1977–85, vol. 1: 240), but Woolf had been interested in his work for some time (he used to exhibit at events organised by the Friday Club). She sent Vanessa a catalogue of his paintings in April 1918 and must have seen his war art published regularly in newspapers (see Muscogiuri forthcoming). *Paths of Glory*, its openly critical title a quotation from Thomas Gray's 'Elegy Written in a Country Churchyard', made headlines when the War Propaganda Bureau (WPB) censored it in 1918, ordering Nevinson to withdraw it from display. Nevinson did not comply, showing the painting with a strip of brown paper across it with the word 'Censored' written in blue chalk. The episode exposes the crucial question of erasure faced by artists: erasure of the reality of war, of the body and, in particular, dead bodies. Missing bodies, corpses never to be returned to Britain, representative bodies (the one corpse that became the Unknown Warrior), bodies (including living ones, if unacceptable by 'official' standards) and corpses concealed and erased by the censorship of the WPB – unless, that is, the body and the reality of death could be used for propaganda, to gain political support, as exemplified by the propaganda-documentary film *The Battle of the Somme* (1916) shot for the War Office (Sherman 2014: 64–5). Here the WPB took a gamble, and it paid off, but it was the only exception. The WPB kept dead bodies away from the eyes of the civilian population, making it even harder to come to terms with personal losses in a war fought mainly far from the national soil.

Woolf was a member of that marginalised civilian population without first-hand experience of 'the War', suffering loss of friends and relatives without seeing the battlefields. She was a constant at the hospital bedside of her brother-in-law Philip Woolf who, having volunteered for the 20th Hussars, as does Miss Edwards's brother in *Jacob's Room* (Woolf 1922: 140), narrowly survived his injuries from the same shell that killed his brother Cecil Woolf in the Battle of Cambrai, 27 November 1917 (Woolf 1977–85, vol. 1: 83, 123). Her liminal position nevertheless crucially charges Woolf's coastal seascapes with an historiography of Empire and the Great War. Her often metaphoric treatment of the sea does not obliterate maritime history but subverts the visual rhetoric prescribed by the WPB to official war artists. Woolf was not on the front line, but she refused not to see what had happened: she transmuted the margin into a threshold for both writer and reader, challenging the erasures made by the establishment.

Jacob's Room rewrites two major official events to disrupt the phallogocentric discourses of nationalism and war heroism: the erection of the Cenotaph in Whitehall and the final sea crossing of the Unknown Warrior from Boulogne to Dover. Of the war dead Jacob Flanders, the novel returns not the corpse but his life before the war, however short-lived, as the final brief chapter attests. Marvelling in the middle of the room Jacob left, '"with everything just as it was . . . his letters strewn about for anyone to read"', Bonamy muses on the misplaced optimism of anyone crossing the Channel to war: '"What did he expect? Did he think he would come back?"' (Woolf 1922: 289). Jacob, whose *unknown* life the novel attempts to piece together, to make it 'known' or 'knowable', rather than celebrate his '[g]lorious', depersonalising death, is a self-consciously fractured, failing composite evocation of uncountable unknown, unknowing, soldiers who depart for war never to return, whether or not expecting to return. The very sea crossing of the Unknown Warrior is shrewdly recreated in the novel through evocative images that subtly replace the permanent, honoured burial place of the Unknown Warrior in Westminster Abbey with the suggestion of a vague, indeterminate coastal grave, so indefinite that it could be equally located ashore or in the sea, only marked, if at all, by the drooping smoke of cottages and a seagull's flight, glimpsed from a boat by a naked Jacob 'looking at the Land's End': 'But imperceptibly the cottage smoke droops, has the look of a mourning emblem, a flag floating its caress over a grave. The gulls, making their broad flight and then riding at peace, seem to mark the grave' (78, 77).

What is left of Jacob for friends and family at the close is a much more personal and fleeting kind of Cenotaph (which literally means 'empty tomb'), namely his 'empty room', which of course will not stay empty. This elegiac image appears in a refrain on his university room in chapter 3, and again on the last page of the novel in the room where his mother holds up his old shoes:

> Listless is the air in an empty room, just swelling the curtain; the flowers in the jar shift. One fibre in the wicker arm-chair creaks, though no one sits there. (61)

> Listless is the air in an empty room, just swelling the curtain; the flowers in the jar shift. One fibre in the wicker arm-chair creaks, though no one sits there. (289–90)

Hence the primary national war memorial is polemically replaced in the novel by a private, personal dimension filled with memories of life.

But if *Jacob's Room* recreates the life of one Unknown Warrior whose 'body' remained 'for ever ... concealed' in 'some corner of a foreign field', as Brooke's 'The Soldier' has it (see Sherman 2014: 81), *Mrs Dalloway* inscribes the life of one of the many soldiers – like the protagonist, Septimus Smith – who has re-crossed the Channel, returning shell-shocked, a reality largely concealed from the general public and that required medical 'normalisation'. The portentous figurative grave circled by gulls that was glimpsed by Jacob from the Channel looms closer to the imperialist metropolitan centre in *Mrs Dalloway*:

> All down the Mall people were standing and looking up into the sky. As they looked the whole world became perfectly silent, and a flight of gulls crossed the sky, first one gull leading, then another, and in this extraordinary silence and peace, in this pallor, in this purity, bells struck eleven times, the sound fading up there among the gulls. (Woolf 2015: 19)

The 'silence and peace' may mark the government's commemorative two-minute armistice silence first introduced at 11 a.m. on 11 November 1919 at the Cenotaph (Bradshaw 2002: 117). In *Jacob's Room* the Cenotaph, having become a permanent monument in Whitehall by 1920, is only elliptically satirised in allusions to the fleetingly 'empty room'. In *Mrs Dalloway* it becomes an overt target, as Peter Walsh watches the ceremony of 'weedy' uniformed boys 'carrying guns' who

> marched with their eyes ahead of them, marched, their arms stiff, and on their faces an expression like the letters of a legend written round the base of a statue praising duty, gratitude, fidelity, love of

England ... Now they wore on them unmixed with sensual pleasure or daily preoccupations the solemnity of the wreath which they had fetched from Finsbury Pavement to the empty tomb. They had taken their vow. The traffic respected it; vans were stopped. (Woolf 2015: 46)

Walsh feels, according to Bradshaw, the '"Hegelian" pull' of these gullible boy soldiers whose dutiful limbs are worked by the 'one will' (Bradshaw 2002: 111). The same metaphoric gull-flown seascape of *Jacob's Room* that counters the 'thanatopolitics' (Agamben 1981: 122) or 'necrolatry of the state' (Bradshaw 2002: 107) invested in the Cenotaph also returns in *Mrs Dalloway* in Septimus's 'visions. He was drowned, he used to say, and lying on a cliff with the gulls screaming over him. He would look over the edge of the sofa down into the sea ... until suddenly he would cry that he was falling down, down into the flames!' (Woolf 2015: 126). He sees himself repeatedly as 'a drowned sailor, on the shore of the world' (83) but in fact, like Jacob, Septimus was a soldier, not a sailor. Yet, their shipwreck is metaphorical – Eliot's *The Waste Land* comes to mind – reprising the old metaphor of the sea crossing as voyage of life. The war brought to a massive shipwreck a whole generation. Bloody seas were both literal and metaphoric. *To the Lighthouse*, which completes Woolf's Great War trilogy, focuses on the civilian population that could only endure the losses. Seascape merges history with vision, allusion to sunken military vessels with the bloodshed following the explosion of the shell that kills Andrew Ramsay (whose death is mentioned parenthetically immediately before this description of the seascape), and indeed, with all wars, past and future. These doleful associations are insinuated by vivid submarine colours and the passing of 'an ashen-coloured ship': 'there was a purplish stain upon the bland surface of the sea as if something had boiled and bled, invisibly, beneath' (Woolf 1927: 207).

Occurring far from the national soil, that carnage was not visible to most people (happened 'invisibly'), yet it is there 'beneath' the surface. Allusion to past wars is strongly suggested by the careful word choice. Woolf's diction is never casual, always 'full of echoes, of memories, of associations' (Woolf, 'Craftsmanship', 1937; 1986–2011, vol. 6: 95). The 'purplish stain' on the sea, the boiling and bleeding beneath, strongly suggests a further, deeper layer of allusions which, through this specific image, ultimately relate this death to all deaths in the context of any war and any empire. This is a recurrent topos in classical (specifically Latin) historical epic and literature: that 'sea stained purple by Punic blood' about which Horace writes repeatedly in *The Odes*, suddenly changing their lyric tone to epic and bestowing on them a tragic cast. Writing of 'the blood-stained eddies' during those wars, which saw the Roman Republic fighting the Carthaginian Empire, Silius Italicus reports how 'pervaded by the war the sea boiled'. On 18 June 1915 allies on both sides of the Channel were acutely aware of the centenary of the Battle of Waterloo, itself in Flanders, rendering the Great War quite literally a palimpsest, where now the French and English, *'foes of a hundred years ago are brothers-in-arms against a common enemy* [the Germans]' (*The Times* 1915: 9, italics in original). Hence *Jacob's Room*, whose publication 'more or less coincided with the seventieth anniversary of [Wellington's] death on 14 September 1852' (Bradshaw 2003: 26), teems with barbed references to 'the battle of Waterloo' (Woolf 1922: 135, 183, 273) and its victor, the Duke of Wellington (60, 81, 105 111, 252, 274), everywhere commemorated in London's streets and monuments.

Woolf's 'palimpsest of war' here is dual: her first three novels of the 1920s repeatedly rewrite the war from ever differing perspectives – of those whose lives, voices, bodies were normally erased by official historiography and official war art; and then, diachronically, through its association with the bloody seas, these texts connect the recent war with wars of the past: 'Truly, a deep sea, the past, a tide which will overtake and overflow us' ('Reading', 1919; Woolf 1986–2011, vol. 3: 141). In her trilogy, this image of the past as a profound, rising and inundating sea exceeds the private sphere and redefines history, turning official historiography on its head, as personal memory and awareness of history become political. Woolf makes a palimpsest of war written on water: elusive, maybe, but permeated by spectral visions, bearing witness to the reality of war and the war dead, echoing erased voices, making 'the invisible visible', attesting to the visibility of bodies 'not present in flesh and blood' (Derrida and Stiegler 2002: 115), referencing, too, the political dead, also called by Derrida the *'revenant'* (Derrida 1993: 96), literally the one who returns, who is dead but keeps coming back – to haunt us. Woolf's spectral aesthethics haunt the reader, insisting on bridging gulfs, crossing abysses, forging cross-Channel connectedness, pacifism.

Acknowledgements

In memory of Jo Cox (1974–2016), haunting presence, and for Liu Xiaobo (1955–2017), become forever waves. To Jane Goldman goes my deepest gratitude for brilliant editing of this essay and generous suggestions.

Bibliography

Agamben, Giorgio (1981), *Homo Sacer: Sovereign Power and Bare Life*, Stanford, CA: Stanford University Press.
Anand, Mulk Raj (1940), *Across the Black Waters*, London: Jonathan Cape.
Beechey, James (1996), 'Introduction' to Richard Shone [1975], *The Friday Club 1905–1922*, London: Michael Parking Gallery.
Bell, Clive (1923), *On British Freedom*, London: Chatto & Windus.
Bishop, Edward L. (2004), 'Mind the gap: the spaces in *Jacob's Room*', *Woolf Studies Annual*, 10: 31–49.
Bradshaw, David (2002), '"Vanished like leaves": the military, elegy and Italy in *Mrs. Dalloway*', *Woolf Studies Annual*, 8: 107–26.
Bradshaw, David (2003), *Winking, Buzzing, Carpet-beating: Reading Jacob's Room*, Southport: Virginia Woolf Society of Great Britain.
Brooke, Rupert (1915), *1914 and Other Poems*, London: Sidgwick and Jackson.
Coward, Thomas (1915), 'Crowing pheasants and the North Sea battle', *The Manchester Guardian*, 10 February 1915. https://www.theguardian.com/environment/2015/feb/08/pheasants-north-sea-battle-1915 (last accessed 14 October 2019).
Das, Santanu (2018), *India, Empire, and First World War Culture: Writings, Images, and Songs*, Cambridge: Cambridge University Press.
Derrida, Jacques (1985), *The Ear of the Other: Otobiography, Transference, Translation*, ed. Christie V. McDonald and Avital Ronell, trans. Peggy Kamuf, New York: Schocken Books.
Derrida, Jacques (1993), *Specters of Marx: The State of the Debt, the Work of Mourning, & the New International*, trans. Peggy Kamuf, London: Routledge.
Derrida, Jacques and Bernard Stiegler (2002), *Echographies of Television* [1996], trans. Jennifer Bajorek, Cambridge: Polity.
Fleming, Peter (2011), *Operation Sea Lion: Hitler's Plot to Invade England* [1957], London: Tauris.
Forster, E. M. (1953a), 'Me, them and you' [1926, misdated as 1925], in E. M. Forster, *Abinger Harvest*, London: Edward Arnold & Co.
Forster, E. M. (1953b), 'Our graves in Gallipoli' [1922], in E. M. Forster, *Abinger Harvest*, London: Edward Arnold & Co.
Goldman, Jane (2004), *Modernism, 1910–1945: Image to Apocalypse*, Basingstoke: Palgrave Macmillan.
Gough, Paul (2013), '"An epic of mud": artistic interpretations of Third Ypres', in *Passchendaele in Perspective: The Third Battle of Ypres*, ed. Peter H Liddle, Barnsley: Pen & Sword Military, pp. 409–21.
Hardy, Thomas (1976), *The Complete Poems of Thomas Hardy*, ed. James Gibson, London: Macmillan.
Herbert, A. P. (1943), *Bring Back the Bells*, London: Methuen.

Humm, Maggie (2009) 'Editing Virginia Woolf and the arts: Woolf and the Royal Academy', in *Woolf Editing / Editing Woolf*, ed. Eleanor McNees and Sara Veglahn, Clemson, SC: Clemson University Digital Press, pp. 154–9.
Hussey, Mark (2016), 'Clive Bell, 'a fathead and a voluptuary': conscientious objection and British masculinity', in *Queer Bloomsbury*, ed. Brenda Helt and Madelyn Detloff, Edinburgh: Edinburgh University Press.
Khan, Douglas (1999), *Noise, Water, Meat: A History of Sound in the Arts*. Cambridge, MA: MIT Press.
Liddell, H. G. and Robert Scott (1889), *An Intermediate Greek–English Lexicon*, Oxford: Clarendon Press.
London, Bette (2010), 'Posthumous was a woman: World War I memorials and Woolf's Dead Poet's Society', *Woolf Studies Annual*, 16: 45–69.
Maughan, Philip (2015), '"I think the dead are with us": John Berger at 88', *The New Statesman*. https://www.newstatesman.com/culture/2015/06/i-think-dead-are-us-john-berger-88 (last accessed 11 October 2019).
Muscogiuri, Patrizia A. (forthcoming 2020), 'Matchsticks out of their boxes, from Arthur Melbourne-Cooper to Virginia Woolf', in *Modernist Objects*, ed. Xavier Kalck and Noëlle Cuny, Clemson, SC: Clemson University Press.
Owen, Wilfred (1985), *Selected Letters*, ed. John Bell, Oxford: Oxford University Press.
Owen, Wilfred (1994), *The War Poems of Wilfred Owen*, ed. Jon Stallworthy, London: Chatto & Windus.
Owen, Wilfred (2013), *The Complete Poems and Fragments*, ed. Jon Stallworthy, 2 vols, London: Chatto & Windus.
Porter, Whitworth, Charles Moore Watson and W. Baker Brown (1952), *History of the Corps of Royal Engineers: The Home Front, France, Flanders and Italy in the First World War*, London: Institution of Royal Engineers.
Pulling, Alexander (ed.) (2018), *Defence of the Realm Manual*, 5th edn (*Manuals of Emergency Legislation*), London: HM Stationery Office.
Russolo, Luigi (1986), *The Art of Noises*, trans. Barclay Brown, New York: Pendragon Press.
Sassoon, Siegfried (1917) *The Old Huntsman and Other Poems*, London: Heinemann.
Sassoon, Siegfried [1918] (1920), *Counter-Attack and Other Poems*, New York: Dutton.
Sherman, David (2014), *In a Strange Room: Modernism's Corpses and Mortal Obligation*, Oxford: Oxford University Press.
Speck, Catherine (2014), *Beyond the Battlefield: Women Artists of the Two World Wars*, London: Reaktion Books.

Stalla, Heidi (2012), 'Woolf and anti-Semitism: is Jacob Jewish?', in *Virginia Woolf in Context*, ed. Bryony Randall and Jane Goldman, Cambridge: Cambridge University Press.
The Times (1915), 'Waterloo Day', *Times*, 18 June 1915, p. 9+, The Times Digital Archive. http://tinyurl.galegroup.com/tinyurl/BP2iM7 (last accessed 19 July 2019).
Woolf, Virginia (1919), *Night and Day*, London: The Hogarth Press.
Woolf, Virginia (1922), *Jacob's Room*, London: The Hogarth Press.
Woolf, Virginia (1927), *To the Lighthouse*, London: The Hogarth Press.
Woolf, Virginia (1929), *A Room of One's Own*, London: Hogarth Press.
Woolf, Virginia (1938), *Three Guineas*, London: The Hogarth Press.
Woolf, Virginia (1941), *Between the Acts*, London: The Hogarth Press.
Woolf, Virginia (1975–80), *The Letters of Virginia Woolf*, ed. Nigel Nicolson assisted by Joanne Trautmann, 6 vols, London: The Hogarth Press.
Woolf, Virginia (1977–85), *The Diary of Virginia Woolf*, ed. Anne Olivier Bell, assisted by Andrew McNeillie, 5 vols, London: The Hogarth Press.
Woolf, Virginia (1985), *The Complete Shorter Fiction of Virginia Woolf*, ed. Susan Dick, London: The Hogarth Press.
Woolf, Virginia (1986–2011), *The Essays of Virginia Woolf*, ed. Andrew McNeillie and Stuart N. Clarke, 6 vols, London: The Hogarth Press.
Woolf, Virginia (2015), *Mrs Dalloway* [1925], ed. Anne E. Fernald, Cambridge: Cambridge University Press.
Wynn, Stephen (2016), *City of London in the Great War*, Barnsley: Pen & Sword Military.

Index

Note: Page numbers for figures appear in italics. The suffix n signifies an endnote.

Abbott, Berenice, 171
Abravanel, Genevieve, 163
Adam, George, 121
Adam, Mrs H. Pearl, 120, 121
Afromodernists, 158
Albright, Daniel, 71
Allégret, Marc, 167, 172–4, 175, 177, 179
Anand, Mulk Raj, *Across the Black Waters*, 230
Ansermet, Ernest, 73
Archer, Ethel, 104
Arnold, Matthew, 'Dover Beach', 156–7
Aron, Robert, 178
Art and Letters (journal), 75, 78
artist's models, 99, 100, 107–10, 111, 123
Athill, Diana, 66n3, 125–6
Auriol, Jean George, 167
Austen, Jane, 59

Back, Kurt, 92
Bacon, Francis, 97
Baker, Josephine, 158, 173
Bakst, Léon, 185
Balázs, Béla, 176
Ballets Russes, 16, 22, 69, 73, 98, 172, 185–6, 195n7

Balzac, Honoré de, *Splendeurs et misères des courtisanes* (*A Harlot High and Low*), 129–30
Banks, George, 31
Banville, John, 207
Banville d'Hostel, Lucien
  'L'inventoriée', 26
  'Midi', 27
Barry, Idris, 165
Baudelaire, Charles, 37
  Les Fleurs du mal, 37
  'N'importe où hors de ce monde', 233
  'The Painter of Modern Life', 147
Beach, Sylvia, 170, 171–2, 173, 174
Beckett, J. C., 200
Beckett, Samuel, 14
Beddington, Violet (Violet Schiff), 69–70, 74, 81
Bell, Clive, 8, 74, 191, 218, 235
  Peace at Once, 222
Bell, Vanessa, 8, 9, 97, 188, 189, 191, 193, 194n5, 216, 235
Benda, Julien, 33
Benjamin, Walter, 94, 123, 149
Bennett, Arnold, 3, 75, 172, 182n22, 187

Berger, John, 215, 217
Bergson, Henri, 21–4, 31, 32–5, 36–7, 38–40
   Durée et simultanéité, 39
   Essai sur les données immédiates de la conscience (*Time and Free Will*), 33–5, 39
   Le Rire, 39
   Matière et mémoire, 39
Bernstein, Sidney, 165
Betts, Ernest, 177
Blakeston, Oswell, 165
Bloomsbury Group
   cross-Channel relations, 8–9, 172, 186, 188
   Friday Club, 216, 235
   and music, 184–5, 193
   pacifism and dissent, 3, 191, 222; *see also* Woolf, Virginia: representations of war
   see also Omega Workshops
bohemian life, 3, 96, 97, 100, 102, 106
Boudot-Lamotte, Emmanuel, 85
Bowen, Elizabeth, 199–212
   and channel crossings, 200–1, 202–12
   and Deleuzian theory, 206, 208, 210, 212
   national identity, 199–200, 202–3, 208
   wartime experiences, 200
   WORKS
   A Time in Rome, 202
   Encounters, 202
   Pictures and Conversations, 201, 202–3, 207
   The House in Paris, 201, 204–11, 212
Bradshaw, David, 238
Brett, Dorothy, 6
Bridgman Metchim, Donald, 223
Britzolakis, Christina, 124
Brockington, Grace, 185, 186, 191
Bronfen, Elizabeth, 107
Brooke, Joceyln, 83–4
Brooke, Rupert, 186, 227, 237
Brooker, Peter, 102, 105–7, 133n8
Broom (journal), 168–9
Brown, Ford Madox, 50, 57–8, 62
Brown, Spencer Curtis, 202
Browning, Robert, 'My Last Duchess', 157
Bryher (Annie Winifred Ellerman), 162, 163, 165, 166, 167, 170–3, 176, 179–80, 181n13
   Film Problems of Soviet Russia, 162
   The Heart to Artemis, 170–1, 172–3
Bunting, Basil, 64, 101
   Briggflatts, 101
Bussy, Dorothy, 172

cadence, 56–7, 63
Cahiers d'Art (journal), 167
Carco, Francis, 26–7, 43n23, 124, 127, 128
   'Aix-en-Provence', 37
   'Les huit danseuses', 27
   Perversité, 128
Carlyle, Thomas, 5
Carr, Helen, 127
Carrington, Dora, 105
Carter, Huntly, 21–2, 23, 31–2, 35
   The New Spirit in Drama and Art, 41n5
Caughie, Pamela, 7
Caws, Mary Ann, 8–9
Chamson, André, 171–2
Chaplin, Charlie, 175, 177
Chevalley, Freddy, 177–8
Ciné pour tous (journal), 167, 176–7
Cinéa (journal), 167, 176–7

cinema culture, 162–80
  the close up, 175–6
  silent film, 163, 164, 178
  sound film, 163, 164, 177–8, 180
  COUNTRIES
  Britain, 162, 163, 165–7, 177
  France, 162, 166, 167, 173–8
  Germany, 162, 166, 173, 178–9
  Netherlands, 178
  Soviet Union, 162, 166, 170
  Switzerland, 162, 166, 178
  United States (Hollywood), 163
Clair, René, 177–8
Close Up (journal), 162–80
  contributors, 162, 164, 165–6, 169–70, 173, 177–9
  editors and editorial focus, 162–3, 165, 169–70, 172
  and film production, 174, 179
  French-language articles, 175, 177–8, 179
  German-language articles, 178–9
  on silent and sound film, 163, 164, 177–8, 180
Clutton-Brock, Arthur, *Simpson's Choice*, 190
Cocteau, Jean, 97, 172
Cohen, Margaret, 9, 201
Colette, 127, 167, 170–1
Collins, Judith, 185, 187, 191
Connolly, Cyril, 193
Conrad, Joseph
  admiration for French prose, 50, 52–3, 56
  collaboration with Ford, 52–60
  French speaking style, 63–4
  and Gide and Allégret, 172, 173
  and Impressionism, 52, 62
  translational model of writing, 52, 58
  WORKS
  Almayer's Folly, 52
  Romance (with Hueffer (Ford)), 52, 56, 59–60
Contact (magazine), 170
Contact Editions, 170
Copeau, Jacques, 181n17, 185, 188, 192
Corcoran, Neil, 208
Cork, Richard, 110–11
Cowley, Malcolm, *Exile's Return*, 168
Crane, Stephen, 50, 62
Crevel, René, 178
Criterion (journal), 69, 77, 79
Crossthwaite, Arthur, 'Ennui', 26
Crowley, Aleister, 97, 104
cummings, e. e., 64, 181n11
Curtiss, Mina, 83

Dante Alighieri
  Divine Comedy, 139
  Inferno, 151n4
Darantière (printer), 170
Darwin, Charles, 40
Das, Santanu, 230
Davie, Donald, 58
Debussy, Claude, 184–94
  and Bloomsbury Group/Omega Workshops, 184–94
  and marionettes, 187–8, 191
  reception in Britain, 184, 193
  and rhythm, 28–9, 31, 35
  WORKS
  Jeux, 185–6
  La Boîte à Joujoux, 185–92, 194
  La Damoiselle élue, 194
  La Mer, 184, 193–4
  L'Après-midi d'un faune, 194
  Pelléas and Mélisande, 184, 185, 192, 194
Debussy, Emma, 184
Delaunay, Sonia, 98
Deleuze, Gilles, 206, 208, 210, 212
Delius, Frederick, 69
Delluc, Louis, 167, 175

Derain, André, *28*
Derrida, Jacques, 215, 218, 223, 224, 239
  Specters of Marx, 215
'Desforges', 25–6
Dever, Carolyn, 9, 201
Diaghilev, Sergei, 69, 71, 97, 98, 172, 195n7
Dickinson, Goldsworthy Lowes, *War and Peace: A Dramatic Fantasia*, 186, 191
Dismorr, Jessie, 29
Doolittle, Hilda (H.D.), 64, 162, 164, 166, 169, 170, 171, 172, 174, 176, 180
  Sea Garden, 171
Dorré, Gina M., 131
Doucet, Henri, 188
Dreschfeld, Violet, 123
Dryden, John, 55
du Maurier, George, *Trilby*, 124
Dumas, Alexandre, *Count of Monte Cristo*, 140
Duncan, Isadora, 22, 27

Ede, H. S., 110, 111
  Savage Messiah, 110, *111*, 113
Eisenstein, Sergei, 162, 169
Eliot, T. S., 14, 69–70, 75, 79
  'The Love Song of J. Alfred Prufrock', 181n11
  The Waste Land, 228, 238
Ellerman, Annie Winifred *see* Bryher
Ellerman, John junior, 172
Ellerman, Sir John, 170, 172
Ellmann, Maud, 208, 212n2
English Review, 64, 168
Epstein, Jacob, 105
Epstein, Jean, 175–6
exile, 148
Experimental Cinema (journal), 163

fashion and modernism, 91–4
Faure, Elie, 175

feminist modernism, 99, 107, 218
Fergusson, J. D., 22, *24*, 41n5
Figaro, 19, 40
film culture *see* cinema culture
Film Society (London), 165
Filmliga (journal), 178
First World War
  air raids, 115–16
  commemorations and depictions in art, 111, 112, 231–6
  conscription, 197n25
  Defence of the Realm Act (DORA), 221–2
  official war artists, 216, 231, 234–5
  pacifism and dissent, 3, 191, 222; *see also* Woolf, Virginia: representations of war
  propaganda and censorship, 50, 63, 162, 216, 218, 221–4, 231–2, 234, 235
  Unknown Warrior, 160, 217–18, 229–30, 236–7
Flaubert, Gustave, 50, 52–6, 57, 60, 62, 127, 170
  'Félicité' (*Trois Contes*), 54–5
  Madame Bovary, 52, 63
Ford, Ford Madox, 50–65
  admiration for French prose, 50, 51, 52–6, 57, 60, 62
  and cadence, 56–7, 63
  collaboration with Conrad, 52–60
  cultural internationalism, 64–5
  family heritage and education, 50, 51
  'Ford's nights', 125
  and Impressionism, 54–5, 60–4
  as journal editor, 64, 167–8
  languages, 51, 57–8
  and *le mot juste*, 52–6, 63
  parodies, 60–1
  on Proust-Joyce meeting, 74
  and Rhys, 58, 63, 120, 121, 122, 126, 127, 128, 129

and translation, 51–8
translational model of writing ('translationese'), 52, 58–61, 65, 127
use of critical terminology, 63
WORKS
A History of Our Own Times, 65
Between St Dennis and St George (as Hueffer), 54–5, 63
Collected Poems, 63
Great Trade Route, 65
'Impressionism – Some Speculations', 63
It Was the Nightingale, 65
Joseph Conrad: A Personal Remembrance, 52–3, 56, 57, 59
'On Impressionism', 63
Parade's End, 59, 64
Provence, 65
Return to Yesterday, 62, 65
'Rive Gauche', 126
Romance (as Hueffer, with Conrad), 52, 56, 59–60
The English Novel, 51
The Good Soldier, 8, 50, 51
The March of Literature, 51, 65
'The Scaremonger', 221
Forster, E. M., 218, 233–4
Foucault, Michel, 210
France, Anatole, 58, 64, 127
Freud, Sigmund, 171, 217
Fry, Margery, 188
Fry, Roger, 8–9, 14, 97, 109–10, 118, 185, 188, 190, 193
Futurists, 70, 221, 235

Gambrell, Alice, 126, 127
Gance, Abel, 166, 167
Gargoyle (journal), 168
Garnett, Constance, 7, 51
Garnett, David, *The Flowers of the Forest*, 187
Garnett, Edward, 51

Gaudier-Brzeska, Henri, 75, 109–15, 116
Dancer, 101
Hieratic Head of Ezra Pound, 116–17
Singer (Chanteuse), 117
Torso and other torsos, 93, 97, 98, 100–2, 107, 109–15, 117
Gaudier-Brzeska, Sophie, 110, *113*
Gertler, Mark, 105
gestural modernism, 97
Gide, André, 170, 172, 173
Retour du Tchad, 173
Voyage au Congo, 173
Gill, Winifred, 186, 188, 189, 190, 191
Grant, Duncan, 8, 184–5, 188, 190, 191, 192, 193
Great War *see* First World War
Gromaire, Marcel, 29
Gros, Frédéric, *The Philosophy of Walking*, 200

H.D. *see* Doolittle, Hilda
Halpern, Barbara Strachey, 184
Hamnett, Nina, 96–118
as academic tutor, 108–9, 111, 112
alternative personae, 103–4
as artist's model (life drawing), 100, 107–9, 114–15
birth and childhood, 102–3
and Bloomsbury Group/Omega Workshops, 97, 98, 109–10, 118, 186, 187
bohemian life, 96, 97, 100, 101, 102, 105–6
clothes and fashion, 98, 103
drawings and sketches, 108, 109, 110, 114–15
and Gaudier-Brzeska, 97, 98, 100–2, 104, 107, 109, 110–18

Hamnett, Nina (*cont.*)
  gestural modernism, 97, 99–100, 105
  portraits and self-portraits, 104–5, 114
  reputation as artist, 96–7, 105–7
  and Roald Kristian, 186, 187, 188, 190
  wartime experiences, 115–16, 190
  WORKS
  Is She a Lady? 101
  Laughing Torso, 96–107, 108, 113, 114–18, 134n9
Hardy, Thomas, 227, 228
  'Channel Firing', 228
Harrison, Jane, *Themis*, 221
Harrison, William, *A Description of England in Shakespeare's Youth*, 6
Heap, Jane, 168
Hecht, Anthony, 'The Dover Bitch', 156–7
Hellé, André, 187, 188, 191, 192
Hemingway, Ernest, 50, 63, 64, 171, 181n11
  The Sun Also Rises, 134n9
Herring, Robert, 165, 166, 167, 173, 177
Hooker, Denise, 107, 109, 110
Hübener, Gustav, 23, 33, 45n42
Hudson, Stephen *see* Schiff, Sidney
Hueffer, Ford Madox *see* Ford, Ford Madox
Hüffer, Franz (Ford's father), 50, 51
Hughes, Langston, 158
  The Big Sea, 155, 158–9
Hugnet, George, 168
Hulme, T. E., 105
Humm, Maggie, 231–2

Huxley, Aldous, 70, 84

Impressionism, 52, 54–5, 60–4
  see also Post-Impressionism
Ireland
  Bowen's relationship with, 199–200, 208
  departure from (in Joyce), 138–50
Irish Channel (St George's Channel), 200–1, 202–8

Jackson, Holbrook, 24, 34
James, Henry, 50, 55, 62, 63–4
John, Augustus, 97, 106, 108
John, Gwen, 64, 100
Jolas, Eugene, 169
Journal du Ciné-club, 167
journals and magazines *see Broom; Cahiers d'Art; Ciné pour tous; Cinéa; Close Up; Contact; Criterion; English Review; Experimental Cinema; Filmliga; Gargoyle; Journal du Ciné-club; La Nouvelle Revue française; La Revue du cinéma; L'art cinématographique; Le Crapouillot; Le Film; Le Navire d'argent; Le Rythme; Les Nouvelles littéraires; Mercure de France; New Age; Nouvelle Revue française; Pagany; Photociné; Poetry; Rhythm; Tambour; The Athenaeum; The Little Review; This Quarter; transatlantic review; transition*
Jouve, Pierre Jean, *Men of Europe*, 190

Joyce, James, 138–50
  and Bryher, 170, 171
  on departure as betrayal, 138–50
  and Ford, 62, 64
  meeting with Proust, 69, 73–4
  and Rhys, 132
  WORKS
  A Portrait of the Artist as a Young Man, 138–50
  Dubliners, 138, 141, 152n14
  Finnegans Wake, 14, 74, 132, 144, 181n11
  Stephen Hero, 141, 151n4
  Ulysses, 14, 71, 74, 144, 170

Kappers-den Hollander, Martien, 120
Keown, Edwina, 201
Keynes, John Maynard, 185
  The Economic Consequences of the Peace, 8
Kipling, Rudyard, 231
Kirkcaldy, Peggy, 120
Kraszna-Krausz, Andor, 178–9
Kristian, Roald, 186–8, 190, 191

La Nouvelle Revue française, 174
La Revue du cinéma, 167
Lacan, Jacques, 148–9
Larbaud, Valery, 64, 174
Larinov, Michel, 73
L'art cinématographique (journal), 167
Le Crapouillot (journal), 174
Le Film (journal), 167
le mot juste, 52–6, 63
Le Navire d'argent (journal), 174, 175
Le Rythme (journal), 24–32
Leblanc, Georgette, 31, *32*
Lecornu, G., *25*, 28
Lenauer, Jean, 177, 178

Lenglet, Jean (Edward de Nève), 120–1, 122
Les Nouvelles littéraires (journal), 174
Levenson, Michael, 97
Lewis, Wyndham, 69, 75, 84–5, 105
  The Apes of God, 84–5
Lion, Flora, 231–2
London, Bette, 218
Lopokova, Lydia, 185
Lukács, Georg, 132

McAlmon, Robert, 170, 171, 172
Macpherson, Kenneth, 162, 163, 164, 165, 169, 173, 174, 176, 177, 179
Maeterlinck, Maurice, 31–2
  Blue Bird, 31, 32
  Monna Vanna, 31
magazines *see* journals and magazines
Mallarmé, Stéphane, 37, 40, 127, 170, 171
Man Ray, 64, 169, 171, 172
Mansfield, Katherine, 6, 7, 69, 74, 75, 128
Marinetti, Filippo, 70, 221
marionettes, 186–8, 191
Martindale, Elsie, *Stories from De Maupassant*, 51
Masterman, C. F. G., 63
Maupassant, Guy de, 50, 52–3, 62, 127
  'Mademoiselle Fifi', 127
Maurois, André, 19, 167
  Climats, 19
Mayor, H. A., 177
Mellor, Katherine, 100
Mercure de France (journal), 32, 168
Messager, André, 73
Miller, Joshua L., 16, 17

Modigliani, Amadeo, 75, 97, 98, 103
Monnier, Adrienne, 171, 174
Montagu, Ivor, 165, 178
Morrell, Ottoline, 3, 185
Morrison, Mark S., 168
Murry, John Middleton, 22, 23, 27, 35, 43n19, 69, 167
music
  and Ford's family background, 51
  as inspiration for Gaudier-Brzeska, 111
  and rhythm, 28–9, 34–5, 36, 37–40
  see also Debussy, Claude; Delius, Frederick; Stravinsky, Igor
Myers, Rollo H., 28–9, 31

Nève, Edward de (Jean Lenglet), 120–1, 122
  Les Verrous (*Barred*), 122
Nevinson, Christopher, 216, 234–5
New Age (magazine), 21, 23, 31–2
Nicolson, Harold, 114–15
Nijinska, Bronislava, 73
Nijinsky, Vaslav, 185
North, Michael, 163, 169
Nouvelle Revue française (NRF), 32–3, 76, 79, 167

O'Faolain, Sean, 199, 201
Oliver, Lois, 100, 112
Omega Workshops, 184–94
  children's art and toy design, 188–91
  and Hamnett, 97, 98, 109, 118
  musical and theatrical activities, 185–94
  publications, 190
  see also Bloomsbury Group
Orpen, Sir William, 123, 233

Osborn, Susan, 208
Owen, Wilfred
  'A New Heaven', 215, 217, 226–7, 229
  'Dulce Et Decorum Est', 234, 235
  'The Kind Ghosts', 226, 227

Pabst, G. W., 170, 173
pacifism and dissent, 3, 191, 222; see also Woolf, Virginia: representations of war
Pagany (journal), 168
Parnell, Charles Stuart, 140, 144
Parsons, Deborah L., 122, 131
Paul, Elliot, 169
Philippe, Charles-Louis, 132
Photociné (journal), 167
Picasso, Pablo, 64, 69, 97, 186, 193
Piette, Adam, 14
Pissarro, Lucien, 105
Pizzichini, Lilian, 121, 123, 127
Poetry (magazine), 63
Poirier, Léon, 173
Polignac, Prince Edmond de, 72
Polignac, Princesse de (Winnaretta Singer), 71–2
POOL group, 162, 169, 170, 174
  see also *Close Up*
Post-Impressionism, 8–9, 14, 62, 186, 189, 193, 216 see also Impressionism
Postle, Martin, 107–8, 109–10, 111–13
Potamkin, Harry Alan, 166, 169
Poulaille, Louis, 175
Pound, Ezra, 14, 40, 50, 51, 58–9, 63, 64, 79, 97, 100, 101, 112, 117
  Homage to Sextus Propertius, 58
  'Ode Pour L'Election De Son Sepulchre', 115
  'Papyrus', 111
  The Cantos, 58

Poynter, Sir Edward, 123
Pre-Raphaelism, 62
Prévost, Jean, 173, 174–5
Priest, Alfred, 231, 232
Probyn, Elspeth, 206
prostitution, 127–8, 130, 145
Proust, Marcel, 69–85
  meeting with Joyce and Stravinsky, 69, 73–4
  Schiff's promotion of, 70–1, 74–9, 85
  translation into English, 79–85
  WORKS
  À la recherche du temps perdu, 39–40, 81
  Du côté de chez Swann, 51, 70, 75, 81, 83
  À l'ombre des jeunes filles en fleurs, 75–6
  Le Côté de Guermantes, 80
  Sodome et Gomorrhe, 71, 74, 76
  Albertine disparue, 70, 79
  Le Temps retrouvé, 82–4
puppetry, 186–8, 191

queer poetics, 3–5, 156

Racine, Jean, Bérénice, 191
Radford, Andrew, 9
Rainsford, Dominic, 9
Ransome, Arthur, 102
Reid, John, 231, 232
Reid, Victoria, 9
Rhys, Jean, 120–32
  as artist's model, 123
  and Ford, 58, 63, 64, 120, 121, 122, 126, 127, 128, 129
  and Jean Lenglet (Edward de Nève), 120–1, 122
  and Mrs Adam, 120, 121
  portrayal of English and Americans, 124–6, 129–31
  and translation, 122, 127, 128
  use of French speech and writing, 128, 131
  use of literary allusions, 128–32
  WORKS
  Good Morning, Midnight, 124, 130–1
  'La Grosse Fifi', 127
  'Night Out 1925', 130
  Quartet, 126, 127, 129
  Smile Please, 121, 127
  'The Blue Bird', 125
  The Left Bank, 124, 126, 127
  'Tout Montparnasse and a Lady', 124–5
  Triple Sec, 121
  Voyage in the Dark, 134n11
  Wide Sargasso Sea, 120
rhythm, 19–41
  and Bergson, 21–2, 23–4, 31, 32–5, 36–7, 38–40
  and film, 177, 178
  French and English understandings of, 21–41
  and music, 28–9, 34–5, 36, 37–40
Rhythm (journal), 22, 24–9, 31, 34, 37, 114, 167
Richardson, Dorothy, 43n25, 64, 164, 165, 171
  Pilgrimage, 43n25, 171
Rimbaud, Arthur, 127
Robert, Clémentine, 70
Rodgers, Gail, 16, 17
Rodker, John, 50
Rogers, Gilbert, 234
Rossetti, Dante Gabriel, 62
Rossetti, William Michael, 51
Rothermere, Viscountess, 69, 79
Royal Academy of Arts, 218, 231–4
Ruffy, Hall, 'The Death of Devil', 26
Russell, Bertrand, 218, 222

Sachs, Curt, 36
Sachs, Hanns, 173
Sackville-West, Vita, 1–4, 8, 14
Sage, Robert, 169
St George's Channel (Irish Channel), 200–1, 202–8
Sargent, John Singer, 231, 233–5
Sassoon, Siegfried
  Counter-Attack and Other Poems, 227
  The Old Huntsman and Other Poems, 227
Schiff, Sidney, 69–85
  as cosmopolitan society and literary host, 69–71
  promotion of Proust in England, 70–1, 74–9, 85
  translation of Proust into English, 79–85
  WORKS (as Stephen Hudson)
  A True Story, 85
  'Celeste', 77
  Prince Hempseed, 71
  Richard Kurt, 71
  Richard, Myrtle and I, 77–8
  'Témoignage d'un romancier', 78
Schiff, Violet (née Beddington), 69–70, 74, 81
Schneider, Louis, 73
Schuwer, Camille, 24
Scott Moncrieff, Charles, 69, 79, 80–2
  Marcel Proust: An English Tribute, 76–7
Second World War, 179–80, 200, 222, 227
Sedgwick, Eve Kosofsky, 3
Segalen, Victor, 184
Sewell, Anna, *Black Beauty*, 130–1
Shakespear, Olivia, 97, 100, 112
Shakespeare and Company, 171
  see also Beach, Sylvia

Shaw, George Bernard, 187
Sheehan, Elizabeth M., 92
Sherman, David, 217, 229–30
Sickert, Walter, 97, 105, 108, 109, 187, 235
Singer, Winnaretta (Princesse de Polignac), 71–2
Smiles, Samuel, *Life of a Scottish Naturalist*, 56–7
Smythies, Major Raymond, 110, 112
Soupault, Philippe, 64, 169, 175
Souza, Robert de, 'Rythme en français', 33
Stanislavski, Constantin, 32
Stein, Gertrude, 50, 64, 159, 168, 170, 171
  Autobiography of Alice B. Toklas, 97, 159
Stendhal, 14, 50, 170
Sterne, Laurence, 9–10
Stewart, Susan, 124
Strachey, James, 186
Strachey, Lytton, 8, 186
Strachey, Oliver, 184
Strauss, Richard, 184
Stravinsky, Igor, 69, 193
  Renard, 69, 71–3
  The Rite of Spring, 71, 73
Suarès, André, 35
Suggia, Madame, 186
Sutton, Emma, 184
Swinburne, Algernon, 181n11
  'A Channel Passage', 156
Sydney-Turner, Saxon, 184, 186
Symons, Arthur, 69, 181n11

Tambour (journal), 168
Taylor-Batty, Juliette, 128
Thackeray, William Makepeace, *Vanity Fair*, 60
The Athenaeum (journal), 231

The *Little Review*, 168
The Times, 51, 121, 123, 184, 218, 239
The Tyro (journal), 77
theatre
  audiences, 25–6
  comparison with film, 178
  and Bloomsbury Group, 185, 186, 188, 192; see also Omega Workshops: musical and theatrical activities, 185–94
  and rhythm, 31–2
This Quarter (journal), 168
Thomas, Dylan, 97, 101
Todd, Ruthven, 101
Toklas, Alice B., 159 *see also* Gertrude Stein
transatlantic review, 64, 65, 121, 168
transition (journal), 168–70
translation
  'domesticating' and 'foreignising', 58
  Dryden's three levels of, 55
  and Ford, 51–8 *see also* translational model of writing ('translationese')
  and modernism, 14–17
  of Proust's *À la recherche du temps perdu*, 79–84
  on reading and being read in translation *see* Woolf, Virginia: 'On Not Knowing French'
  and Rhys, 122, 127, 128
  and understandings of rhythm, 38–9
translational model of writing ('translationese'), 52, 58–61, 65, 127
Trevelyan, R. C., *Lucretius on Death*, 190
Turgenev, Ivan, 55

Unknown Warrior, 160, 217–18, 229–30, 236–7

Vaughan, William, 107–8, 109–10, 111–13

Waidner, Isabel, *We Are Made of Diamond Stuff*, 160
Warner, Marina, 55
Wells, H. G., 62, 75, 187
Whitehead, Alfred North, 159
Whitman, Walt, 174, 181n11
Williams, William Carlos, 64, 74, 170, 181n11
Wise, Pyra, 70, 87n25
Woolf, Cecil, 235–6
Woolf, Leonard, 8
Woolf, Philip, 235–6
Woolf, Virginia, 215–39
  and art, 216, 231–3, 235
  and Hamnett, 97, 105
  and music, 184, 193
  queer poetics, 3–5, 156
  representations of war, 215–39
  and translation, 14, 19
  and Vita Sackville-West, 1–4, 8
  WORKS
  A Room of One's Own, 97, 99, 107, 113, 217–18
  'Anon', 6
  Between the Acts, 227
  'Character in Fiction', 5
  'Craftsmanship', 238
  Flush: A Biography, 4–5
  general essays, articles and reviews, 7, 9–10, 184, 227
  'Heard on the Downs', 218–19, 220–5
  Jacob's Room, 217, 219–20, 224, 225, 229–30, 235, 236–7, 238, 239
  Kew Gardens, 224, 225

Woolf, Virginia (*cont.*)
  Mrs Dalloway, 224–5, 237–8
  'On Not Knowing French', 19–20, 22–3, 36, 40–1
  Orlando: A Biography, 1, 2, 4, 8, 40
  'Portents at Home', 221
  Radclyffe Hall, 1
  'The Mark on the Wall', 221
  'The Royal Academy', 215, 231–3
  'The War from the Street', 223
  Three Guineas, 223, 232
  'To Spain', 225–6, 227, 228, 229
  To the Lighthouse, 19, 157–8, 238
  The Waves, 4, 230
Wright, Sarah Bird, 8–9
Wyndham, Francis, 121, 133n2

Yeats, W. B., 'The Lake Isle of Innisfree', 60

Zadkine, Ossip, 103
Zola, Émile, 127
  Nana, 134n11

EU representative:
Easy Access System Europe
Mustamäe tee 50, 10621 Tallinn, Estonia
Gpsr.requests@easproject.com

www.ingramcontent.com/pod-product-compliance
Lightning Source LLC
Chambersburg PA
CBHW071830230426
43672CB00013B/2808